GERMAN IDEALISM AND
THE QUESTION OF SYSTEM

THE COLLECTED WRITINGS OF JOHN SALLIS
Volume III/4

GERMAN IDEALISM AND THE QUESTION OF SYSTEM

John Sallis

Edited by Mark J. Thomas

Indiana University Press

This book is a publication of

Indiana University Press
Office of Scholarly Publishing
Herman B Wells Library 350
1320 East 10th Street
Bloomington, Indiana 47405 USA

iupress.org

© 2024 by John Sallis

All rights reserved
No part of this book may be reproduced or utilized in any form or by any means, electronic or mechanical, including photocopying and recording, or by any information storage and retrieval system, without permission in writing from the publisher. The paper used in this publication meets the minimum requirements of the American National Standard for Information Sciences—Permanence of Paper for Printed Library Materials, ANSI Z39.48-1992.

Manufactured in the United States of America

Collected Writings of John Sallis printing 2024

Based on the lecture course of 2016–17 at Boston College, with supplementary material from the lecture courses of 2006 and 2010 at Boston College.

Cataloging information is available from the Library of Congress.

ISBN 978-0-253-06970-2 (hdbk.)
ISBN 978-0-253-06971-9 (pbk.)
ISBN 978-0-253-06972-6 (web PDF)

Contents

	Key to Citations	*vii*
1	Beginnings	*1*
	1. Guiding Questions	*1*
	2. Kant and a New Beginning	*2*
	3. German Idealism and the End of Philosophy	*6*
	4. Additional Remarks on Kant	*7*
	5. The Oldest Systematic Program of German Idealism	*12*
2	Reception of the Critical Philosophy	*16*
	1. The Garve-Feder Review	*16*
	2. Jacobi's Critique of Reason and the Thing in Itself	*18*
	3. Reinhold's Internal Criticism and Development of Kant's Philosophy	*20*
	4. Schulze's Skeptical Attack	*25*
3	The Genesis of Fichte's Thought	*29*
	1. Kantian Beginnings and the Professorship in Jena	*29*
	2. Fichte and the Early Reception of Kant's Philosophy	*32*
	3. The Concept of the *Wissenschaftslehre*	*37*
	4. Introducing the *Wissenschaftslehre*: Its Aim, Beginning, Course, and Method	*41*
4	The Fundamental Principles of the *Wissenschaftslehre* (Fichte's *Grundlage*, Part I)	*49*
	1. The First, Absolutely Unconditioned Fundamental Principle (§1)	*49*
	2. The Second Fundamental Principle (§2)	*56*
	3. The Third Fundamental Principle (§3)	*58*
	4. Additional Points concerning the Three Principles	*61*
5	The Foundations of Theoretical and Practical Knowledge (Fichte's *Grundlage*, Parts II–III)	*64*
	1. The Initial Syntheses (Sections A–D of Part II)	*64*
	2. Fichte and Spinoza	*71*

3. Introducing Section E of Part II ... 74
  4. The Problem of Finitude and the Stages of Idealism-Realism ... 78
  5. On Imagination ... 85
  6. The Deduction of Presentation ... 87
  7. The Practical *Wissenschaftslehre* ... 89
  8. Conclusion ... 93

6 The Early Development of Schelling's Thought ... 95
  1. Philosophical Beginnings ... 96
  2. Introduction to the *System of Transcendental Idealism* ... 99
  3. Imagination and Art ... 104
  4. The Break with Fichte and Collaboration with Hegel ... 108

7 Schelling's Treatise on Human Freedom ... 115
  1. Beyond Absolute Identity: The *Freiheitsschrift* and the Progression of German Idealism ... 115
  2. The First Introduction (SW VII, 336–38) ... 119
  3. Schelling's Opposition to Fichte ... 120
  4. The Second Introduction (SW VII, 338–57) ... 121
  5. The Possibility of Evil (SW VII, 357–73) ... 126

Conclusion: The Question of System ... 133

Editor's Afterword ... 137

Appendix 1: Structure of the Initial Syntheses in Fichte's *Grundlage*, Part II ... 139

Appendix 2: Interplays and Independent Activities (Fichte's *Grundlage*, §4, Section E) ... 141

Appendix 3: Formal Structure of Fichte's *Grundlage*, §4, Section E ... 143

Appendix 4: Outline of Fichte's *Grundlage*, §4, Section E (FW I, 151–217) ... 145

Bibliography ... 161

Index ... 165

Key to Citations

Anthologies

Between Kant and Hegel: Texts in the Development of Post-Kantian Idealism (**BKH**). Translated and edited by George di Giovanni and H. S. Harris. Rev. ed. Indianapolis: Hackett, 2000.
Philosophy of German Idealism (**PGI**). Edited by Ernst Behler. New York: Continuum, 1987.

Kant's Works

Gesammelte Schriften (**AA**). Edited by the Preußische Akademie der Wissenschaften. Berlin: De Gruyter, 1900–.
Critique of Pure Reason. Translated by Norman Kemp Smith. New York: St. Martin's Press, 1965. Cited by the pagination in the 1781 German first edition (**A**) and the 1787 second edition (**B**).
Critique of Practical Reason (**CPrR**). Translated by Lewis White Beck. Indianapolis: Liberal Arts, 1956.
Critique of Judgment (**CJ**). Translated by Werner S. Pluhar. Indianapolis: Hackett, 1987.
Prolegomena to Any Future Metaphysics (**PFM**). Edited by Lewis White Beck. Indianapolis: Liberal Arts, 1950.
Foundations of the Metaphysics of Morals (**FMM**). Translated by Lewis White Beck. Indianapolis: Liberal Arts, 1959.

Fichte's Works

Sämmtliche Werke (**FW**). Edited by I. H. Fichte. 8 vols. Berlin: Veit, 1845–46.
Early Philosophical Writings (**EPW**). Translated and edited by Daniel Breazeale. Ithaca, NY: Cornell University Press, 1988.
The Science of Knowledge (**SK**). Edited and translated by Peter Heath and John Lachs. Cambridge: Cambridge University Press, 1982.

Schelling's Works

Sämmtliche Werke (**SW**). Division I: 10 vols. (= I–X); Division II: 4 vols. (= XI–XIV). Edited by Karl Friedrich August Schelling. Stuttgart: Cotta, 1856–61.

The Unconditional in Human Knowledge: Four Early Essays, 1794–1796 (**UHK**). Translated and edited by Fritz Marti. Lewisburg, PA: Bucknell University Press, 1980.
System of Transcendental Idealism (1800) (**STI**). Translated by Peter Heath. Charlottesville: University Press of Virginia, 1978.
Philosophical Investigations into the Essence of Human Freedom (**PI**). Translated by Jeff Love and Johannes Schmidt. Albany: SUNY Press, 2006.

Hegel's Works

Werke in zwanzig Bänden: Theorie-Werkausgabe (**HW**). Edited by Eva Moldenhauer and Karl-Markus Michel. Frankfurt: Suhrkamp, 1969–71.
Phenomenology of Spirit (**PhS**). Translated by A. V. Miller. Oxford: Oxford University Press, 1977.

Heidegger's Works

Gesamtausgabe (**GA**). Frankfurt: Klostermann, 1975–.

GERMAN IDEALISM AND THE QUESTION OF SYSTEM

1. Beginnings

1. Guiding Questions

Before we begin, it is appropriate to set down some very general questions, guiding questions situated at the horizon of our study of German Idealism.

First, what is the relation of German Idealism to the previous philosophical tradition? In what ways does it resume the tradition and in what ways does it go beyond the tradition? Especially important is its relation to modern metaphysics. To what extent does it complete what was begun by Descartes? To what extent does it remain (or surpass) a philosophy of the cogito? How does it transform the concept of substance that is so crucial in early modern philosophy?

Second, what is the genuine outcome of German Idealism? Here we need especially to call into question the usual view that the outcome is simply the philosophy of Hegel and that Fichte and Schelling are important only as a bridge between Kant and Hegel, that is, only as stages in a development brought to completion by Hegel. In this context, we should mention Heidegger's book on Schelling, in which he attempts to present Schelling as "the genuinely creative and farthest-reaching thinker of this whole age of German philosophy."[1] He thereby presents Schelling as the one who most decisively brings German Idealism to its completion. Nevertheless, Heidegger carries out such a re-interrogation of German Idealism only in *one* respect, with respect to the question of freedom. It needs to be carried out in other respects as well—for example, with respect to the question of finitude in Fichte and the question of the philosophy of nature in Schelling.

Third, whatever its outcome, German Idealism came to an abrupt end—and there is perhaps no transition in Western thought that is greater (or more problematic) than the transition from German Idealism to what followed in the second half of the nineteenth century and the twentieth century. We therefore need to ask: In what sense did German Idealism come to an end? Was its end a fulfillment or a collapse—or perhaps both? Here let me cite Heidegger:

> What makes the situation of Europe all the more catastrophic is that this enfeeblement of the spirit originated in Europe itself and—though prepared by

---

1. Martin Heidegger, *Schellings Abhandlung Über das Wesen der menschlichen Freiheit (1809)*, ed. Hildegard Feick, 2nd ed. (Tübingen: Niemeyer, 1995), 4; Martin Heidegger, *Schelling's Treatise on the Essence of Human Freedom*, trans. Joan Stambaugh (Athens: Ohio University Press, 1985), 4.

earlier factors—was definitively determined by its own spiritual situation in the first half of the nineteenth century. It was then that occurred what is popularly and succinctly called the "collapse of German Idealism." This formula is a kind of shield behind which the already dawning spiritlessness, the dissolution of the spiritual energies, the rejection of all original inquiry into grounds and men's bond with the grounds, are hidden and masked. It was not German Idealism that collapsed; rather, the age was no longer strong enough to stand up to the greatness, breadth, and originality of that spiritual world. (GA 40, 49)[2]

Fourth, the end of German Idealism points to a final question: What is the significance of this end for our attempt to understand what philosophy can be today? How does German Idealism bear upon our attempt to philosophize today?

2. Kant and a New Beginning

We will begin with the beginnings of German Idealism. But even before that, let us begin with the *sense* of beginning, the orientation to beginning that animated German Idealism from its beginning. From the start, there was a strong and persistent sense that philosophy was engaged in carrying out a new beginning. In fact, more than a decade after the inception of German Idealism, this sense of a new beginning continued to be operative and to find expression. Furthermore, it had by then broadened to such an extent that the new beginning and all that it was to bring about was taken as a transformation of spirit itself and of the world as shaped by spirit. One of the most celebrated expressions is in the preface to Hegel's *Phenomenology of Spirit*:

> It is not difficult to see that our time is a time of birth and of transition to a new era. Spirit has broken with the previous world of its existence and representations and is prepared to make it sink into the past, indeed in the labor of its own transformation. . . . But just as the first breath drawn by a child after its long, quiet nourishment breaks the gradualness of mere quantitative growth—there is a qualitative leap—and the child is born, so likewise the spirit in its formation matures slowly and quietly into its new shape, dissolving bit by bit the structure of its previous world. . . . The gradual crumbling that left unaltered the face of the whole is interrupted by the sunrise, which, in one flash, illuminates the features of the new world. (HW 3, 18–19; PhS §11)

But in the initial phase of German Idealism, the sense of a new beginning did not yet have quite the comprehensive scope it would come to have in Hegel's mature work. Rather, it was still the sense primarily of a new beginning *in philosophy*—or, more broadly, in *science* (Wissenschaft—ἐπιστήμη: systematic, rigorously grounded knowledge). Now, German Idealism is usually taken as

---

2. Martin Heidegger, *Introduction to Metaphysics*, trans. Ralph Manheim (New Haven, CT: Yale University Press, 1959), 45.

having itself begun in the aftermath of Kant's critical philosophy—that is, in the reception, criticism, and reformulations of Kant's *Critiques*. To this extent, it does not—strictly speaking—constitute a beginning but rather a furthering of the beginning made by Kant. In fact, within four or five years after the publication of the third *Critique*, Kant's successors began composing and publishing their earliest works. Several were in communication with Kant and produced many of their major works before Kant's death in 1804. So, though they acknowledged that Kant had made the initial breakthrough, they had a sense that they, too, were engaged in actually carrying out the new beginning.

The new beginning launched by Kant has several distinct aspects. This multiplicity is especially evident if one takes into account all three *Critiques*. But the sense of beginning that is most decisive is that which Kant expresses from the very beginning of the *Critique of Pure Reason*. Here the new beginning has to do with metaphysics; in other words, it has to do with the endeavor to gain knowledge by means of pure reason—that is, without relying at all on sense experience, on our experience of objects. Such knowledge is what Kant calls a priori knowledge. This is the kind of knowledge that metaphysics has always sought to gain. Kant, however, interrupts this search: he maintains that before it can be carried out scientifically, it is necessary to interrogate reason itself—that is, to ask whether, how, and within what limits reason can gain a priori knowledge. So, with the critical philosophy, there is to be a break with the metaphysics of the past (that is, the exploits of pure reason) in order to make a new beginning in which—through the critical appraisal of reason—knowledge would be scientifically grounded.

This break, this new beginning is necessary because, as Kant says, metaphysics hitherto has been a "battlefield of endless controversies" (A viii). He says: "It has not yet had the good fortune to enter upon the secure path of science" (B xiv). For this reason, Kant issues "a call to reason to undertake anew the most difficult of all tasks, namely, that of self-knowledge" (A xi). A tribunal must be instituted: "This tribunal is no other than the critique of pure reason" (A xii). We should also note the title of the book published two years after the *Critique of Pure Reason* to explain his work in a more popular way: *Prolegomena to Any Future Metaphysics Which Will Be Able to Come Forth as a Science*.

It is this Kantian, critical beginning that the German Idealists take up. This taking up of the Kantian project is the way in which each of them makes his own beginning:

(1) Even before the *Critique of Judgment* appeared, Reinhold undertook to rebuild the critical philosophy in a form that was thoroughly systematic and based on a first principle. In the period 1789–93, Reinhold gained a reputation as the definitive expositor of Kant—indeed, he virtually replaced Kant as the recognized spokesman for the critical philosophy.

(2) Starting in 1794, Fichte made a similar beginning by taking up the critical philosophy. In his *First Introduction* (1797), he explains the conclusion to which he

came, having become acquainted with the Kantian *Critiques*: "Not a single one of [Kant's] numerous followers perceives what is really being said. Believing that I did, I decided to dedicate my life to a presentation, quite independent of Kant, of that great discovery, and will not relent in this determination" (FW I, 419; SK 3).

(3) In his first publication, *On the Possibility of a Form of All Philosophy* (1794), Schelling begins by referring to his study of the *Critique of Pure Reason*—and to the efforts made to elaborate it by Reinhold and Fichte. His second work, *Of the I as Principle of Philosophy* (1795), is more expansive in this regard: he says that in this work he attempts to depict the results of the critical philosophy through a regression to a fundamental principle. On the other hand, he charges that "the way of the *Critique of Pure Reason* cannot possibly be the way of philosophy as science" (SW I, 153; UHK 65). At the beginning of the book, he goes on to enumerate several criticisms of the form that critical philosophy takes in the first *Critique*. He proposes to give "an exposition of Kant's philosophy based on superior principles" (SW I, 154; UHK 66)—an exposition that uncovers "the still more original sense of his thoughts" (SW I, 155; UHK 66). In this spirit, then, he speaks of the need "to follow the great new lead which philosophy is beginning to take . . . to map a new course for the human mind" (SW I, 158; UHK 68). He offers then a striking image of this new beginning, this taking up and extending of the Kantian beginning: "Nature has wisely provided for human eyes the device of dawn as a transition to broad daylight. Small wonder then that wisps of fog remain in the lower regions while the mountain peaks already shimmer in the radiance of the sun. But once the first blush of morning appears, the sun cannot fail" (SW I, 159; UHK 69). He goes on to speak of bringing about "the beautiful day of knowledge" (SW I, 159; UHK 69).

We have noted that the new beginning that Kant launches is a critical interrogation of pure reason. The German Idealists take up the results of this critique but then proceed in two directions that they regard as going beyond Kant. On the one hand, they carry out a regress to a fundamental principle, a ground, of all knowledge. Though Kant did not entirely fail to carry out such a regress, this principle (ground) remained indeterminate. On the other hand, the German Idealists renewed the endeavors of metaphysics as it had been made possible by critique. These two developments came together in the mature work of Schelling and Hegel, especially Hegel's *Science of Logic*. This marks their apogee, yet it involves a comprehensive and fundamental transformation of both developments.

Let us return now to Kant. We have already seen that the primary task of the *Critique of Pure Reason* is to show how purely rational knowledge is possible. In other words, the task is to show how there can be knowledge that is *not* gained through experience of objects, knowledge that does not in any way rely on experience (on what is presented to or through our senses)—that is, knowledge gained purely through reason, a priori knowledge. So the primary task of the *Critique* is to show how a priori knowledge of objects is possible. Such a demonstration required a kind of revolution—a basic shift in the very conception of knowledge and objects.

Kant draws a comparison with the revolution that had occurred in astronomy, the one initiated by Copernicus. Thus the *Critique of Pure Reason* is said to carry out a kind of Copernican revolution. All the German Idealists will consider this revolution as a decisive moment in the new beginning launched by Kant. Here is Kant's description of it:

> Hitherto it has been assumed that all our knowledge must conform to objects. But all attempts to extend our knowledge of objects by establishing something in regard to them *a priori*, by means of concepts, have, on this assumption, ended in failure. We must therefore make trial whether we may not have more success in the tasks of metaphysics, if we suppose that objects must conform to our knowledge. This would agree better with what is desired, namely, that it should be possible to have knowledge of objects *a priori*, determining something in regard to them prior to their being given. We should then be proceeding precisely on the lines of Copernicus' primary hypothesis. Failing of satisfactory progress in explaining the movements of the heavenly bodies on the supposition that they all revolved round the spectator, he tried whether he might not have better success if he made the spectator to revolve and the stars to remain at rest. A similar experiment can be tried in metaphysics, as regards the *intuition* of objects. If intuition must conform to the constitution of the objects, I do not see how we could know anything of the latter *a priori*; but if the object (as object of the senses) must conform to the constitution of our faculty of intuition, I have no difficulty in conceiving such a possibility. (B xvi–xvii)

What is the point of the analogy? Copernicus explained the apparent movement of the planets by taking into account the movement of the observer—that is, of the earth. In other words, the apparent movement is treated as the resultant of two movements: the actual movement of the planet *and* the movement of the observer (the earth).

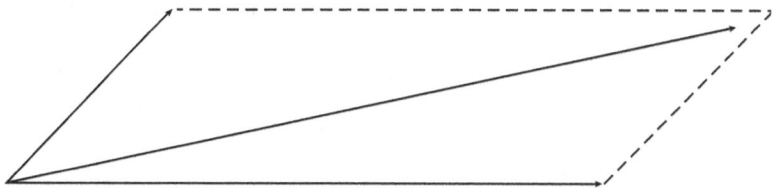

Analogously, in the *Critique of Pure Reason*, the object as experienced (the "appearance") is treated as the "resultant" of the object itself (the "thing in itself") *and* that which is contributed (bestowed on the thing) by the subject. In other words, the constitution of the object (as it appears, as an appearance) is determined in part by the thing itself (as it is apart from any experience of it) *and* in part by what is contributed to it by the subject.

Now there is one further step. By reflection on itself, the subject can determine what it contributes to the appearance (to the object as it appears). Specifically, it can recognize that it confers (projects) on objects certain structures that the objects otherwise would not have. Then, if indeed this structure is projected on every appearance, I know a priori that every appearance must have this structure—and I know this independently of any experience of objects. Kant says, "We can know *a priori* of things only what we ourselves put into them" (B xvii).

3. German Idealism and the End of Philosophy

With Kant and the German Idealists, there was not only the sense of a new beginning; there was also a sense that this beginning was so decisive, so radical that by carrying it through, philosophy would be brought to a certain *end*—in both senses of the word. It involves the *termination* of the futile or incomplete efforts of the past but also a *fulfillment* in the sense that finally, philosophy will have come into its own. Thus it is in German Idealism that a discourse on the end of philosophy first appears. It is a discourse that continues in our time in thinkers such as Heidegger and Derrida—and in my own work. This sense of a new beginning so decisive that it promises an imminent end is already voiced in 1781 by Kant at the end of the *Critique of Pure Reason*: "If the reader has had the courtesy and patience to accompany me along this path, he may now judge for himself whether, if he cares to lend his aid in making this path into a high-road, it may not be possible to achieve before the end of the present century what many centuries have not been able to accomplish; namely, to secure for human reason complete satisfaction in regard to that with which it has all along so eagerly occupied itself, though hitherto in vain" (A 856/B 884). This is expressed more vigorously and assuredly in 1807 by Hegel in the preface to the *Phenomenology of Spirit*: "To help bring philosophy closer to the form of science, to the goal where it can lay aside the title 'love of knowledge' and be actual knowledge—that is what I have set myself to do" (HW 3, 14; PhS §5).

Merleau-Ponty puts most succinctly the view that with German Idealism, something comes to an end. In a lecture at the Collège de France in 1958–59 that was addressed to "the question of the possibility of philosophy today," he said: "With Hegel something comes to an end. After Hegel there is a philosophical void."[3] Here the "end" is not, as with Hegel, a matter of fulfillment, of achieving

---

3. Maurice Merleau-Ponty, *Themes from the Lectures at the Collège de France, 1952–1960*, trans. John O'Neill (Evanston, IL: Northwestern University Press, 1970), 100.

the level of science but rather a kind of termination, a kind of exhaustion that left a void in place of philosophy.

In conclusion, let me cite two declarations by Heidegger regarding German Idealism. The first comes from his text on negativity in Hegel (1938–39). He speaks of a so-called common view, a prejudice regarding German Idealism: "What we encounter here is the common view that . . . German Idealism in general always remained the extravagant speculation of some fanciful minds and thus stood 'outside' of so-called life. To that one must respond that German Idealism as a whole . . . unfolds a historically effective force whose extent and limits we today cannot yet fathom because we are flooded by it from all directions without recognizing it" (GA 68, 7–8).[4] The second is the already cited passage from Heidegger's 1935 lectures *Introduction to Metaphysics*. Here he speaks about the so-called collapse of German Idealism. He refers to the spiritual situation in the first half of the nineteenth century, then writes: "It was then that occurred what is popularly and succinctly called the 'collapse of German Idealism.' This formula is a kind of shield behind which the already dawning spiritlessness, the dissolution of the spiritual energies, the rejection of all original inquiry into grounds and the human bond with the grounds, are hidden and masked. It was not German Idealism that collapsed; rather, the age was no longer strong enough to stand up to the greatness, breadth, and originality of that spiritual world" (GA 40, 49).[5] The question—for Heidegger and for us today—is whether we can gather the strength to reenter that spiritual world, even if from a certain distance.

4. Additional Remarks on Kant

Before continuing with the development of German Idealism, let me make several additional points regarding Kant. First, we have seen that appearances are compounded from two very different kinds of components: (1) That which derives from the thing itself—that is, sensations that result from the way the thing affects our senses. This is the material moment. (2) Forms that have their source in the subject. There are two kinds of forms: (i) Intuitive forms: these are the forms in which appearances are placed (namely, as one after another or as one next to another—that is, in order of succession or of coexistence, cf. Leibniz).[6]

---

4. Martin Heidegger, *Hegel*, trans. Joseph Arel and Niels Feuerhahn (Bloomington: Indiana University Press, 2015), 6–7.

5. Heidegger, *Introduction to Metaphysics*, 45.

6. [Editor's note: see Leibniz's view, as stated in his letter to Samuel Clarke: "Space is that order which renders bodies capable of being situated and by which they have a situation among themselves when they exist together, just as time is that order with respect to their successive position." Gottfried Wilhelm Leibniz, *The Leibniz-Clarke Correspondence*, ed. H. G. Alexander (Manchester: Manchester University Press, 1956), 42. See also the discussion in John Sallis, *Kant and the Spirit of Critique*, ed. Richard Rojcewicz (Bloomington: Indiana University Press, 2020), 27–28.]

Kant calls these the forms of pure intuition and identifies them as *space* and *time*. (ii) Rational or categorial forms: These are the forms by which appearances are structured or ordered (such that there are properties belonging to substances, for example) and not just a swarm of sensations. These moments are the *categories*. In the *Critique of Pure Reason*, Kant carries out a deduction whereby he shows that there are twelve categories, grouped under four headings: quantity (e.g., unity and plurality), quality (e.g., reality), relation (e.g., substance and accident, cause and effect), and modality (e.g., possibility and necessity).

Second, both intuitive and categorial forms originate from the subject—but what is the subject? The key lies in Kant's statement: "It must be possible for the 'I think' to accompany all my representations" (B 131). This means that in any experience, it is always possible to be aware of myself as the subject of the experience. This identifies two features that define the subject: (1) All representations involve an "I think." In other words, for every representation, there is an I that is the subject of the representation. Note that "representation" (*Vorstellung*) is a generic term, designating both intuition (*Anschauung*) and thinking (*Denken*). If there is an intuition, for example, there must be an I that intuits. Accordingly, the subject is the I that is the agent *of* every representation. (2) Yet the I does not represent (e.g., intuit) without being conscious of itself *as representing*. That is, in any experience, it is always possible for me to be aware of myself as subject of the experience. In other words, the subject is an I that is (or can always be) aware of itself, self-conscious.

So the subject is an I that is (1) conscious of every object that is experienced and (2) conscious of itself—that is, self-consciousness.

This dual character of the subject or I—that it is both consciousness and self-consciousness—is absolutely decisive for German Idealism. Fichte's entire *Wissenschaftslehre* proceeds from this dual character of the I: this is what is expressed in his three fundamental principles.

Third, we have seen that for an object to appear, it must embody the forms (intuitive and categorial) bestowed on it by the subject. But this entails that we can have no knowledge of things as they are in themselves, that is, as they are apart from the forms imposed on them by the subject. Thus things in themselves must be declared unknowable. This becomes a major point of controversy in the early development of German Idealism—and eventually in the debate between Fichte and Schelling/Hegel.

Fourth, we have focused so far on Kant's first *Critique*, which deals with reason in its full *theoretical* range, determining its possibility and limits. But the first *Critique* deals with reason *only* in its theoretical employment, not in its practical (moral) employment—that is, as determining will and action rather than objects. For the development of German Idealism, the second *Critique* (the *Critique of Practical Reason*) is hardly less important than the first. Its importance for German Idealism lies not so much in the moral principles that it grounds but rather in certain other accomplishments. Most importantly, Kant here gives his defense of freedom.

In the *Critique of Pure Reason*, the question of freedom versus determinism is taken up, but the result is an antinomy (the third): Whether everything takes place by natural causality *or* there is a causality through freedom—this question cannot be resolved by theoretical reason. All that can be shown is that freedom is possible. In the *Critique of Practical Reason*, Kant begins with what he calls a *fact of reason*. This fact is that we are bound by the moral law. This law is what Kant designates as the categorical imperative, one formulation of which reads: "Act only according to that maxim by which you can at the same time will that it should become a universal law" (AA 4, 421; FMM 38). It is on this basis that Kant establishes the reality of freedom: one can be bound by the moral law (i.e., obligated to act in accordance with it) *only if* one is free and not determined by natural causality. In other words, the moral law (= fact of reason) presupposes freedom—which is therefore real. "But freedom, among all the ideas of speculative reason, is the only one whose possibility we know a priori. We do not understand it, but we know it because it is the condition of the moral law, which we do know" (AA 5, 4; CPrR 4). In the same context, Kant writes: "All other concepts (those of God and immortality) which, as mere ideas, are unsupported by anything in speculative reason now attach themselves to the concept of freedom and gain, with it and through it, stability and objective reality" (AA 5, 4; CPrR 3). These ideas Kant calls "practical postulates." They cannot be proven by theoretical reason (as the *Critique of Pure Reason* shows). But if the reality of freedom is granted, then it is necessary to postulate immortality and the existence of God. (Kant shows this by a thorough, complex analysis of what it means to be bound by the moral law and yet to exist in the world of sense.) Finally, Kant writes: "The concept of freedom, insofar as its reality is proved by an apodictic law of practical reason, is the keystone of the whole architecture of the system of pure reason and even of speculative reason" (AA 5, 3–4; CPrR 3). For all the German Idealists, the centrality of the concept of freedom is decisive—even more than for Kant.

Fifth, as a result of the critical philosophy and its development in German Idealism, certain shifts take place in basic philosophical parameters. These alter the shape of philosophical thought once and for all—a transition without return. One decisive shift occurs with respect to reason itself. Whereas in the Enlightenment, the confidence in reason was virtually unlimited—the confidence in the capacity of reason to answer fundamental questions, to reshape society, and to replace myths and religion—reason is now submitted to critique, interrogated with respect to its possibilities and limits. In some ways, the force of reason will be retained and even critically enhanced in German Idealism. But, at the same time, the critical scrutiny of reason will serve to bring to the center another human power that in the Enlightenment had been regarded largely in a negative way: imagination.

This shift toward the imagination was already foreshadowed by Rousseau, who writes in *Émile*: "It is imagination that extends for us the limits of the possible."[7] It is unmistakable in the *Critique of Pure Reason*: "Synthesis in general [especially of thought and intuition, i.e., reason and sense] is the mere result of the power of imagination . . . without which we would have no knowledge whatsoever" (A 78/B 103). Imagination is even more prominent in the *Critique of Judgment*: it is at the center of the experience of beauty—both of art and of nature.

One of the results of the shift toward imagination is to emphasize the relation between philosophy and art. In German Idealism, art will turn out to have enormous significance for philosophy. In a later phase, that of Hegel's Berlin period (1820s), Hegel's lectures on the philosophy of art will constitute what Heidegger calls "the most comprehensive reflection on art that the West possesses" (GA 5, 68).[8] Also, in its earliest phase, the new philosophical beginning in German Idealism occurred in greatest proximity to the new beginning in poetry and literary theory: Sturm und Drang, German Romanticism. There were not only intellectual ties but also, in most cases, close personal ties among Fichte, Schelling, and Hegel *and* Goethe, Schiller, Hölderlin, Schlegel, and Novalis. We can therefore consider the imagination as one of the major parameters determining the orientation of the new beginning.

Sixth, as we have seen, another such parameter is freedom. But, along with the emphasis on freedom, the question of nature came to be posed in a new way. Previously (and still in the first *Critique*), freedom and nature were seen as utterly opposed, since nature was identified as the realm governed entirely by mechanical causality. But largely through the influence of Kant's *Critique of Judgment*, nature came to be regarded also—even primarily—in terms of beauty. As beautiful nature, it displays (according to the *Critique of Judgment*) a certain accord

---

7. Jean-Jacques Rousseau, *Emile or On Education*, trans. Allan Bloom (New York: Basic Books, 1979), 81.

8. Martin Heidegger, "Origin of the Work of Art," in *Basic Writings*, ed. David Farrell Krell, rev. and exp. ed. (New York: HarperCollins, 1993), 204.

with our freedom—it even provides "traces" in which something about the spirit could be discovered. Schelling will call nature "visible spirit" (SW II, 56; PGI 202). In this way, the modern Romantic conception of nature arose, expressed perhaps most beautifully and succinctly in Hölderlin's *Hyperion*. He writes of being placed "into the arms of nature, the changeless, quiet, and beautiful" (*in die Arme der Natur, der wandellosen, stillen, und schönen*).[9]

Finally, we saw above that the subject (the I) has a double character. On the one hand, the I is the subject of all my representations—that is, it is consciousness of all appearances (on which it confers intuitive and categorial forms). On the other hand, the I is also aware *of itself* as subject of all representations—that is, it is self-consciousness. In Kant's more fundamental analysis, the I is characterized as transcendental apperception. In this formulation, what Kant stresses is the unity of the I, its identity throughout the course of experience—and, as a result, the unity or coherence of appearances: "There can be in us no modes of knowledge, no connection or unity of one mode of knowledge with another, without that unity of consciousness which precedes all data of intuitions, and by relation to which representation of objects is alone possible. This pure original unchangeable consciousness I shall name *transcendental apperception*" (A 107). This theme is developed extensively in the *Critique of Pure Reason*.[10] But rather than following this treatment in all its intricacies, let us look at the broader question of self-knowledge—of its possibilities and limits.

Kant describes the manner in which the self is given (is experienced) in the inner intuition of oneself, that is, when we simply look within ourselves. As given in this way, the self is already determined by the forms projected on all objects (inner or outer) as they appear—specifically, by the pure intuition of time as well as the categories. Thus, in the intuition (hence in the concrete givenness) of oneself, the self is presented only as an appearance, not as it is in itself, not as self-in-itself. "Consciousness of self according to the determinations of our state in inner perception is merely empirical, and always changing. No fixed and abiding self can present itself in this flux of inner appearances" (A 107). Such consciousness Kant calls *inner sense* or *empirical apperception*. Through inner sense, the self does not appear to itself as it is but only as it appears.

Such consciousness (inner sense or empirical apperception) Kant contrasts with consciousness of the I as transcendental apperception. The unity of experience, the unity of the manifold of experiences, is the accomplishment of transcendental apperception, which consists in the I's referring of this manifold back to itself. "It must be possible for the 'I think' to accompany all my representations"

---

9. Friedrich Hölderlin, *Hyperion*, trans. Willard R. Trask, in *Hyperion and Selected Poems*, ed. Eric L. Santner (New York: Continuum, 1990), 3.

10. Cf. John Sallis, *The Gathering of Reason*, 2nd ed. (Albany: SUNY Press, 2005), 69–76.

(B 131). This statement—the very making or uttering of it—expresses, indeed enacts, the I's referring of the manifold back to itself. Yet this referring does not provide self-knowledge. Let me quote a decisive passage: "In the transcendental synthesis of the manifold of representations in general, and therefore in the synthetic original unity of apperception, I am conscious of myself, not as I appear to myself, nor as I am in myself, but only that I am. This *representation* is a *thinking*, not an *intuiting*" (B 157). We can formulate this in terms that bring us closer to German Idealism. The I refers the manifold back to itself. In other words, the I thinks or posits itself as that to which all representations belong and by which they are unified. In short, one can say regarding the I of transcendental apperception: it occurs as a *positing of itself*. With this, we arrive at the first principle of Fichte's *Wissenschaftslehre*.

5. The Oldest Systematic Program of German Idealism

In 1913, a single unsigned page with writing on both sides was put up for auction in Berlin. It came from the literary estate of Friedrich Förster, who had been a student of Hegel's and later one of the leaders of the *Freundeskreis Hegels*. At the auction, it was described as being by Hegel and was purchased by the Preußische Staatsbibliothek. Then, in 1917, it was published, with commentary, by Franz Rosenzweig with the title (added by Rosenzweig) "Das älteste Systemprogramm des deutschen Idealismus" ("The Oldest Systematic Program of German Idealism"). Ever since its publication, there has been enormous controversy about it, both philological and philosophical. All the research and discussion have been brought together in the volume *Mythologie der Vernunft*, edited by Christoph Jamme and Helmut Schneider.[11]

Much of the discussion concerned the authorship. The text is indisputably in Hegel's handwriting. However, Rosenzweig could not square the ideas expressed in the fragment with Hegel's ideas. In particular, what is said about the state and about the supremacy of the aesthetic and of poetry is quite different from Hegel's published views. Rosenzweig thought that these ideas were also different from Hegel's earlier ideas, though at the time not much was known about Hegel's early development. So Rosenzweig argued that Schelling was the author and Hegel merely copied it. Indeed, several things said in the fragment are suggestive of Schelling: the transformation of metaphysics into ethics, the supremacy of the aesthetic, and the emphasis on myth.

However, in 1926, Wilhelm Böhm and others showed that these apparently Schellingean ideas were not, in fact, Schelling's concern at the time the fragment was written. At this time, Schelling was still Fichtean, and the aesthetic did not

---

11. Christoph Jamme and Helmut Schneider, eds., *Mythologie der Vernunft: Hegels "ältestes Systemprogramm des deutschen Idealismus"* (Frankfurt: Suhrkamp, 1984).

yet have the significance for him that it would come to have. Böhm argued that the author was Hölderlin. As evidence, he mentions Hölderlin's aesthetic Platonism, attested—for example—by a letter in which Hölderlin tells of his plans for an essay on aesthetic ideas, which will take the form of a commentary on Plato's *Phaedrus*. This letter also mentions that at the time of the fragment, beauty was Hölderlin's central systematic idea. Nonetheless, it is still maintained by Böhm that Hegel merely copied down the fragment—that Schelling got it from Hölderlin and loaned it to Hegel.

Finally, in 1965, Otto Pöggeler proposed and argued that the author was Hegel. This is the most widely held view, and it is maintained by Jamme and Schneider. Pöggeler was able to make his case because of the thorough, rigorous research on Hegel's early development that was carried out in the 1950s and 1960s at the Hegel Archive. Among other things, Pöggeler shows that the concept of myth, of a mythology of reason expressed in the fragment can be attributed to no one else but Hegel—though an earlier, more Romantic Hegel. Pöggeler's case was strengthened in 1975 when Dieter Henrich showed that very probably the fragment had come from Hegel's own *Nachlaß*.

On the fragment there is no date. Obviously, in the dispute about authorship, the dating was important. The watermark on the paper allowed scholars to identify the manufacturer and even the approximate date when the paper was produced: 1796–97. This is confirmed by a comparison of the handwriting with the text of a poem and three letters written by Hegel during this time.

An important question is whether the page was simply written from the beginning as a single page. In this case, the first words, "eine Ethik," could be taken to be a kind of title. But if this is a fragmentary page that has been detached, then these words would form the end of a sentence carried over from the previous page. Jamme and Schneider argue for the second alternative. They mention that in Hegel's manuscripts, there is no other example of a title written in lowercase letters. Also, there are numerous other fragments of Hegel's that begin with partial sentences carried over from a preceding page. What, then, might one presume was the sentence that was carried over and ended in "eine Ethik"? Jamme and Schneider suggest that it probably had to do with the question: What can metaphysics still mean after Kant? The answer would be: an ethics. This would clarify the first sentence, which begins, "Since all metaphysics will henceforth fall into morals . . ." and immediately thereafter mentions Kant and the practical postulates (PGI 161).

Let us now look at the fragment from a more philosophical perspective. It outlines a progression similar to what is found throughout German Idealism—especially in such works as Schelling's *System of Transcendental Idealism* and Hegel's *Phenomenology of Spirit*. Here it is a progression through "a complete system of all ideas." We should note two things here: (1) The text calls this systematic progression "ethics" or "morals." It says that it is into this that metaphysics henceforth falls. (2) The text says that the system of ideas is equivalent to all the practical postulates.

Now, this system (the new metaphysics) is *ethics*—not primarily in the sense of providing principles of conduct or the means for making moral decisions but rather in the sense determined by Kant's *Critique of Practical Reason*, that is, as a metaphysics of the absolutely *free* subject. Specifically, it is a metaphysics that (1) begins with the absolutely free subject, just as Kant's practical philosophy begins with that fact of reason that attests to the freedom of the subject—namely, the moral law or our being bound by moral law. It is also a metaphysics that (2) moves from the free subject—determining what must be true granted the freedom of the subject. These truths are what Kant called practical postulates. Hence we see why the fragment identified ideas (through which it progresses) as practical postulates. The fragment notes that Kant has given only an example of these. In other words, he has not developed the complete system of practical postulates or ideas. Most of the fragment is devoted to tracing out this system of ideas. It begins with the concept of the self as an absolutely free being. Then it moves through a series of ever-higher ideas until finally it reaches the highest idea: the idea of beauty.

Let me trace the progression in more detail. Just as with Kant, freedom is the starting point from which he advances to the practical postulates, so in the fragment, the progression begins with freedom: "The first idea is naturally the conception of *my self* as an absolutely free being" (PGI 161). It is also characterized as a "self-conscious being." As in Kant, the self is free *as* self-determining, giving the law to itself, and thus as self-related. The German Idealists will radicalize this self-relatedness.

Secondly, there is the world or nature. Or, more precisely, nature emerges simultaneously (*zugleich*), along with the free, self-conscious self. So it is not as though the self first exists *and then* creates the world but rather the world emerges simultaneously. (Here the question arises: What is the character of this simultaneity—this correlation that is also creation? It is not necessarily temporal.) The text says that in physics (in investigating the natural world), the question will be "How must a world be constituted for a moral being?" In other words, the world will be regarded (hypothetically at least) as having a character that would be in accord with the character of the subject (as a free, moral subject).[12] Alluding to Schiller, the text adds that we would give our physics wings again. (But this would not, of course, relieve it of the need for experimentation.)

Then comes man's work (*Menschenwerk*). This means primarily: the political, that is, the state. What is remarkable about this idea (that of the state) is

---

12. Cf. Kant's discussion of the "purposiveness of nature" in the third *Critique*, AA 5, 195–96; CJ 36–37. See also his discussion of intellectual interest in the beautiful, AA 5, 300–301; CJ 167–68.

that it is *not* an idea: "There is no idea of the *state* because the state is something mechanical" (PGI 161). Here the machine exemplifies what is opposed to freedom (cf. Schiller and Fichte). Since "only that which is the object of freedom is called idea" and since the state embodies the opposite of freedom, it is *not* an idea. The text concludes: "We must therefore go beyond the state!" In other words, the state "should cease." In this connection, the text mentions "eternal peace" (a reference to Kant's "perpetual peace") and says that this is subordinate to a higher idea (PGI 162). However, the text does not say explicitly what this higher idea is. It could be the "idea of a moral world," which is mentioned at the next, higher stage. The text also mentions "the principles for a history of the human race." This would not be a stage in the progression but a negative undertaking, an exposing of such miserable work as the state. The text does not say what—if anything—is to replace the state. We can therefore pose the question: Could there be a form of community that, unlike the state and all its institutions, would not be mechanical? Would such a form of community represent a stage in the progression that is being sketched here?

The text then proceeds to the higher ideas—of a moral world, deity, immortality (here again we encounter Kant's practical postulates). These we carry within ourselves: God and immortality are to be sought not outside but within each of us.

At last, the progression reaches its culmination: "Finally, the idea which unites all, the idea of *beauty*, the word taken in the higher Platonic sense" (PGI 162). Correspondingly, the highest act of reason is an *aesthetic* act, and thus "the philosopher must possess just as much aesthetic power as the poet" (PGI 162). The text also mentions that "truth and goodness are united like sisters only in beauty." In other words, both theoretical reason ("truth") and practical reason ("goodness") are born from the aesthetic or poetic. (Here we see a rethinking and ordering of the three Kantian *Critiques*.)

Finally, the text addresses the question of a *sensual* religion (*eine sinnliche Religion*) and declares that this is needed both by the multitude and by philosophy: "Monotheism of reason and the heart, polytheism of the imagination and art—that is what we need" (PGI 162). Thus the text refers to a *mythology of reason* in which our ideas will be made aesthetic and concludes by declaring that this will be "the last and greatest work of mankind" (PGI 163). So here again, in this *beginning*, there is an anticipation of the *end* that will be reached by following through what here begins.

2. Reception of the Critical Philosophy

THE CONTEXT IN which German Idealism arose was determined by Kant and the reception—often critical—of Kant in the 1780s and early 1790s. Both Fichte and Schelling began as Kantians, and their first major works were aimed at developing Kant's critical philosophy in a more rigorous way. The need to develop Kant's thought in this way arose largely from the criticism leveled against Kant by such figures as Jacobi, Reinhold, and Schulze. But before we consider these three, let me say a few words about the early reception of the first *Critique*.

1. The Garve-Feder Review

The *Critique of Pure Reason* appeared in May 1781. Initially, it had almost no effect—no reviews of it appeared in 1781. The only responses that Kant received were complaints that it was obscure, indeed unintelligible. In the *Prolegomena*, Kant complains that it had been "honored by silence" (AA 4, 380; PFM 129). One of the earliest expositors later said that it was initially regarded as "a sealed book" consisting of nothing but "hieroglyphics."[1] However, at the beginning of 1782, the silence was broken. An anonymous review appeared in an obscure journal called *Göttingische gelehrte Anzeigen*. This was not only the first but also what would become the most notorious review of the first *Critique*.

From its beginning, the review is polemical—indeed, quite negative. Kant's work "exercises the understanding of its readers—even if it does not always instruct it." It "often strains their attention to the point of exhaustion," and so forth.[2] The basic charge that it makes against the first *Critique* (at first mainly by implication, but then more and more directly) is that Kant's transcendental idealism is basically the same as Berkeley's subjective idealism, which reduces all things to mere representations in the mind. The claim is that Kant, like Berkeley, regards experience as a mere tissue of representations, and so he makes it impossible to distinguish what is actual from what is merely imagined or possible. Thus the *Critique* has the effect of destroying our belief in the reality of the

---

1. Johann Schultz, *Erläuterungen über des Herrn Professor Kant Critik der reinen Vernunft* (Königsberg: Dengel, 1784), 6, 7. See Frederick C. Beiser, *The Fate of Reason: German Philosophy from Kant to Fichte* (Cambridge, MA: Harvard University, 1987), 172.

2. "The Göttingen Review," in *Kant's Early Critics: The Empiricist Critique of the Theoretical Philosophy*, ed. Brigitte Sassen (Cambridge: Cambridge University Press, 2000), 53.

external world. As the review says at the end, according to the *Critique*, "everything of which we can know and say something is merely representation and law of thought."³

Kant was outraged at the review since he thought that he had been deliberately misunderstood and distorted. It was largely because of this review that Kant decided to reformulate his position in what became the *Prolegomena* (1783). It also led Kant to write the section "Refutation of Idealism" in the second edition of the *Critique of Pure Reason* (1787). In the *Prolegomena*, there is a long "Appendix" as well as several independent sections ("Remarks") and notes that are addressed to this review. (For the comments in the "Appendix," see AA 4, 372–73; PFM 121–22.) Throughout, Kant's reply is that he does *not* deny the existence of things outside the subject's representations: he affirms the existence of things in themselves and denies only that we can know them. For example, in "Remark II" at the end of part I, he refers to the idealism (viz. Berkeley's) that regards only representations—and not external objects—as existing. He then continues: "I, on the contrary, say that things as objects of our senses existing outside us are given, but we know nothing of what they may be in themselves, knowing only their appearances, that is, the representations which they cause in us by affecting our senses. Consequently I grant by all means that there are bodies outside us" (AA 4, 289; PFM 36). Now, one could see a subtle shift, at least of emphasis: whereas the first edition of the *Critique* stresses that objects of experience are appearances and not things in themselves, the *Prolegomena* stresses that they are appearances *of* things in themselves.

Who wrote the review? When Kant wrote the *Prolegomena*, he still did not know, but there he demanded that the author reveal himself and take responsibility. In July 1783, a few months after the *Prolegomena* appeared, Kant received a letter from Christian Garve. He admitted to writing the review, but he disowned the published version on the grounds that it had been thoroughly mutilated by the journal editor. Garve pleads that the published version contains "only some phrases" from his original.⁴ He does not name the editor—but Kant would have known it was Johann Georg Heinrich Feder. Ever since, this has been known as the Garve-Feder review.

In his letter replying to Garve, Kant is polite, though he condemns the editor for filling the review with "the breath of pure animosity" (AA 10, 337).⁵ Kant stresses that "it is not at all metaphysics that the *Critique* is doing but an entirely new science, never before attempted, namely, the critique of . . . reason"

---

3. "The Göttingen Review," in *Kant's Early Critics*, 58.
4. See Beiser, *The Fate of Reason*, 175–76.
5. Kant to Christian Garve, August 7, 1783, in Immanuel Kant, *Correspondence*, trans. Arnulf Zweig (Cambridge: Cambridge University Press, 1999), 196.

(AA 10, 340).⁶ He argues that the *Critique* should not be judged by whether or not it agrees with this or that metaphysics. In any case, the review and Kant's response brought the critical philosophy to the attention of philosophers throughout Germany. It became clear to all parties that the critical philosophy was something to be reckoned with.

2. Jacobi's Critique of Reason and the Thing in Itself

Friedrich Heinrich Jacobi was one of the first philosophers in Germany to make a frontal attack on the ideals of the Enlightenment, especially the confidence in reason. In 1787 he published *David Hume on Belief, or Idealism and Realism*. It is cast as a dialogue between two persons designated simply as "I" and "he." Most importantly, it has an appendix "On Transcendental Idealism." In the dialogue, Jacobi defends Hume's skepticism regarding reason—that by reason we cannot prove causal connection or even the persisting identity of the self. However, Jacobi does not simply endorse Hume's skeptical conclusions. Rather, he argues that they indicate the limits of reason and so point to the need for something other than reason.

In this book, he also relates his discovery, years earlier, of Spinoza. The lesson he learned from Spinoza was negative: he says that what Spinoza demonstrated for him was that reason necessarily leads finally to atheism and fatalism. He refers to Spinoza's denial of human freedom and to Spinoza's God, which consists of the single universal substance of which everything else is merely a mode. This is a naturalistic, completely immanent, impersonal God that could not be responsive to humans—so that, for Jacobi and many others, the affirmation of such a God is tantamount to atheism. Furthermore, Jacobi maintained that Spinoza is the paradigm of metaphysics—that is, that speculative reason inevitably leads to the same conclusions as Spinoza. Thus we are faced with the choice: either follow reason and become atheists and fatalists *or* accept an irrational faith that allows us to affirm God, freedom, and all else that rational skepticism undermines.

In *David Hume*, Jacobi also contrasts idealism and realism. The idealist is the one who follows reason and is inevitably led to become a skeptic—or what Jacobi calls a *nihilist* (he first gave the word currency). This is the one who is driven to deny the existence of all reality independent of his own sensations (such as external objects, God, other subjects, and even his own persisting self). The antithesis to this is the realist, who believes in independent existence. But this position cannot be demonstrated: it is a matter of faith (and not only in a narrow religious sense).

---

6. Kant to Christian Garve, August 7, 1783, in Kant, *Correspondence*, 198.

To *David Hume*, Jacobi added an appendix titled "On Transcendental Idealism." The criticism that he aims here at Kant has to be seen against the background of his more general attack on the aspirations of reason. Already here he begins to see Kant rather than Spinoza as the one in whom the consequences of following reason become most evident. This theme he picks up in the 1799 *Letter to Fichte*. There it is the Kantian philosophy as developed by Fichte that represents the final consequence of rational idealism: "A pure, that is, completely immanent philosophy, a philosophy all of a piece, a genuine system of reason, is only possible in the Fichtean manner" (PGI 126). Jacobi's general criticism of Kant—and later of Fichte—is that in these systems we remain caught inside the circle of our own consciousness, which represents nothing existing outside. (So his criticism, up to this point, goes in the same direction as the Garve-Feder review.) Yet Jacobi acknowledges (unlike the Garve-Feder review) the importance of the thing in itself for Kant. However, he regards the thing in itself as a final, desperate effort by Kant to keep his philosophy from falling into nihilism—an effort that ultimately failed.

Let us turn to Jacobi's specific—very famous—criticism of the Kantian thing in itself. It proceeds in two steps. First, he criticizes Kant's assumption that objects are the causes of our representations. Empirical objects (appearances) cannot be taken as such, because Kant says that they are nothing but representations, that is, nothing outside our representations. Transcendental objects (as he calls the things in themselves) cannot be affirmed to be such causes, for Kant says that we cannot have any knowledge of them, hence we cannot know that they are the causes of representations.

Second, if it is thus inconsistent for Kant to assume that objects are the cause of our representations, it is also necessary for him to make this assumption, because he assumes that our sensibility is passive—that is, acted on by something. So the assumption that objects—in particular, things in themselves—cause our representations is inconsistent with Kant's system and yet necessary to it. As Jacobi puts it in his famous statement from the appendix: "Without this assumption I could not enter the system, but with this assumption I could not remain inside it."[7]

Let me mention a final passage by Jacobi from a long (and famous) letter to Moses Mendelssohn from November 1783: "As I see it, the first task of the philosopher is to disclose and to reveal existence [*Dasein zu enthüllen und zu offenbaren*]. Explanation is only a means, a way to this goal: it is the first task, but it is never the last. The last task is what cannot be explained: the irresolvable, immediate,

---

7. Friedrich Heinrich Jacobi, "On Transcendental Idealism," in *Kant's Early Critics*, 173. Original edition: *David Hume über den Glauben, oder Idealismus und Realismus, ein Gespräch* (Breslau: Löwe, 1787), 223.

and simple."[8] Let me highlight two points in this passage. First, Jacobi's reference to what cannot be explained, to the irresolvable, is echoed later in his *Letter to Fichte*: "By the true, I understand something which is prior to and outside of knowing; which first gives knowing and the capacity for knowing, for reason a value.... With his reason, the human being is not given the capacity for a science of the true, but merely the feeling and consciousness of his ignorance thereof: *presentiment* of the true" (PGI 131). Note that in these passages Jacobi does not simply oppose reason and faith; instead, he hints at a function of reason that, instead of just leading to nihilism, would have a more positive—even Socratic role.

Second, the passage from the letter to Mendelssohn also indicates a positive function of philosophy in another direction: philosophy's task is not to explain (which is at best a means) but to *reveal* and *disclose* that which actually exists. In both of these respects—though Jacobi does not acknowledge it—Fichte will take up and develop what Jacobi merely suggests.

3. Reinhold's Internal Criticism and Development of Kant's Philosophy

Whereas Jacobi's criticism of Kant is external, from a position completely outside the critical philosophy, Karl Leonhard Reinhold's criticism is internal. His criticisms are not meant to refute the critical philosophy but to expose ways in which it needs to be developed further.

Yet initially Reinhold is more a spokesman for the critical philosophy than a critic of it. He first read the first *Critique* in autumn 1785 and immediately became a disciple of Kant. In fact, he set out to write a book explaining Kant's philosophy. The result was *Letters concerning the Kantian Philosophy* (*Briefe über die kantische Philosophie*), which appeared in installments beginning in August 1786 and as a book in 1790. In the *Letters* he praised Kant: the *Critique of Pure Reason* is "the greatest masterpiece of the philosophical spirit."[9] Even later, when he went beyond simply explaining Kant's philosophy, Reinhold still expressed this enormous respect for Kant. For example, in *The Foundation of Philosophical Knowledge* (1791), he said that in Kant are combined the spirits of Leibniz, Hume, Locke, and Newton. Kant "made advances such as were never made by any single thinker before" (BKH 61).[10] In his *Letters*, Reinhold focused especially on Kant's relevance for current ethical and religious debates, including that waged by

---

8. Quoted in Beiser, *The Fate of Reason*, 67. Original edition: Friedrich Heinrich Jacobi, *Über die Lehre des Spinoza in Briefen an den Herrn Moses Mendelssohn* (Brelau: Löwe, 1785), 31–32.

9. Karl Leonhard Reinhold, *Briefe über die kantische Philosophie*, vol. 1 (Leipzig: Göschen, 1790), 106. See Beiser, *The Fate of Reason*, 234.

10. Karl Leonhard Reinhold, *Ueber das Fundament des philosophischen Wissens* (Jena: Mauke, 1791), 55.

Jacobi. He presented Kantian practical reason as a middle ground between theoretical reason and mere faith or feeling.

Letters was an immediate and enormous success. This book, even more than Kant's own, was responsible for making the critical philosophy the center of philosophical attention in Germany. Reinhold wrote to Kant and asked him whether he would publicly acknowledge that Reinhold's book embodies a correct understanding of the critical philosophy. Kant was very pleased with the Letters and wrote back to Reinhold in December 1787 praising the book. In January 1788 Kant's essay "On the Use of Teleological Principles in Philosophy" appeared, in which he publicly praised the Letters as "a contribution to the common cause of speculative and practical reason" (AA 8, 183).[11]

On the basis of the Letters, Reinhold received a professorship at the University of Jena. There he held lectures on Kant's philosophy before huge audiences, and Jena gained a reputation as a center of Kantianism in Germany. Reinhold taught there from 1788 to 1794 and was succeeded by Fichte (1794–99), Schelling (1798–1803), and Hegel (1801–6). Let me briefly sketch what was happening in Jena during this time. Hegel and Schelling launched the Critical Journal of Philosophy (1801–2). Friedrich Schlegel also taught philosophy at Jena. In 1798 he and his brother August Wilhelm launched the journal Athenäum, the most important vehicle of early German Romanticism. A. W. Schlegel began translating Shakespeare into German. Schiller was a professor of history at Jena. Hölderlin was there, studying with Fichte. Twenty-five kilometers away was Weimar, where the intellectual-artistic circle around Goethe was located (including Herder and Wieland). Seldom has there been such a concentration of major thinkers and poets, and seldom such creative productivity. Dieter Henrich writes of this period in Jena: "We can compare its richness of productivity to that which occurred between the death of Socrates in 399 BC and the death of Aristotle seventy-seven years later."[12]

Let us return to tracing Reinhold's development. By 1787 he began to think that the critical philosophy, as Kant had presented it, needed to be recast in a more systematic form, with an emphasis on representation (Vorstellung). So in 1789 Reinhold published Attempt at a New Theory of the Human Power of Representation (German: Versuch einer neuen Theorie des menschlichen Vorstellungsvermögens). He refined his theory in two subsequent books: Contributions to the Rectification of Misconceptions Hitherto Held by Philosophers (1790) and Foundations of Philosophical Knowledge (1791). He called his system Elementarphilosophie, a term taken from Kant's Elementarlehre. In the first Critique, Kant had

---

11. See Beiser, The Fate of Reason, 236.
12. Dieter Henrich, Between Kant and Hegel: Lectures on German Idealism, ed. David S. Pacini (Cambridge, MA: Harvard University Press, 2003), 76.

identified "elements" as concepts that are pure (not empirical) and fundamental (not derivative) (A 64/B 89).

Reinhold sent his *Attempt* to Kant. This time, Kant was less enthusiastic. In his letter to Reinhold on September 21, 1791, he writes that he will be happy to acknowledge that the book "constitutes a great contribution to the critique of reason. I plan to acknowledge this publicly one of these days, as soon as I can get clear about those parts that are still obscure to me" (AA 11, 288).[13] Then he goes on to say, in effect, that the critique really does not need to be recast more systematically.

Reinhold's most general criticism of Kant was that he had not put his philosophy on a firm foundation. In other words, he had not developed it as a system derived from a single fundamental principle. Reinhold refers to Kant's deductions of the categories as an example of his lack of systematic methodology: Kant does not derive the twelve categories from a single principle but simply picks them up from the traditional table of logical judgments.

Reinhold also criticizes Kant's treatment of the concept of representation (*Vorstellung*). In the first *Critique*, this is the generic concept under which there are specific forms: intuitions (pure and sensible), concepts of the understanding, and ideas of reason. As expressed succinctly by Reinhold in his *Attempt*: "The term *representation* encompasses in its wider sense sensation, thought, intuition, concept, idea, in a word everything which occurs *in our consciousness* as an immediate effect of sensing, thinking, intuiting, comprehending."[14] His criticism is that Kant did not investigate representation as such but only the specific forms, which he consequently treated in isolation rather than in their systematic connection. Reinhold thought that much of the dispute and misunderstanding regarding the critical philosophy was a result of this lack.

Now in *The Foundation of Philosophical Knowledge*, Reinhold indicates that there are two basic moves that must be made in order to go from critical metaphysics (as in Kant) to the system (*Elementarphilosophie*) by which the critique would first be systematized and grounded. First comes the move from objects of knowledge to the faculty (power) of knowledge. This is necessary because what is determined regarding objects of knowledge can be grounded only by investigating the faculties of knowledge.

> This science, which Kant did not establish, would have to be distinguished from the *metaphysics* he did establish thus: whereas the latter is the science of the characteristics (determined *a priori*) of *objects proper*, the former would

---

13. Kant to Karl Leonhard Reinhold, September 21, 1791, in Kant, *Correspondence*, 390.

14. Karl Leonhard Reinhold, *Essay on a New Theory of the Human Capacity for Representation*, trans. Tim Mehigan and Barry Empson (Berlin/New York: De Gruyter, 2011), 96; book 2, §IX. Original edition: *Versuch einer neuen Theorie des menschlichen Vorstellungsvermögens* (Prague and Jena: Widtmann and Mauke, 1789), 209.

> have to be the science of the characteristics (determined *a priori*) of *mere representations*. The metaphysics has as its object the objects of experience, i.e., what can be cognized *a posteriori* by being represented through the *a priori* forms of sensible representation and of the concepts; the other science would have for its object those very forms, but precisely as what is originally knowable *a priori*. Or again, one is the science of empirical nature inasmuch as this can be known *a priori*; the other would be the science of the empirical faculty of cognition, which is made up of sensibility and understanding. (BKH 67)[15]

We should note that Kant recognized this to some extent in that he referred not only to an objective deduction but also to a subjective deduction (cf. A xvi–xvii). But, especially in the second edition of the *Critique*, he stressed the primacy of the objective deduction.

The second move is from the faculty of knowledge to the faculty of representation. The faculties of empirical knowledge are sensibility and understanding. The faculty of pure knowing is reason. The faculty of the practical is desire, defined in the second *Critique* as "the faculty of causing through its ideas the reality of the objects of these ideas" (AA 5, 9n; CPrR 9n). All these are specific forms of the faculty of representation, and their systematic connection can be established only by regressing to the faculty of representation.

> This science of the *faculty of cognition* would have to be *preceded* by another that establishes its foundation. This other science too would be a science of sensibility, understanding and reason—not, however, inasmuch as these are identical with the faculty of cognition, but inasmuch as they stand in common at its foundation (and indeed, at the foundation of the *faculty of desire* as well). It would be the science of the *a priori* form of *representing* through sensibility, understanding and reason; on this form depends the form of knowledge, as well as that of desire. In a word, it would be the science of the *entire faculty of representation as such*. (BKH 67)[16]

How, then, is the *Elementarphilosophie* actually carried out? It begins with a single, foundational, self-evident first principle—a fundamental principle (*Grundsatz*). This principle is a description of a self-revealing fact of consciousness: "The concept of representation can only be drawn from the CONSCIOUSNESS of an *actual fact*. This fact alone, *qua fact*, must *ground* the foundation of the Philosophy of the Elements—for otherwise the foundation cannot rest, without circularity, on any philosophically demonstrable proposition" (BKH 70).[17] The principle puts aside all metaphysical presuppositions regarding the nature of the subject and object—even those that Kant continued to assume in the *Critique of Pure*

---

15. Reinhold, *Ueber das Fundament des philosophischen Wissens*, 70–71.
16. Reinhold, *Ueber das Fundament des philosophischen Wissens*, 71.
17. Reinhold, *Ueber das Fundament des philosophischen Wissens*, 77–78.

Reason, such as the dualism of sensibility and understanding (the "two stems") and the unknowability of the thing in itself.

The principle is stated in a slightly indirect way in *Foundation*: "It is not through any inference of reason that we know *that in consciousness representation is distinguished through the subject from both object and subject and is referred to both*, but through simple *reflection* upon the actual fact of consciousness" (BKH 70).[18] The formulation in *Contributions* is a bit clearer: "Representation is distinguished in consciousness by the subject from the subject and the object, and is referred to both."[19] This is called the principle of consciousness (*der Satz des Bewusstseins*). Though there are other fundamental principles, Reinhold contends that "*only one absolutely fundamental explanation* [i.e., principle] *is possible in philosophy*" (BKH 80).[20]

The sense of the principle can be explained as follows. First, the subject refers (relates) representation to itself, in the sense that representation is possible only if there is a subject who has it and is aware of having it. Representation must be *for someone*. Second, the subject refers its representation to an object, in the sense that representation must be a representation *of* something—that is, there must be something that it represents. Third, the subject distinguishes the representation from the object, in the sense that the representation cannot be (identical with) what it represents. If representation were indistinguishable from its object, then it would not represent it. Fourth, the subject distinguishes representation from itself: one who represents is not the same as the representation itself. These four moments are included in the following diagram:

1) Subject ⟵——— Representation   Object

2) Subject   Representation ———⟶ Object

3) Subject   Representation ≠ Object

4) Subject ≠ Representation   Object

From this fundamental principle, Reinhold then goes on to further principles that can be deduced from it, including (1) the principle that representations

---

18. Reinhold, *Ueber das Fundament des philosophischen Wissens*, 78.
19. Karl Leonhard Reinhold, *Beyträge zur Berichtigung bisheriger Missverständnisse der Philosophen*, vol. 1 (Jena: Mauke, 1790), 167.
20. Reinhold, *Ueber das Fundament des philosophischen Wissens*, 101.

consist of *form* (by which they are related to the subject) and *content* (by which they relate to objects); (2) the principle that the faculty of representation consists of an active and a passive capacity; and (3) the principle that there can be no representation of the thing in itself (since the object of representation is transformed by the active capacity of the subject). Thus, like Kant, Reinhold retains the thing in itself to explain the origin of the content of representations.

With his *Elementarphilosophie*, Reinhold believed he had established the critical philosophy as science, thus bringing the critical breakthrough to its completion:

> Because it only paved the way for the Philosophy of the Elements without actually laying it down, *critical* philosophy could only premise its proofs and arguments with incomplete expositions. But the complete expositions of the Philosophy of the Elements could never have been discovered if these very arguments drawn from the *Critique*'s incomplete expositions had not *come first*. The work of the *critical philosophy* could be—and had to be—brought to *completion* only with the fundamental explanation of representation. With the establishment of that, however, philosophy ceases to be *critical*, and the *science of the foundation of the philosophy which is philosophy* WITHOUT EPITHETS [OHNE BEINAMEN] begins.[21] This is the Philosophy of the Elements. It is the last on the road leading to science, yet the first on the side of science itself. (BKH 81–82)[22]

4. Schulze's Skeptical Attack

In 1792 there appeared anonymously a book titled "Aenesidemus or Concerning the Foundations of the Philosophy of the Elements Issued by Prof. Reinhold in Jena together with a Defense of Skepticism against the Pretensions of the Critique of Reason." The main title "Aenesidemus" is the name of an ancient skeptic. The original Aenesidemus was so radical that he accused all previous skeptics of being dogmatists, because they made the dogmatic claim that there is no knowledge—that is, they claimed to know that there is no knowledge.

The identity of the author of *Aenesidemus* remained unknown for more than a year. When Fichte wrote his famous review of the book, he did not know who the author was and simply called him Aenesidemus. Eventually, it came out that the author was Gottlob Ernst Schulze. He was unknown at the time, though he had connections with the Göttingen circle, especially with Feder, his father-in-law.

---

21. A *Beiname* is an epithet or a characterizing word accompanying the name of something (e.g., "far-shooting Apollo"), thus something added on. A philosophy *ohne Beinamen* is therefore a philosophy without any qualifications.
22. Reinhold, *Ueber das Fundament des philosophischen Wissens*, 104–5.

As the extended title indicates, the book is mainly a critical examination of Reinhold's *Elementarphilosophie*, carried out largely from the standpoint of Hume's skepticism. But it is also a forceful skeptical attack on Kant. The book claims to be the record of the correspondence between Hermias, who is a recent convert to the critical philosophy, and Aenesidemus, who tries to dissuade him from his faith in the critical philosophy. The main attack on Reinhold is found in a treatise appended to Aenesidemus's second letter (the third letter in the entire series). This appended treatise in fact constitutes at least three-quarters of the book as a whole. Here Schulze cites verbatim a series of thirty-six propositions from Reinhold and critically examines them. In the treatise, there are separate sections devoted to Kant, and it is clear that Schulze recognizes that Kant's system and Reinhold's are not identical.

Schulze's criticisms of Reinhold range widely. Let me mention the two major areas of criticism. First, Schulze attacks Reinhold's principle of consciousness in various ways. He charges that the principle is hopelessly vague and ambiguous, especially its use of the terms "refer" (*beziehen*) and "distinguish" (*unterscheiden*). Another criticism is that the principle is not universal: there are states of consciousness for which it is not valid. Schulze claims that intuition is such a state, because in intuition the subject is not self-conscious but focuses all his attention on the object. Further, he charges that since the principle is a "fact of consciousness," it must be empirical, and so it cannot be—as is required of the principle—certain and necessary. (But here one could object to Schulze by referring to Kant's "fact of reason" in the second *Critique*, which also is not empirical. See AA 5, 42–43; CPrR 43–44.)

A second group of criticisms is directed at Reinhold's argument for the existence of a faculty of representation. Here Schulze bases his criticism on a crude, psychologistic interpretation of the critical philosophy: he takes Reinhold as beginning with representations and then positing the faculty of representations as the *cause* of the representations. Then he can criticize Reinhold for applying the category of causality to the faculty of representation, since this is not an object of experience (and categories are applicable only to objects of experience). In fact, Schulze directs this same criticism at Kant: in order to explain how a priori synthetic propositions are possible, Kant simply applies the concept of causality and declares that the mind is their cause. Here again we see the crudeness of Schulze's interpretation: he makes no distinction between natural, causal explanation and an account that regresses to the conditions of the possibility.

Nonetheless, this does link up with a more cogent and serious criticism of Kant. The criticism is this: any explanation of the origin and conditions of experience must violate the critique's own standard of knowledge—for these origins and conditions do not themselves appear within experience. Schulze expresses this in relation to the question of whether the necessity that belongs to experience derives from the mind (as Kant and Reinhold maintain) or from external things (i.e., things in themselves). "Deriving what is necessary and universally valid in our cognition from the mind does not make the presence of such necessity in the least more comprehensible than deriving it from objects outside us and from their mode of operation. For since we know nothing of what the mind is in itself, as the *Critique of Reason* also concedes, by choosing one derivation over the other we do nothing more than substitute one form of non-knowledge for another" (BKH 118).[23] More generally, the question is: How do we have access to the origin and conditions of knowledge, granted that these are not themselves objects of experience? Even if we can *think* the possibility of experience only by referring it to the mind, how do we know that it *actually is* dependent on the mind?

> From the fact, therefore, that we are incapable of representing to ourselves, or to think, how the necessary synthetic judgments found in our knowledge are possible, except by deriving them from the mind, the *Critique of Reason* proves that they must originate in it in actual fact too, or *realiter*. It thus infers the objective and real constitution of what is to be found outside our representations, from the constitution of the representations and thoughts present in us; or again, it proves that something must be constituted *realiter* in such and such a way because it cannot be thought otherwise. But it is precisely the validity of this kind of inference that Hume questioned. (BKH 116)[24]

Aenesidemus had a major impact, and the supporters of the critical philosophy recognized that this skeptical attack had to be answered. Even Fichte expressed a certain appreciation for it. In November or December 1793 (only a month or two before he finally finished his review of the work), Fichte wrote the following in a letter to Johann Friedrich Flatt, a Tübingen professor renowned as a Kantian: "*Aenesidemus*, which I consider to be one of the most remarkable products of our decade, has convinced me of something which I admittedly already suspected: that even after the labors of Kant and Reinhold, philosophy is still not a science" (EPW 366). In fact, it was primarily Fichte who engaged and largely answered the skeptical critics in his famous review of *Aenesidemus*, published in February 1794.

One of the long-term effects of *Aenesidemus* was to inject into the development of the critical philosophy a lively discussion of skepticism. This came to fruition in Hegel, for whom there is a moment of skepticism within the movement of philosophy as a whole. On the other hand, Hegel was anything but respectful

---

23. *Aenesidemus, oder über die Fundamente der von dem Herrn Prof. Reinhold in Jena gelieferten Elementar-Philosophie, nebst einer Verteidigung gegen die Anmaaßungen der Vernunftkritik* (1792, no indication of publisher or place of publication), 145–46.
24. *Aenesidemus*, 140.

of Schulze. Eight years after *Aenesidemus*, Schulze published a book titled *Critique of Theoretical Philosophy*, in which he developed and systematized the criticisms of Kant first presented in *Aenesidemus*. In 1803, Hegel published a review of Schulze's new book in the *Critical Journal of Philosophy*. Hegel exposes at every turn the crudeness of Schulze's interpretation of Kant. He says that Schulze could understand the thing in itself only as "a rock under snow." He adds: "What happens here is not what the devil asked of Christ, the changing of stones into bread; instead, the living bread of reason is transformed forever into stone" (HW 2, 220; BKH 318).

3. The Genesis of Fichte's Thought

LET US TURN now to Fichte and his development of the first major system in German Idealism. We need to see (1) how Fichte allied himself very closely with Kant, (2) how he engaged critically with the major figures in the Kantian reception (Reinhold, Schulze, and Jacobi), and (3) how, in and through this engagement, Fichte's *Wissenschaftslehre* emerged.

1. Kantian Beginnings and the Professorship in Jena

Fichte was working as a private tutor in Leipzig when, in summer 1790, he discovered Kant's writings. He immersed himself in the three *Critiques*. In a letter to his fiancée, he described this time as "the most blissful days of my life" and continued: "And all that I write for the next few years at least will be concerned with this philosophy."[1] Fichte's discovery of Kant thus brought about a revolution in his way of thinking—and, as he wrote in another letter to his fiancée: "[I engaged in] hurling myself head over heels into the Kantian philosophy."[2]

In spring 1791, he took another position as a private tutor in Warsaw. Then—so the story goes—he walked all the way from Warsaw to Königsberg to meet Kant. His first meeting with Kant did not go all that well, so Fichte decided to get his attention by submitting some written work. He chose a topic that Kant had not yet dealt with but that would lend itself to treatment in the manner of the critical philosophy: the nature of divine revelation. He began by positing the *fact* of divine revelation and then inquired into the conditions of the possibility of this fact. Thus proceeding in a strictly Kantian manner, he deduced a negative criterion for revelation: no legitimate revelation can contradict either the laws of nature or the moral law. The result was his manuscript *Attempt at a Critique of All Revelation*.

When he sent it to Kant, the older philosopher was so pleased with it that he recommended it to his own publisher, who brought it out in the spring of 1792. But something odd happened: in the first copies Fichte's name was omitted from the title page. Also omitted was his preface, where he explains the word *Attempt* by saying that he had not yet reached such maturity as would allow him to set

---

[1]. Letter to Johanna Rahn, September 5, 1790. Quoted in EPW 5.
[2]. Letter to Johanna Rahn, August 12, 1790. Quoted in EPW 6.

forth sure results. He adds: "Honorable men judged it kindly" and encouraged him to publish it (FW V, 12).[3] Now, since Kant's book on religion was expected, everyone believed that the book was Kant's. The book received high praise and glowing reviews. Kant came forward and explained that the book was not his but Fichte's. Almost overnight, Fichte became famous. Jens Baggerson, a friend of Reinhold's, wrote to his friend of "the most shocking and astonishing news— something which, of all impossible things, is the most impossible of all to believe, that Kant is not the author of the *Critique of All Revelation*. Forgive me, but I would have bet not merely my life, but my immortal soul that nobody but Kant could have written this book." He continues by referring to "this amazing news of a third sun in the philosophical heavens."[4] And thus Fichte is placed third in the line of philosophical "suns": Kant, Reinhold, Fichte.

In summer 1793, Fichte moved to Zurich, home of his soon-to-be wife. The period in the fall and winter of 1793–94 was crucial in the development of Fichte's own system. Much of it was first worked out in a long, unpublished manuscript on Reinhold and in his famous review of *Aenesidemus*. As he says in a letter to Flatt, "*Aenesidemus* has shaken my own system to its very foundations, and, since one cannot very well live under the open sky, I have been forced to construct a new system."[5] During this same period (through 1793), Fichte also wrote some political essays defending freedom of speech and championing the ideals of the French Revolution. These, along with his outspoken views on religious issues, earned him many enemies. One critic (Johann Benjamin Erhard) wrote: "God forbid that Fichte should be persecuted, or else there might very well emerge a Fichtianity a hundred times worse than Christianity."[6]

In January 1794, primarily through Goethe's recommendation, Fichte was offered the chair in Jena that was being vacated by Reinhold. During his final months in Zurich, Fichte wrote a short book describing the character of his new philosophy. This book was to serve as an introduction and prospectus to his lectures at Jena: "On the Concept of the *Wissenschaftslehre*." It was here that he began using the term *Wissenschaftslehre*—"Theory (or Doctrine) of Science"—instead of "philosophy." Once he arrived in Jena, he was a great success. His more popular public lectures were attended by hundreds. In his "private lectures" for advanced philosophy students, he presented his *Wissenschaftslehre*. As he worked out the system, he had the text printed in installments and delivered to the students. The result was the *Grundlage der gesammten Wissenschaftslehre*

---

3. Johann Gottlieb Fichte, *Attempt at a Critique of All Revelation*, ed. Allen Wood, trans. Garrett Green (Cambridge: Cambridge University Press, 2010), 3.
4. Letter of September 11, 1792. Quoted in EPW 9.
5. "Draft of a Letter to Flatt, November or December 1793," translated in EPW 366.
6. Letter to Niethammer, June 16, 1796. Quoted in George Armstrong Kelly, *Idealism, Politics, and History: Sources of Hegelian Thought* (Cambridge: Cambridge University Press, 1969), 187–88.

("Foundation of the Entire *Wissenschaftslehre*"). In subsequent years in Jena, he elaborated other parts of his system on the basis of the *Grundlage*:

1795—*Outline of the Distinctive Character of the Wissenschaftslehre with respect to the Theoretical Faculty*
1796—*Foundations of Natural Right*
1797—*[First] Introduction to the Wissenschaftslehre, Second Introduction to the Wissenschaftslehre*
1798—*The System of Ethical Theory*

In Jena, Fichte was controversial. More conservative professors and members of the court opposed him as an atheist and revolutionary. This reached a climax in 1798. A Kantian named Friedrich Karl Forberg submitted to Fichte's journal an essay on religion, which dismissed all theoretical discussion of religious topics. Fichte asked him to withdraw the essay, but when Forberg persisted, Fichte decided that he would add an essay of his own on the same topic, lest people take Forberg's views to be his. Fichte's essay, "On the Foundation of Our Belief in a Divine Government of the Universe," identifies God with the moral world order. In other words, Fichte maintains that the same duty that obliges us to act morally also obliges us to acknowledge the reality of God—a position that is not so far from Kant's practical postulates.

The two articles quickly became the object of intense public controversy. Fichte's conservative enemies appealed to the prince (Karl August, the Duke of Saxe-Weimar-Eisenach), who issued an edict condemning the volume of the journal containing the two articles and threatening punishment to the authors. Thus there erupted the *Atheismusstreit*, which captured the attention of all of Germany. Fichte's reply to the charges could hardly have been less diplomatic. He rejected the accusation of atheism. He also declared that he would accept no censure, adding that if he were censored, he would have no choice but to resign. He had badly miscalculated. In March 1799, the court authorities sent him a letter repeating the earlier edict and accepting Fichte's offer to resign. Despite protests from all over Germany and petitions and demonstrations by students at Jena, Fichte—whom Hölderlin had called "the soul of Jena"—left in June 1799.

One of the results of the Atheism Controversy was that it provoked a very unpleasant affair between Kant and Fichte. Up to that time, they had remained on good terms—and, indeed, Fichte's admiration for Kant was unbounded. For instance, in September 1793 (just before he was offered the chair in Jena), Fichte wrote in a letter to Kant: "No, great man, you who are of such importance for the human race, your work will not perish! It will bear rich fruits. It will give mankind a fresh impetus; it will bring about a total rebirth of man's first principles, opinions, and ways of thinking. Believe me, there is nothing that will be unaffected by the consequences of your work, and your discoveries have joyous prospects" (EPW 365). But when Fichte was forced to resign in Jena, Kant completely dissociated himself from Fichte. In fact, he published a declaration against Fichte: "I hereby declare that I regard Fichte's *Wissenschaftslehre* as a totally indefensible system.... May God protect us from our friends, and we shall watch out for our enemies ourselves" (AA 12, 370–71).[7]

Fichte felt that he owed too much to Kant to attack him. So he wrote a letter to his friend Schelling, which Schelling then published. Fichte's reply to Kant was restrained:

> It is only to be expected, dear Schelling, that just as the defenders of the pre-Kantian metaphysics have not yet ceased telling Kant that he is occupying himself with fruitless subtleties, Kant should say the same to us. It is only to be expected that, just as they assert against Kant that their metaphysics still stands undamaged, unimprovable, and unalterable in all eternity, Kant should assert the same about his against us. Who knows where even now the young fiery head may be at work who will go beyond the principles of the *Wissenschaftslehre* and try to prove its errors and incompleteness.[8]

The irony is that this "young fiery head" proved to be Schelling himself.

2. Fichte and the Early Reception of Kant's Philosophy

In the preface to the *First Introduction*, Fichte writes: "My system is nothing else than the Kantian; this means that it contains the same view of things, but is in method quite independent of the Kantian presentation [*Darstellung*]" (FW I, 420; SK 4). Likewise, in the *Second Introduction*, he says that his *Wissenschaftslehre* "is perfectly in accordance with the teaching of Kant and is nothing other than Kantianism properly understood" (FW I, 469; SK 43). However, Fichte was convinced that Kant had *not* been properly understood: he thought that nearly all of Kant's followers, as well as his critics, had failed to understand what Kant was really saying and had relapsed from critical philosophy into dogmatism.

So Fichte proposed a "complete reversal of current modes of thought" (FW I, 421; SK 4). This reversal would renew critical philosophy. It would, in effect, carry out *again* what Kant had carried out only to have it corrupted (and ultimately reversed) by his followers: the Copernican revolution. Here is how Fichte formulates it: "The object shall be posited and determined by the cognitive

---

7. "Declaration concerning Fichte's *Wissenschaftslehre*" (August 7, 1799), in Kant, *Correspondence*, 559–60.

8. Fichte to Schelling, [no date] 1799, in *Fichte-Schelling Briefwechsel*, ed. Walter Schulz (Frankfurt: Suhrkamp, 1968), 66–67. Quoted in Walter Kaufmann, *Hegel: A Reinterpretation* (Notre Dame, IN: University of Notre Press, 1978), 105. See discussion in John Sallis, *Spacings—Of Reason and Imagination in Texts of Kant, Fichte, Hegel* (Chicago: University of Chicago Press, 1987), 160–61.

faculty, and not the cognitive faculty by the object" (FW I, 421; SK 4). Thus Fichte claims to take up the *spirit* of Kant's philosophy. He says that the spirit and innermost heart of Kant's philosophy is also the spirit and heart of the *Wissenschaftslehre* and that this lies in the achievement "of having first knowingly diverted philosophy away from external objects and directed it into ourselves" (FW I, 479; SK 52).

In carrying out again the Kantian reversal, in developing an independent presentation of the Kantian system, Fichte takes up critically and productively the reception, criticism, and transformation of Kant's thought by Reinhold, Schulze, and Jacobi. Fichte's review of *Aenesidemus* is especially important, for here he engages both Reinhold and Schulze. Moreover, Fichte always retained great respect for Jacobi. We will see that the way Jacobi marks the limits of theoretical knowledge is not entirely alien to Fichte.

A. Reinhold

Fichte agrees entirely with Reinhold's insistence that the critical philosophy must be developed as a system derived from a single fundamental principle. Fichte grants (like Reinhold) that Kant did not really derive the categories and forms of intuition from a single higher principle. Yet Fichte says that "Kant envisaged such a system," even if he provided only fragments (FW I, 478; SK 51). In fact, Fichte maintains that Kant even identified a fundamental principle—even if he did not go on to develop the system from it. That fundamental principle is *pure apperception*. This designates consciousness that is the subject of all representations *and* is conscious of itself (self-consciousness). So Fichte says: "Hence, for Kant, the possibility of all consciousness will be conditioned by the possibility of the I or of pure self-consciousness, exactly as in the *Wissenschaftslehre*" (FW I, 476–77; SK 50).

Granted Fichte's identification of the fundamental principle (both for Kant and in the *Wissenschaftslehre*) as self-consciousness, it is not surprising that Fichte is critical about what Reinhold took to be the fundamental principle, namely, the principle of consciousness: "Representation is distinguished in consciousness by the subject from the subject and the object, and is referred to both."[9] In Fichte's review of *Aenesidemus*, he addresses Reinhold's principle, agreeing with Schulze that it is vague and ambiguous. In particular, Fichte insists that the concepts of distinguishing and referring can be rigorously determined only by means of the concepts of identity and opposition. (Note that these are the concepts that will enter into Fichte's principle.)

---

9. Karl Leonhard Reinhold, *Beyträge zur Berichtigung bisheriger Missverständnisse der Philosophen*, vol. 1 (Jena: Mauke, 1790), 167.

On the other hand, Fichte does not simply reject Reinhold's principle of consciousness. What he rejects is merely the claim that it is the fundamental principle of philosophy. But he grants that it is a "theorem" based on another (truly fundamental) principle and that it can be rigorously demonstrated a priori from that fundamental principle. Thus Fichte rejects entirely Schulze's attempt to refute the principle of consciousness by producing empirical counterexamples. Moreover, just as Reinhold's principle of consciousness is to be referred beyond to a more fundamental principle, so Fichte suggests that there must be a more fundamental concept than that of representation. (In fact, in the *Grundlage* there is a "Deduction of Representation.")

Fichte suggests that what misled Reinhold into taking the principle of consciousness as the fundamental principle was his conviction that the fundamental principle should be based on a fact of consciousness. In Fichte's view, this was right as far as it went. The first principle needs to express not some formal or abstract concept but something immediately evident. But, says Fichte, it does not have to express an actual fact (*Tatsache*) but can express a deed (act, performance—*Tathandlung*).

B. Schulze

There is irony in the descriptive term Fichte applies to Schulze/Aenesidemus: "This skepticism leans toward a very presumptuous dogmatism" (FW I, 10; BKH 143). Fichte knows that the last thing a skeptic wants to be called is a dogmatist. Yet for Fichte, it is justified because Schulze's criticisms of Reinhold and Kant are driven by his dogmatic belief in the existence of things independent of consciousness— that is, things in themselves. We see this, for example, in Schulze's argument that Reinhold infers a *faculty* of representation by applying—illegitimately, of course—the category of causality. He charges Reinhold with saying, in effect, that behind representation there must be a cause, namely, the faculty of representation. Here is Fichte's rejoinder in his review:

> This reviewer, or anyone else with a penchant for being amazed, would not wonder any less at the skeptic for whom, only shortly before, nothing was established except that there are different representations in us, and who now, the moment the words "faculty of representation" hit his ear, cannot think by them anything but a "thing" (Is it round or square?) that exists as thing in itself, *independent* of his *representing* it, and indeed as a thing *that represents*. As the reader will soon see, no injustice is done to our skeptic by this interpretation. The faculty of representation exists *for* the faculty of representation and *through* the faculty of representation. This is the necessary circle in which any finite understanding (and this means, any understanding we can think of) is locked. Whoever wants to escape from this circle does not understand himself. (FW I, 11; BKH 143).

The fallacy is therefore not Reinhold's, who does not take the faculty of representation as a thing in itself that would cause representation. Instead, the error is Schulze's, who completely confuses the cognitive faculties with things existing in themselves and fails to recognize that such a faculty is *for* itself—that being *for* itself is its very way of being. Note especially Fichte's reference in the quotation to *finite* understanding and its necessary circle. The point is that we cannot jump out of the circle of our own understanding to gain access to things as they presumably would be outside our understanding of them. Because he ignores this, Schulze's skepticism is both presumptuous and dogmatic.

But aside from the presumptuously dogmatic way in which Schulze presses his criticisms, there is (as we saw) a more serious issue: How can we explain the origin and conditions of experience without violating the very restrictions imposed by the *Critique of Pure Reason*, namely, that there can be no knowledge beyond the limits of experience (and its possible objects)? In other words, how do we have access to the fundamental condition(s) (ground) of experience, since knowledge is limited to objects of experience *and* this condition is not itself an object of experience? This amounts to asking: How is critique or transcendental philosophy possible?

In response to this question, Fichte introduces *intellectual intuition*, the act by which the I (as self-consciousness) intuits itself. Such an act provides, says Fichte, a genuine grasp of the I, in contrast to mere inner sense, in which the I is given only as appearance. By giving genuine access to the I as self-consciousness, this act thus gives access to the conditions of the possibility of experience, which in systematized critical philosophy derive from the I as self-consciousness. Now Fichte maintains that this is something entirely different from what Kant condemned under the name "intellectual intuition" (i.e., the intuition of the thing in itself). Moreover, Fichte insists that, though Kant did not introduce it, intellectual intuition in the legitimate sense has a place in Kant's system: it is the kind of consciousness that is found in the consciousness of the moral law. Such a consciousness is immediate, received, not reached by thinking—thus "intuition." And yet it is not sensory—hence "intellectual."

C. Jacobi

Jacobi was just as important for Fichte's development as Reinhold and Schulze. To see how, we need to go back to Fichte's review of *Aenesidemus*. There he shows in various ways that Schulze is still thoroughly caught up in the old belief in things in themselves. He says that the "old mischief about a thing in itself . . . is at the origin of all the skeptical as well as the dogmatic objections raised against critical philosophy" (FW I, 19; BKH 149). But, regarding this belief, Fichte says that "Kant and Reinhold (as it at least seems to this reviewer) have long declared themselves against it, though not loudly and emphatically enough" (FW I, 19; BKH 149). Then he says that Kant gave the notion a certain authority by distinguishing appearances from things in themselves. Yet this was "a distinction which was certainly intended to hold only provisionally for the general reader" (FW I, 19; BKH 149–50).

It is against this background that we need to interpret Fichte's appeal to Jacobi in the *Second Introduction*. Fichte refers to the famous appendix "On Transcendental Idealism" and says that here (ten years earlier) Jacobi made it clear once and for all that Kant rejected the thing in itself. In fact, Fichte is separating—or putting in sequence—the two conflicting requirements that Jacobi pointed out in the *Critique of Pure Reason*. According to the first requirement, Kant cannot maintain that things in themselves are the causes of our representations. The reason Jacobi gave was that we have no knowledge of things in themselves, according to the first *Critique*. Fichte adds another reason, which was at best only implicit in Jacobi: this would require applying the category of causality beyond the limit of objects of experience. According to the other requirement, Kant must maintain that things in themselves are the causes of our representations because our sensibility is passive and must be acted on by something.

Now Jacobi is usually interpreted as having taken these to be *conflicting* requirements *that Kant could not reconcile*. But Fichte interprets them differently. The second requirement (that things in themselves must cause our representations) is only "provisional and for the general reader"—in other words, for those who have not yet reached the critical standpoint (those who have not yet undergone the Copernican Revolution). This requirement would, then, be something that Kant abandons once he is within the system of the *Critique of Pure Reason*—in order, then, to satisfy the other requirement (that is, to forego assuming that there are things in themselves that cause our representations).

How, then, does Fichte understand the Kantian thing in itself *if not* as something completely outside our experience that causes our sensible intuitions? According to Fichte, Kant took the thing in itself to be merely something that we *add in thought* to appearances—something that we merely *think as* affecting us. This does not mean that the thing in itself results from some fanciful inference that we are free to make or not. Rather, it is a *necessary* addition, which we *must* make in order to be the subjects we are. In this connection, Fichte describes the thing in itself as "something, therefore, which *arises only through our thinking*; but something that exists, not through our *free* thinking, but through a thinking *necessary* on the presupposition of I-hood [*Ichheit*]—and exists, therefore, only *for our thinking*, for ourselves as thinking beings" (FW I, 482–83; SK 55).

This does not mean that Fichte denies affection or receptivity (the passivity of the subject). What he denies (primarily) is affection *by an object*. Granted this, he then allows that "our knowledge all proceeds from *an affection*; but not affection *by an object*. This is Kant's view, and also that of the *Wissenschaftslehre*" (FW I, 488; SK 60). The task is to understand such "affection" not as a causal effect of the thing in itself but as a determinacy, a limitation imposed on the subject (though *not* ultimately grounded in the subject). Thus Fichte insists that if Kant is properly understood, he is an idealist, and there is no remnant of dogmatism in his system.

3. The Concept of the *Wissenschaftslehre*

As a more systematic introduction to the *Wissenschaftslehre*, let us treat the concept of the *Wissenschaftslehre* before turning to its aim, beginning, course, and method. For the concept, we will focus on Fichte's 1794 essay "Concerning the Concept of the *Wissenschaftslehre*."

In the preface to this essay, Fichte draws a direct connection between his work and Kant's: "I realize that I will never be able to say anything which has not already—directly or indirectly and with more or less clarity—been indicated by Kant" (FW I, 30; EPW 95–96). Fichte's purpose is to lay out the general form that the *Wissenschaftslehre* must take—in its relation to other sciences and human knowledge as such. The essay itself is merely hypothetical. It is therefore *not* the *Wissenschaftslehre* or a part of it but rather a kind of critique preceding the *Wissenschaftslehre* itself (critique in the Kantian sense of establishing the possibility and limits of that to which it is addressed). Yet the essay was also meant as a kind of prospectus for the lectures that Fichte would give in 1794–95 when he arrived in Jena. So it preceded the formal presentation of the *Wissenschaftslehre* (i.e., the *Grundlage*) by only a few months.

Part I of the essay begins with something on which all (he says) would agree: philosophy is a *science*. The question is, then: What is science? Fichte answers: "A science possesses systematic form. All the propositions of a science are joined together in a single first principle [*Grundsatz*, i.e., fundamental or grounding principle], in which they unite to form a whole. This is also generally admitted." Then Fichte poses the question: "Is this enough to exhaust the concept of science?" (FW I, 38; EPW 101).

Fichte goes on to show that systematic form alone does not suffice to define the concept of science. Rather, in a science—for it to be a science—there must be at least one proposition that is *certain*. Strictly speaking, a science may consist simply of a single certain proposition. But normally, a science contains additional propositions and is such that the certain proposition (the fundamental principle: *Grundsatz*) imparts its certainty to all the other propositions. All the propositions thus share the same certainty and constitute a single science. Thus systematic form is not the aim of science (it is, rather, certainty) but only an incidental means toward that aim (in a science that consists of several propositions). Every science must have a fundamental principle. But it can have only one. If it had more, it would be several sciences.

Within a science, there are two things that cannot be proved, two things that are presupposed by the very possibility of proof in that science: (1) the fundamental principle (it must already be established as certain prior to the system); (2) the form of connection with the fundamental principle by which other propositions are imparted their certainty. Fichte expresses these presuppositions as questions: "In short, how can *the certainty of the first principle itself* be established? And what is *the warrant for that specific kind of inference by which we infer the certainty of other propositions from the certainty of the first principle*?" (FW I, 43; EPW 105). The science that answers these questions would be a science of science as such. This science of science is the *Wissenschaftslehre*.

Here we should note two things. First, Fichte illustrates his concept of science by means of the architectonic metaphor—exactly the same as in Kant. Science is a building. The foundation must be sound (this is the *Wissenschaftslehre*). But one cannot live on the mere foundation, so, as protection, one adds walls and a roof. If these are attached to a sound foundation, then the entire building will be safe and sound.

Second, Fichte says that the nation that has discovered this science of science (the nation of Kant, Reinhold, and himself) deserves to give it a name in its own language. And so, for what previously was called "philosophy," Fichte introduces the name *Wissenschaftslehre*. A note adds: "Thereby this language itself, as well as the nation that speaks it, would gain a decisive superiority over all other languages and nations" (FW I, 44–45; EPW 106). Here we see a very decisive turn in the relation of philosophy to its language: rather than simply taking over the language handed down ultimately from antiquity (Latin), there is now a sense of the need to take up philosophical thought in *one's own language*. Then there is gain both for thinking and that language. Here Fichte broaches the aspiration that Hegel will later express in speaking of his aim to teach philosophy to speak German.[10] (Some also hope to teach philosophy to speak English.)

With respect to other sciences, the *Wissenschaftslehre* has two principal tasks. The first concerns their fundamental principles: it must ground the possibility of a fundamental principle as such—that is, it must show how something can be certain and what it means to be certain. Moreover, it must go on to prove the fundamental principles of all possible sciences. As its second task, it has to ground the systematic *form* for all possible sciences.

---

10. Cf. "Luther made the Bible speak German, and you have done the same for Homer . . . I may say of my endeavor that I wish to try to teach philosophy to speak German." Hegel to Johann Heinrich Voss, March 1805, in *Hegel: The Letters*, trans. Clark Butler and Christiane Seiler (Bloomington: Indiana University Press, 1984), 107.

However, the *Wissenschaftslehre* is itself a science. It therefore must have a fundamental principle that cannot be proved within it but is presupposed for its very possibility as a science. But this fundamental principle cannot be proved in any higher science. So the fundamental principle is utterly incapable of proof—that is, it cannot be traced back to any higher principle. It therefore must be certain *in and through itself*: it must be immediately certain. This principle will then be the ground of all certainty, of all science. Moreover, insofar as the *Wissenschaftslehre* is a science and consists of several propositions (which are the first principles of other sciences), it must also have a systematic form. But determination of this form cannot be obtained from any other science. The *Wissenschaftslehre* must therefore have this form in itself and must ground it through itself.

Fichte elaborates and illustrates these issues by formulating the distinction between the form and content of a proposition. The *content* is that about which one knows something. The *form* is that which one knows about it. Take, for example, the proposition "Gold is a body." The content is gold and body. The form is that they are, in a certain respect, equivalent. (This "relation" is the form.) Now, no proposition is possible without both form and content, and, in particular, the fundamental principle of the *Wissenschaftslehre* must have both. Accordingly, for the fundamental principle to be certain in and through itself (i.e., immediately certain), its content must determine its form, and its form must determine its content. In other words, its form fits only its content, and conversely.

Just when this schema seems to have been secured (namely, a single fundamental principle imparts its certainty to all other propositions), Fichte complicates it, at least with respect to the *Wissenschaftslehre*. He introduces—though still hypothetically—a pluralizing of the ground, that is, of the fundamental principle: "Should the *Wissenschaftslehre* turn out to have multiple principles [*mehrere Grundsätze*] in addition to this absolute first one, these others can be only partially absolute; they must, however, be partially conditioned by this first and supreme principle—for otherwise there would not be a single principle" (FW I, 49; EPW 109). Fichte goes on to show that there can be only three *Grundsätze*: (1) an absolute *Grundsatz*, which determines itself—that is, its form and content are mutually determining; (2) a *Grundsatz* that is absolute in form but whose content is determined by the absolute *Grundsatz*; (3) a *Grundsatz* that is absolute in content but whose form is determined by the absolute *Grundsatz*.

At this point, we can take a step back and clarify exactly what is meant by "absolute" when Fichte refers to the fundamental principle as absolute. In such a fundamental principle, the form and the content are mutually determining—that is, the fundamental principle is in no way determined by anything other than (outside) itself. Thus something is absolute if it is "absolved" (Latin: *absolvere*) from everything other than or outside itself. So a fundamental principle that is absolute in form (its form not determined by anything else) can be conditioned in content (conditioned by the absolute fundamental principle). Likewise, a fundamental principle that is absolute in content (its content not determined by anything else) can be conditioned in form by the absolute fundamental principle.

At the end of part I of the essay, Fichte observes that the possibility of a *Wissenschaftslehre* (in distinction from the mere exposition of its concept, as undertaken here) presupposes that there really is a system in human knowledge. (Note that this is essential to the very sense of system in German Idealism: *system* refers not primarily to a system of propositions, principles, and inferences but to a system actually operative within human knowledge and experience.) Fichte adds that if there is no such system, then there are two conceivable possibilities. The first is that there is nothing that is immediately certain (hence no fundamental principle). Then our knowledge would consist of infinite chains: "We build our dwelling upon the earth. The earth rests upon an elephant. The elephant stands upon a tortoise. The tortoise? Who knows what it is standing on? And so on, ad infinitum" (FW I, 52; EPW 112). The second possibility is that knowledge would consist of several finite but independent series, each ending in its own fundamental principle. Thus human knowledge would be a "piecework."

If either of these alternatives were the case, we would have no choice but to accept it. And indeed, we cannot decide in advance whether there is a system in human knowledge or whether one of these alternatives prevails. That there is a system in human knowledge can only be shown by actually constructing—or enacting—it.

With respect to part II of the essay, let me briefly develop four points. First, the *Wissenschaftslehre* (as "theory *of* science") is to be a science of sciences. What, then, is its relation to the other sciences? First of all, the *Wissenschaftslehre* provides all sciences with their first principles, as we noted above. So every proposition that constitutes the first principle of a science is also a proposition within the *Wissenschaftslehre*. Furthermore, for a proposition of the *Wissenschaftslehre* to be a principle of a science, something additional is required. Specifically, something that remains undetermined ("free") in the *Wissenschaftslehre* must become determined. For example, the human body can be considered as raw matter, organized matter, or animate matter. But as soon as it is decided (determined) to consider it in just one of these ways, then we have the principle of the physics, chemistry, or biology of the human body.

Second, Fichte raises the question: How can we ever be assured that the account of human knowledge in the *Wissenschaftslehre* is complete or exhaustive? He answers that this is confirmed when the progressive deduction of propositions eventually leads back to the first principle, with which it began: "We require a positive criterion in order to be able to demonstrate absolutely and unconditionally that nothing more can be deduced. This criterion can only be this: that the very principle from which we began is at the same time our final result. It would then be clear that we could go no further without retracing the path we have already taken" (FW I, 59; EPW 117). In other words, it is a matter of a return to the beginning.

A third point concerns the place of logic with respect to the *Wissenschaftslehre*. Logic contains merely the *form* of the propositions of other sciences—in abstraction from all content. For example, if $p \supset q$ and p are both true, then q is true. This is entirely independent of what p and q are; that is, it is independent of content. Thus logic does not belong to the *Wissenschaftslehre*, since propositions of the *Wissenschaftslehre* have both form *and* content. Here Fichte introduces two very important concepts: (1) *Abstraction*. This is the act by which form is separated from content. Logic comes about through such separation. (2) *Reflection*. Though logic concerns the mere form of other propositions, it must nonetheless have some content. What happens is that the form (which has been abstracted) becomes its own content. For example, $(p \supset q) \cdot p \vdash q$ (modus ponens) is not only the form of other propositions; it is also the content of logic. This act in which the form becomes its own content is *reflection*. Fichte declares that no abstraction is possible without reflection, and conversely.

Finally, the *Wissenschaftslehre* is to take up "the acts of the mind" (by reflective abstraction) and cast these into a scientific system. The problem is that there are no rules for doing this, and thus the philosopher can proceed only by blindly groping along. At first, he is guided only by an obscure feeling. Then Fichte adds in a note: "This makes it clear that the philosopher requires an obscure feeling for what is right [i.e., for the right way to proceed] or genius, to no less extent than does, for instance, the poet or the artist" (FW I, 73; EPW 128). Note how Fichte is extending the concept of genius. In the third *Critique*, Kant develops this concept only in reference to the artist. Fichte extends it to the philosopher. So there is not only the artistic genius but also the philosophical genius. (Kant is no doubt the paradigm.)

4. Introducing the *Wissenschaftslehre*: Its Aim, Beginning, Course, and Method

In considering the (A) aim, (B) beginning, (C) course, and (D) method of the *Wissenschaftslehre*, we will draw primarily on the *First* and *Second Introductions*. These were written as introductions not to the *Grundlage* (1794–95) but to the *Attempt at a New Presentation of the Wissenschaftslehre* (1797). Fichte undertook this project because the *Grundlage* had been written under pressure and thus more hastily than he would have liked. However, Fichte actually wrote only a very brief part of *Attempt*. There are themes in the *Introductions* that are not found as such in the *Grundlage*—perhaps most notably, the concept of intellectual intuition.

A. *The Aim of the* Wissenschaftslehre

We can fill out the (formal) concept of the *Wissenschaftslehre* by focusing on its task, as Fichte presents this at the beginning of the *First Introduction*. Fichte begins: "Attend to yourself; turn your attention [*Blick*—"look"] away from everything that surrounds you and toward your inwardness [*dein Inneres*]; this is the first demand that philosophy makes of its disciple" (FW I, 422; SK 6). So philosophy is initiated by a radical break with one's ordinary comportment toward things—by turning one's vision away from things and back upon oneself, one's own inwardness (inner state). We should notice here Fichte's peculiar rhetoric: he places a demand on his reader, a demand for a certain deed. This rhetorical form points to the essential role that enactment plays for Fichte. A philosophical system is not just a set of propositions to be learned (or written, or read); it is instead a deed (turning inward) to be enacted—a deed that the propositions merely trace, like outward reminders of inner deeds. This is why Fichte says that "a philosophical system is not a dead piece of furniture that we can reject or accept as we wish; it is rather a thing animated by the soul of the person who holds it" (FW I, 434; SK 16).

What is most immediately revealed when one makes the inward turn that Fichte demands? Various modifications of one's consciousness, that is, presentations (*Vorstellungen*). (We see that Fichte is initially setting up the problematic at the same level as Reinhold, that is, at the level of presentations.) Among these, there are two distinct kinds: (1) Some appear as completely dependent on our freedom. We do not believe that there is anything outside us corresponding to them. Fichte mentions phantasy (*Phantasie*, not *Einbildungskraft*—"imagination") and will as sources of such presentations. (2) Others we refer to a reality that we take to be independent of us. In determining (forming) these presentations, we are limited by the condition that they must correspond to this reality. These are the kind of presentations that constitute *knowledge*. Fichte sums up: some presentations are accompanied by a feeling of freedom, others by a feeling of necessity.

Regarding presentations that depend on freedom, there can be no question why they are determined as they are. They are so because I have freely determined them. But the situation is different with the other kind. Here there is a genuine question: "What is the ground [*Grund*] of the system of presentations which are accompanied by the feeling of necessity, and of this feeling of necessity itself?" (FW I, 423; SK 6). It is the task of philosophy to answer this question. In fact, philosophy is nothing but the science that answers this question. This system of presentations is called "experience" (*Erfahrung*). So the task of philosophy—that is, the task of the *Wissenschaftslehre*—is to furnish the *ground* of all experience.

However, the ground of something, by its very concept, falls *outside* that which it grounds. So the ground of experience necessarily lies outside all experience. The *Wissenschaftslehre* is therefore utterly removed from all empiricism. It is not based on experience but rather has as its object the ground of experience, which lies outside experience.

But how is such an undertaking possible? (This is the problem that arose, historically, from Schulze's criticism.) How can one raise oneself above experience to consider its ground? Fichte answers: by abstraction. This means that through freedom of thought, one can separate what is conjoined in experience. Specifically, one can leave out of consideration either the thing or the intelligence. What one then obtains is not something in experience but rather the intelligence in itself or the thing in itself. These are the two possible grounds of experience, and they correspond to the two philosophical systems that are possible: idealism and dogmatism. For dogmatism, the thing in itself is the ground of experience. For idealism, it is intelligence, which Fichte also calls the I in itself (*das Ich an sich*)—not "self," as *Ich* is sometimes translated. Moreover, he notes that the I in itself *is not* to be taken as a thing in itself.

Here a comparison can be drawn with Aristotle. In Aristotle, metaphysics as the ἐπιστήμη of being as being has as its aim the discovery and analysis of the truly first (most fundamental) ἀρχή (corresponding to the German *Grund*). When this is pursued along the lines sketched in *Physics* B (for example), the ἀρχαί prove to be form (μορφή) and matter (ὕλη). Both of these fall outside the field of things—in Fichte's terms, outside experience—since nothing is merely form alone or matter alone. Each is thought only by abstraction from things (as, with Fichte, are the intelligence and the thing in itself). Aristotle's investigation shows that the truly first ἀρχή is form—just as Fichte shows that the true ground is the intelligence rather than a thing.

In any case, idealism and dogmatism are the two philosophical systems corresponding to the two possible grounds of experience, according to Fichte. Neither of the two systems can directly refute the other. They disagree about the fundamental principle, and thus their disagreement cannot be resolved by going back to something more fundamental. The question is, then: What motivates a person to accept one position or the other? In other words, what leads a person either to sacrifice the independence of things to that of intelligence or conversely? That is, what is the basis of the decision, since reason provides no means for making it?

Fichte answers that the basis of the difference between idealists and dogmatists is the difference of their *interests*. He explains: "The highest interest and the ground of all others is the interest for oneself" (FW I, 433; SK 15). This means that the highest interest is the interest in not losing oneself, in maintaining oneself.

In this connection, there are two levels of humanity. On the one hand, there are those who have not raised themselves to the full consciousness of their freedom—who thus *find themselves* only in the presentation of things. Fichte says: "Their image is reflected back at them only by things, as by a mirror; if these were taken from them their self [*Selbst*] would be lost at the same time; for the sake of their self, they cannot give up the belief in the independence of things, for they themselves exist only if things do" (FW I, 433; SK 15). These are the dogmatists.

On the other hand, there is the person who is conscious of his freedom and independence from everything outside him. This consciousness is achieved only by making oneself into something independently of everything else—so that one does not need things for support of what one oneself is (for maintaining oneself). This is the idealist. Thus Fichte concludes: "What sort of philosophy one chooses depends . . . on what sort of person one is" (FW I, 434; SK 16).

It is true that the dogmatist cannot be refuted (in his own mind) to the extent that he is dependent on things and lacks consciousness of freedom. However, to one who has this consciousness, to one who satisfies in himself the precondition required for idealism, dogmatism can be shown to be completely untenable. Idealism can thereby be established as the only possibility. Why is dogmatism untenable? Because it cannot explain what it claims to explain—that is, it cannot explain presentation (*Vorstellung*) on the basis of the influence (affection) of the thing in itself. Note that in the background are both Reinhold's attempt to explain (re)presentations and the concealed dogmatism of Schulze's criticism of Reinhold and Kant.

Let us consider Fichte's argument: "The nature of intelligence consists in the immediate unity of being and seeing" (FW I, 435; SK 17). This means that the intelligence *is* such as to *observe* itself. For example, when I think something, I also appear to myself *as* thinking that something. That is, whatever the intelligence *is*—for example, an act of thinking—it is *for itself*. It sees itself *as* whatever it is. Now one can contrast the intelligence with a *thing*, which lacks this "being for itself." In the case of the intelligence, there is a *double series* of being and seeing, and the essence of the intelligence consists in the unity of these. But a thing has only a single series, that of being.

Dogmatism wants to explain the intelligence and its determinations by means of the principle of causality—to explain presentations as resulting from the causal effect of things in themselves. However, causality holds only for a single series, not a double one. Each member in a causal series transfers an effect to another member outside it. No member of the series reacts upon itself. Expressed in different terms, each member of a causal series is simply identical with itself and simply different from every *other* member. Causality cannot bring about that identity within difference, that unity within duality, which distinguishes intelligence. Thus it is impossible to explain the passage from things to presentations—hence, dogmatism fails.

B. *The Beginning of the* Wissenschaftslehre

Fichte's task is to establish intelligence as the ground of experience. The first principle, with which the *Wissenschaftslehre* begins, is a posing of this ground, a posing of the intelligence—or, as Fichte calls it in the *Grundlage*, the I. In other words, the first principle is a statement (expression) of what the I is, a statement of the concept of the I.

What is the I? Fichte says that it is an *act* or doing or deed (*Tun*). This means two things in general. First, by its nature, the I is active rather than passive. Why is it not passive? Because it is the final ground, preceded by nothing that could account for passivity in it. That is, it cannot be dependent on something else that would act on it and in relation to which it would be passive, dependent—grounded rather than ground. Note that this character of the I will be a crucial pivot for the system of syntheses in the *Grundlage*, for it will turn out that the I *does* contain passivity, even though by its very nature it cannot. The synthesis will proceed as the mediation between the terms of this contradiction.

Second, the I is an act in distinction from being: the I has no being proper or subsistence. The point is that the I is not *something* that is active—as though there were something (a thing in itself) in which activity inheres, a something that would perform the act. To use an example from Nietzsche, when one says, "Lightning flashes," the lightning is nothing other than the flashing.[11] In the same way, the I is simply act and nothing more. Note that this determination of the I determines, in turn, a decisive *dislocation of being* from the central position it has traditionally held. It can be written thus: The I ̶i̶s̶ beyond being. This dislocation pertains to the very essence of transcendental idealism: "The essence of transcendental idealism in general, and of its presentation in the *Wissenschaftslehre* in particular, consists in the fact that the concept of being is by no means regarded as a *primary* and *original concept*, but is viewed merely as *derivative*, as a concept derived, at that, through opposition to activity, and hence as a merely *negative* concept" (FW I, 498–99; SK 69). This is the point where a confrontation between Fichte and Heidegger could be staged.

But what kind of act is the I? Fichte says that this question can be answered by direct demonstration in consciousness: "Think of yourself, frame the concept of yourself; and notice how you do it" (FW I, 458; SK 33). So what do I do when I frame the concept of myself? I turn inward. I make myself an object for myself. That is, what is involved is a self-reverting activity or an act of turning back upon

---

11. Friedrich Nietzsche, *On the Genealogy of Morals*, trans. Walter Kaufmann and R. J. Hollingdale (New York: Random House, 1967), 45; essay 1, §13.

myself. In other words, it is an activity in which there is an immediate identity of subject and object. Accordingly, this is the way the I presents itself to itself—as a self-reverting act. That means this is the way the I *is* for itself. This is its being for itself.

Furthermore, this being-for-itself is not to be contrasted with what the I is *in itself*. Such a contrast would be a remnant of dogmatism—seen, for example, in Schulze. It is not as though the I were first "there," and then it turned back on itself. Rather, it is the activity of turning back on itself—and nothing more. As a self-reverting activity, the I is the act in which "thinking and what is thought are the same" (FW I, 462; SK 37). Fichte says: "The concept of the I is the concept of this act. Both are exactly the same" (FW I, 460; SK 35). Again: "I and self-reverting act are perfectly identical concepts" (*Ich und in sich zurückkehrendes Handeln [sind] völlig identische Begriffe*) (FW I, 462; SK 37).

Now the first principle simply expresses this concept of the I: "Das Ich setzt ursprünglich schlechthin sein eigenes Sein." ("The I originally posits absolutely its own being.") (FW I, 98; SK 99). In a note added in 1802, Fichte provides another formulation: "The I is a necessary identity of subject and object: a subject-object; and is simply so, without further mediation" (FW I, 98; SK 99).

Summing up, we can say that philosophy begins with a reflective turn away from things back upon oneself, upon one's own inwardness. In carrying out this turn (self-reversion), one enacts precisely what one is—namely, an I that is purely act rather than being or substance. Or, more specifically, an I that is such that its being derives solely from its character as a self-reverting act—that is, as posing itself for itself or self-positing. It is the I as thus conceived that the *Wissenschaftslehre* will show to be the ground of experience. Thus the first principle of the *Wissenschaftslehre* simply expresses this concept of the I: "The I originally posits absolutely its own being."

C. The Course of the Wissenschaftslehre

There is one very important indication of the course of the *Wissenschaftslehre* that we need to notice. The I will be shown to be the ground of experience—hence, the condition of the experience of objects outside (other than) the I. *But also*, Fichte says that he must show "that this act [= I] would be impossible without another, whereby there arises for the I a Being [*Sein*] outside itself" (FW I, 458; SK 34). So, on the one hand, the self-reverting act (= I) is the condition of the experience of things outside the I (i.e., of the not-I); on the other hand, the experience of things outside (i.e., of the not-I) is a condition of the self-reverting activity (= I). In short, the I presupposes the not-I, and the not-I presupposes the I. This is the basic circle from which the entire series of syntheses that constitutes the theoretical part of the *Grundlage* proceeds.

D. *The Method of the* Wissenschaftslehre

In §1 of the *Second Introduction*, Fichte sketches the methodological structure that is to be operative in the *Wissenschaftslehre*, in the exhibition of the I as ground. He begins by referring, negatively, to those who simply proceed by means of concepts without any concern for the *origin* of these concepts. They simply analyze concepts and combine them—and the philosophy they concoct is simply a product of their own thought, an artifact. By contrast, the *Wissenschaftslehre* is not concerned with lifeless concepts to be manipulated by thought. Rather, it is concerned with something that manifests itself, something that engenders insight from and through itself—and which the philosopher merely contemplates (rather than manipulating): "But how the object manifests itself is not his [the philosopher's] affair but that of the object itself, and he would be operating directly counter to his own aim if he did not leave it to itself, and sought to intervene in the development of the appearance" (FW I, 454; SK 30).

In different terms, the content of the *Wissenschaftslehre* does not consist of lifeless concepts but rather of thought itself. For those who manipulate concepts, there is only one sequence of thought: that of the meditating philosopher. However, for the *Wissenschaftslehre*, there are two sequences of thought: that of the I that the philosopher observes *and* that of the philosopher himself. This is Fichte's answer to the charge that the *Wissenschaftslehre* is an empty formalism, the mere manipulating of concepts. But this answer is only preliminary: the full methodological structure of the *Wissenschaftslehre* can be seen only in working through the *Wissenschaftslehre*, because method is not something just decided in advance and merely imposed on the matter itself.

Finally, let us consider a concept from the *Introductions* that does not occur in the *Grundlage*, at least not as such—namely, that of intellectual intuition. It seems that the introduction of this concept is a development in Fichte's thought, most likely under the influence of the young Schelling. Fichte begins with the I and asks: To what class of modifications of consciousness is its self-reverting activity to be assigned? Here Fichte has in mind the fundamental Kantian distinction between thought (concepts) and intuition. He answers: this activity is *not* a conceiving (*Begreifen*). It could become such *only* by contrast with a not-I and through the determination of the I within this opposition. That is, conceiving involves determination, which involves negation—hence a contrast with the not-I. So this self-reverting activity is mere *intuition*. And, consequently, it is not, in the strict sense, a consciousness (i.e., experience) since this requires both thought and intuition, according to Kant. So this intuition is not, strictly speaking, a self-consciousness; it provides only the *possibility* of self-consciousness.

This self-reverting activity Fichte calls *intellectual intuition*: it is the immediate awareness that *I* act in my acts. It is something that must occur at every moment of my consciousness. However, it occurs not as a separate act but only in conjunction with sensory intuition and thought. It never occurs in isolation as a complete act of consciousness: "I cannot find myself in action without discovering an object on which I act, in the form of a conceptualized sensory intuition" (FW I, 464; SK 38).

This brings us to the other series or sequence mentioned above—that of the observing philosopher. He intuits the self-reverting act by actually carrying it out. Yet he not only intuits it; he also *conceives* it (thinks it). And, most importantly, the philosopher separates intellectual intuition *as* part from that totality in which it always occurs: "The philosopher thereby discovers this intellectual intuition as a fact [*Factum*] of consciousness (for him it is a fact [*Tatsache*]; for the original I an act [*Tathandlung*]); yet he discovers it, not immediately, as an isolated item in consciousness, but rather by distinguishing what appears in combination in the ordinary consciousness, and resolving the whole into its constituent parts" (FW I, 465; SK 40). In connection with intellectual intuition, Fichte adds, finally, that—beyond the task of distinguishing intellectual intuition—there is the further task of explaining it in terms of its *possibility*. Now, to explain the possibility of intellectual intuition is to explain the possibility of the I as such. How can one do this? Fichte says: in terms of the moral law. In other words, the moral law is the condition of the possibility of the I. This offers a first glimpse of the primacy of the practical.

4. The Fundamental Principles of the *Wissenschaftslehre*

(Fichte's *Grundlage*, Part I)

Let us turn to the *Grundlage der gesammten Wissenschaftslehre* ("Foundation of the Entire *Wissenschaftslehre*"). We should note a couple things at the outset. First, this is not the entire *Wissenschaftslehre* but only its foundation—in something like the way the Kantian *Critiques* are the foundation of metaphysics. The *Grundlage* is divided into three parts. Parts II and III correspond to what, for Kant, are the two main divisions of philosophy: theoretical and practical. Part I is devoted to what is absolutely foundational, which precedes this distinction. We should also note that, historically, this text was the basis for Fichte's lectures when he arrived in Jena in 1794. It was issued to his students in installments—and then elaborated in the lectures.

1. The First, Absolutely Unconditioned Fundamental Principle (§1)

We can begin by calling attention to Fichte's statement in the preface regarding the importance of understanding the *whole*: "It will be necessary first to obtain a view of the whole before any single proposition therein can be accurately determined, for it is their interconnection that throws light on the parts" (FW I, 87; SK 90). There is no place where this is more important than in the treatment of the first fundamental principle (*Grundsatz*): it can be genuinely exhibited as a principle only through working out the whole foundational system. In other words, the fundamental sense of this "beginning" can be explained only at the end. In fact, in the last part of the *Grundlage*, Fichte returns to this principle and explains its most fundamental sense.

We should note, at least in passing, that although the concept of intellectual intuition plays, as such, no role in the beginning of the *Grundlage*, there is clearly a general connection. In the *Second Introduction*, Fichte says that the philosopher separates (distinguishes) intellectual intuition from the totality in which it occurs. He *thinks* it (conceives, determines it). Such a distinguishing (thinking) is what, in general, is accomplished in the treatment of the first principle in part I of the *Grundlage*, though the *Grundlage* follows a different itinerary.

Let us consider the task of §1. Fichte says: "Our task is to discover [*aufsuchen*] the absolutely first, absolutely [*schlechthin*] unconditioned fundamental principle of all human knowledge. This can be neither proved nor determined [*bestimmen*], if it is to be the absolutely first fundamental principle" (FW I, 91; SK 93). This relates back to the formal concept of the *Wissenschaftslehre*: it is a matter of discovering the principle that is absolutely first—in distinction from whatever other fundamental principles there may be, which will be determined in part. There will be two other fundamental principles, determined in part by the first. One will be determined (conditioned) as to content: the second fundamental principle. The other will be determined (conditioned) as to form: the third fundamental principle. But the absolutely first fundamental principle cannot be proved (*beweisen*) because it provides the basis for (hence is presupposed by) all proof within the *Wissenschaftslehre*. Also, it cannot be determined (*bestimmen*) through any other fundamental principle, since it is absolutely first (unconditioned).

Fichte continues by moving from the formal to the material concept: "It [the first principle] is to express that act [*Tathandlung*] which does not and cannot appear among the empirical states of our consciousness, but rather lies at the ground of all consciousness and alone makes it possible" (FW I, 91; SK 93). So the absolutely first principle will express the *ground* of all experience. And, in the manner of idealism, that ground will be identified as an act rather than a being or a fact (*Tatsache*).

How is that act to be "discovered"? Since it does not occur in empirical consciousness (in experience), we can discover it only by rising above experience. This requires *abstraction*, through which we separate out what never occurs separately and as such in experience (cf. the treatment of abstraction in the *First Introduction*, discussed in chapter 3).

But there is also required a *reflection*—hence the exposition of the first principle (in §1) assumes the form of an *abstracting reflection*. We can see clearly what this involves if we consider, in general, what would be required to establish the first fundamental principle *as such* (as the first principle of the *Wissenschaftslehre*). This would require: (1) separating out, distinguishing, and delimiting the relevant act (which will then be expressed in the first principle); and (2) showing that the act distinguished *is* the *grounding* act (so that the expression of it can constitute a *Grundsatz*). For (1), abstraction is required. For (2), reflection is required—specifically, a reflection back from some fact of consciousness to this act as its ground. This *regressive* move is, however, only the initial step: the grounding act (first principle) can be fully established as such only by then *progressing* from it, showing that and how it grounds the entire system of experience.

Near the end of §1, Fichte explicitly relates the first principle to Kant's work: "That our proposition is the absolute fundamental principle of all knowledge, was pointed out by Kant, in his deduction of the categories" (FW I, 99; SK 100). Clearly, Fichte is referring to the principle of transcendental apperception in the first *Critique*. If we recall the Kantian discussion, we can see in outline what Fichte's abstracting reflection (especially the reflective moment) involves. Kant in effect carries out a regress, involving two main steps: a first step *from* presentations (experience) *to* the I, as the self-identical, enduring subject to which all presentations relate back; and a second step *from* the I as mere enduring subject *to* the I as self-consciousness, as unification with itself.[1] Fichte carries out the same regress: *from* a fact of consciousness (corresponding to Kant's presentations—but now something more specific, a determinate presentation) *to* a fundamental fact presupposed by it (the identity of the I), and then *to* a fundamental (i.e., grounding) act (the I as self-positing).

More specifically, the fact with which he begins pertains to the law of identity: A = A. He says that everyone agrees that this is absolutely certain and thus requires no grounding. So we assert absolutely that A is A. This absolute assertion is the fact with which he begins. Then he shows that this assertion presupposes another, more fundamental assertion: "I am I." In other words, it presupposes the identity of the I. The general sense of this presupposing is simple (though Fichte's actual elaboration is complex): to judge that "A is A," the I that judges must remain self-identical throughout the judging ("permanently uniform," "one and the same," FW I, 94; SK 96). This "I am I" is the more *fundamental fact* presupposed by the assertion of the law of identity. Furthermore, since all knowledge presupposes the law of identity (as the basic principle of logic), this fundamental fact is presupposed by all knowledge.[2] But, finally, this fundamental fact is not just a fact but also an act—the self-reverting, self-positing, self-conscious act (= I). To identify A with A, the I must not simply persist (like a thing) but must be aware of itself as the same: it must be self-consciousness. This act, then, is what the first fundamental principle expresses.

Finally, consider who the I is—or, rather, who the I is *not*. First, the I is not the individual human being. The individual is never just sheer self-reverting activity; it is not just self-consciousness but also consciousness of things presented through sensible intuition. The individual I (= person, self) is always set over

---

1. [Editor's note: see John Sallis, *Kant and the Spirit of Critique*, ed. Richard Rojcewicz (Bloomington: Indiana University Press, 2020), 62–68.]

2. In this regard, Fichte is opposed to the rational metaphysics of the Wolffians, who maintained that the principle of identity (or of noncontradiction) is the most fundamental principle, on which all knowledge is based. He also shows, at least in general, that the laws of logic are not fundamental but are based on the principles of the *Wissenschaftslehre*.

against (limited by) a not-I. Even beyond this, the individual I is determined only in distinction from the *thou*—that is, only within intersubjectivity. Second, the I is not God; that is, it is not a pure (absolute) consciousness apart from the empirical consciousness of humans. This is clear in Fichte's criticism of Spinoza. One could say, using Fichte's phrase, that the I is "the pure consciousness given in empirical consciousness" (FW I, 101; SK 101).

Let us now trace in more detail just how Fichte introduces the first fundamental principle. Consider the stages by which he carries out the task. We begin with the proposition "A is A." Everyone will agree that this is absolutely certain. Thus we ascribe to ourselves the power of asserting something absolutely—that is, of asserting something without recourse to further grounds. Note that what Fichte intends to show is that it is precisely this power of asserting (i.e., the act by which the principle of identity is asserted) that is the ground of the logical principle and that is to be expressed in the first principle of the *Wissenschaftslehre*.

What, then, is asserted (posited) in the proposition "A is A"? It does not assert that A *is*. Rather, it says: if A is, then A is. It is a matter not of content (that about which you know something) but of form (what you know about something). So what is asserted (posited) absolutely is the *necessary connection* between "if" and "then." This necessary connection = X.

Now Fichte proceeds to relate the proposition to the I that asserts it: X is *in* the I and is posited *by* the I. What does this mean? To say that something is *in* the I simply means that it is an object for the I as subject. So what really distinguishes X is that it is *posited by* the I. But this follows simply from the fact that X is posited absolutely: it is posited without recourse to any other ground, which is to say that it is simply posited by the I.

Now let us go back to the original proposition and consider what X connects: If A is, then A is.

$$\text{A is} \xrightarrow{X} \text{A is}$$

But "A is" means "A is posited in the I."
So:

$$\text{A is posited in the I} \xrightarrow{X} \text{A is posited in the I}$$

So X connects two positings of A. What is the character of these positings, and how does X connect them? Recall that "A is A" does not say that A is. In other words, it does not tell us whether and how A is actually posited. So the first positing of A is unknown. X then connects this unknown positing to an absolute positing of A. That is, X brings about this connection: if the first positing of A

occurs, then, on the strength of that positing, there is an absolute positing of A—a positing of A without recourse to any further grounds, and thus a positing of A *by* the I.[3]
So:

A is posited in the I   ————— X —————▶   A is posited in the I
(unknown)   *by* the I

We then come to the most crucial step: X is posited *by* the I—that is, the I connects the two positings. What is the condition of the possibility of this connecting? For the positing of A in the I to guarantee that A is in the I (hence, to make possible the absolute assertion of A, i.e., the connecting of the first positing to an absolute positing of A), the I must be the *same with itself.* So Fichte says: "It is asserted that within the I . . . there is something that is permanently uniform, forever one and the same; and hence the X that is absolutely posited can also be expressed as I = I; I am I" (FW I, 94; SK 95–96). Thus the condition of the possibility of the connecting is the identity of the I. If one asserts "A is A," one thereby asserts the identity of the I.

Here there is a further development. X is posited by the I—that is, X is asserted absolutely, unconditionally. But X is equivalent to the proposition "I am I." So "I am I" is absolutely and unconditionally asserted. This means that, unlike "A is A," it does not involve a conditional element (i.e., an unknown positing of the term). As Fichte says, I am I "is valid not only in form but also in content. In it the I is posited, not conditionally, but absolutely, with the predicate of equivalence to itself; hence it really *is* posited, and the proposition can also be expressed as *I am*" (FW I, 95; SK 96).

Now we need to connect this development with our previous considerations in connection to the *Second Introduction.* In the assertion of the law of identity (i.e., as the condition of the possibility of this assertion), the I is asserted absolutely. But to be asserted absolutely means to be asserted without recourse to any further ground outside the assertion itself—that is, it is asserted simply by the I itself. In other words, the I is simply posited by itself, or (in the terms used earlier)

---

3. In von Herrmann's formulation, the second positing is the positing of the A-being of A, of A's identity with itself. Friedrich-Wilhelm von Herrmann, "Fichte und Heidegger," in *Der Idealismus und seine Gegenwart: Festschrift für Werner Marx zum 65. Geburtstag,* ed. Ute Guzzoni, Bernhard Rang, and Ludwig Siep (Hamburg: Meiner, 1976), 233–35. I would instead say that it is the positing of A in connection with the positing of X, since Fichte writes "absoluten Setzen *desselben* A" ("absolute positing of *the same* A," FW I, 94; SK 95, emphasis added). Cf. Fichte's statement: *"If* A is posited, it is naturally posited *as* A, with the predicate A [*als A, mit dem Prädicate gesetzt*]" (FW I, 94–95; SK 96).

the I is the act of positing itself. This act is what is expressed in the first principle: "The I simply [absolutely] posits originally its own being" (FW I, 98; SK 99). And the I so regarded is the absolute subject: "That whose being (essence) consists simply in the fact that it posits itself as being, is the I as absolute subject" (FW I, 97; SK 98).

We now need to add some additional considerations of Fichte's treatment of the first principle so as to put clearly into focus the path followed up to this point. The general task is to *think* the absolutely grounding act (*Tathandlung*), the expression of which will then constitute the first principle. This thinking will do two things. First, it will distinguish the grounding act—that is, separate it out from the total fabric of experience in which it *always* occurs. Second, through the very way of distinguishing, it will be shown that this act must *necessarily be thought as ground*. As ground of what? As ground of that *with* which the distinguishing begins and from which the grounding act is distinguished as its precondition. Eventually, of course, this act is to be exhibited as the ground of experience as such—but this is not something that can be accomplished at the beginning.

In carrying out the task of thinking the grounding act, the general procedure is to begin with a fact of empirical consciousness and then proceed to detach its empirical features until only the pure element, the pure grounding act, remains. Formulated differently, one begins with a fact of empirical consciousness, and then one proceeds to distinguish the grounding act as something presupposed by the fact, as its precondition.

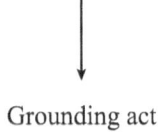

Fact of empirical consciousness

Grounding act

What is the fact of empirical consciousness with which Fichte begins? It is *not*, strictly speaking, the law of identity—that is, it is not this law *regarded as* a thing above and beyond the I who asserts it. Instead, Fichte begins with the fact that we assert the law of identity absolutely, that we are constrained to regard it as absolutely certain. So what he begins with is the absolute assertion of "A is A"; that is, he begins with the absolute *positing* of the principle of identity. What, then, is the grounding act at which Fichte arrives as the precondition of this fact? It is the pure act that we considered in dealing with the *Introductions*: intellectual intuition, self-reverting activity, the sheer activity of positing itself.

We can therefore outline the regress that the "abstracting reflection" makes:

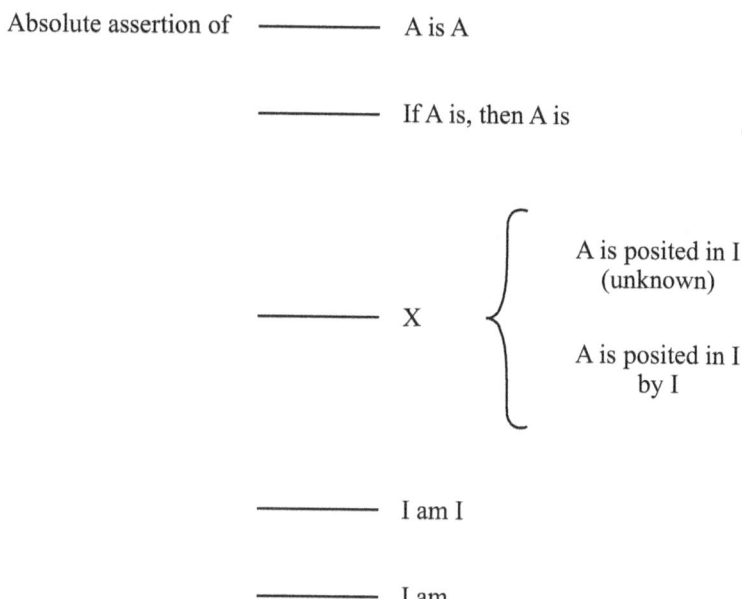

So in the absolute assertion of "A is A," there is already an absolute assertion of "I am"—in other words, an absolute positing of "I am," or a positing in which the I posits itself. This act, the I's positing of itself (of its own being) is the grounding act. It is what is expressed in the first principle: the I simply (absolutely) posits originally its own being.

There is one other feature of the regress that especially needs to be noted. Fichte is able to make the regress only because he goes beyond the concept of identity as mere sameness in a purely formal sense. In the regress, he moves from mere formal sameness to the concept of identity as involving mediation of a thing with itself—a synthesis or unification into unity with itself. We can see this in the first transition:

'A is A' ⟶ 'If A is, then A is'

The course of the regress then exhibits more and more elaborately the structure of identity in this synthetic sense, eventually exhibiting it as the synthesis of distinguishable positings of A in the I. Then, at the most crucial juncture, it is shown that such a synthetic identity (unification into unity with itself) presupposes the self-identity of the I that posits the synthesis. In other words, the identity of the

I is a precondition for all identity. But, in turn, the identity of the I is no mere formal sameness but is unification with itself; that is, the identity of the I is the positing of itself. (On the wider significance of this transformation of the sense of identity, see Heidegger's *Identity and Difference*.[4])

Having reached the grounding principle, Fichte then indicates how other things can be derived from it. Suppose we begin with the terminal point of the regress: "I am" or more precisely, "the I posits absolutely its own being." If we abstract from the specific content (namely the I), then we get the mere form of an inference from being posited to being—*and*, following the regress in the opposite direction, this turns out to be just "A is A." Here we see the relation between the *Wissenschaftslehre* and logic: basic principles of logic arise by abstraction from the content of the principles of the *Wissenschaftslehre*. As Fichte says in "On the Concept," "The essence of logic consists in abstraction from all the content of the *Wissenschaftslehre*" (FW I, 67; EPW 123).

On the other hand, suppose we make a further abstraction from the specific activity of judging and consider only "the general *mode* of action of the human mind that this form presents" (FW I, 99; SK 100). Then we get the category of reality: what is posited in virtue of the simple positing of some thing is the reality or the essence of that thing.

2. The Second Fundamental Principle (§2)

For the second principle, Fichte's procedure is similar to his treatment of the first in §1 of the *Grundlage*. Again, he begins with a fact of consciousness and then carries out an abstracting reflection so as to regress to its fundamental condition. In the very briefest of terms, let us first summarize this procedure. The fact with which he begins is the absolute assertion of the proposition "~A is not equal to A" (~A ≠ A). Here the content is conditioned (determined): for ~A to be counterposited to A, A must be posited. But the form, counterpositing (opposition), is original. Fichte goes on to state the fundamental condition of this fact: "Nothing is posited originally except the I; and this alone is posited absolutely (§1). Hence there can be an absolute opposition only to the I. But that which is opposed to the I = the not-I" (FW I, 104; SK 104). This opposition is what is expressed in the second principle: a not-I is opposed to the I.

Let us now look in greater detail at Fichte's derivation of this second fundamental principle. Here again Fichte proceeds from a fact of empirical consciousness and goes through a similar regress. The fact with which he begins is that we assert absolutely the proposition "~A ≠ A." What do we assert in asserting this proposition? We assert (posit) ~A in its opposition to A.

---

4. GA 11, 27–82; Martin Heidegger, *Identity and Difference*, trans. Joan Stambaugh (Chicago: University of Chicago Press, 1969).

So the question is: How is this asserting possible? That is, how is opposition posited? In other words, how is ~A posited? Or, how does a counterpositing occur? Fichte says that the form of counterpositing is not contained in that of positing. This means that this proposition is not derivable from the principle of identity—that is, opposition is not derivable from identity. Rather, counterpositing and positing are "flatly opposed" (FW I, 102; SK 103). Thus counterpositing must be, as regards its *form*, an absolute, unconditioned act. Since we assert absolutely the proposition "~A ≠ A" (this assertion is a fact of consciousness), there must be (as a condition of this fact) an opposition that is absolute, unconditioned in form.

But the act of opposition is *materially* conditioned (i.e., conditioned as to content). This simply means that for ~A to be posited, A must be posited. Counterpositing is, with respect to its content, essentially *dependent* on a corresponding positing. This dependence brings to light another important feature: "Opposition is possible only on the assumption of a unity of consciousness between the I that posits and the I that opposes" (FW I, 103; SK 104). This unity is necessary for positing and counterpositing to be connected, hence, for one to be able to be dependent on the other. Opposition therefore presupposes unity—that is, it presupposes the identity of the I (expressed in the first principle).

We now come to the most crucial step. Beginning with the fact of consciousness, Fichte has shown that there must be an absolute opposition—that is, an opposition that is not reducible to a position (positing) and thus is not even reducible to (derivable from) the most fundamental positing (the I's positing of itself). How is this possible? Only if the opposition is not included in the scope of that fundamental positing—that is, only if it is an opposition to that positing as such (an opposition to the I). To come back to the most crucial statement (cited above): "Nothing is posited originally except the I; and this alone is posited absolutely (§1). Hence there can be an absolute opposition only to the I. But that which is opposed to the I = the not-I" (FW I, 104; SK 104). The second principle states the outcome: a not-I is opposed absolutely to the I.

So in the case of both principles, Fichte has exercised a regress from logical principles (taken as facts of consciousness) back to the transcendental level, which is the dimension of ground. The first principle expresses the *originary identity* of that dimension. The second principle expresses the *originary difference* (opposition) within that dimension. However, both the position (identity) and the opposition (difference) are *absolute*. How is this possible? More specifically, how can there be an absolute identity that nevertheless admits difference (much less absolute difference)? And how can the dimension of ground involve two opposed absolutes? This is the *fundamental contradiction* on which the entire *Wissenschaftslehre* turns.

Before proceeding to the third fundamental principle, let me make some amplifying remarks on Fichte's account of the first two. We have considered the *abstracting reflection* by which Fichte arrives at the absolutely first fundamental principle. In this move, *abstraction* serves to separate out (distinguish, delimit) the grounding act, which in experience never occurs alone. *Reflection* carries out a regress from a fact of consciousness back to this act as its ground. In other words, it exhibits the act as the ground of the fact of consciousness.

As Fichte carries it out, the abstracting reflection moves from the fact of the *assertion* (on which all agree—which is thus a fact for all, without exception) that A is A (A = A), that is, the assertion that if A is posited, then A is posited. Then comes the decisive move: to assert that A is A (that if A is posited, then A is posited), the I (who makes the assertion) must remain identical with itself. Hence the assertion presupposes that I = I. Yet, in turn, the I that (first) posits A must also *recognize* that it is the same I as the I that (then) posits A. So the I is not only identical with itself; it also is conscious of itself as self-identical. This means that the I has itself as an object (as identical with itself). In other words, the I is such that it turns back on itself and thus is a self-reverting act.

In this regard, there is a very important point to note. Fichte generally uses the term "posit" (*setzen*). For example, something is *posited* in the I. This simply means that it is an object for the I as subject. Here "object" means what in Kant's language is called appearance or phenomenon—not a thing in itself, which would be completely outside the sphere of consciousness. Now we can see something crucial: if the I is an object for the I as subject, then in Fichte's terms, the I is posited by the I—that is, the I posits itself. This positing (self-positing) is the ground that is expressed in the first fundamental principle: "The I originally posits absolutely its own being" (FW I, 98; SK 99).

With respect to the second principle, Fichte's procedure is similar, as we have seen. He begins with the assertion (a fact that all will agree to) that ~A ≠ A—the fact of opposition. Then he regresses to absolute opposition, and this is expressed in the second principle: a not-I is opposed absolutely to the I. Here we can note another important point. The word "oppose" in German is *entgegensetzen*. So to be opposed (counterposited) is precisely *not* to be posited by the I—that is, not to be an object (appearance) for the I as subject. Thus the not-I lies completely outside the circle of the I (subject) and object (appearance). This means the not-I is the thing in itself—though only at this initial stage. So here we see how Fichte is taking up the problem of the thing in itself as it stems from the *Critique of Pure Reason* and as it was critically taken up by Jacobi and Schulze.

3. The Third Fundamental Principle (§3)

Recall that the first principle is absolutely unconditioned (with respect to both form and content). The second principle is unconditioned only in form. Its content is determined by the first principle. (As the principle of the not-I, the *not* is unconditioned and the I is determined—that is, conditioned—by the first principle.) Now the third principle is to be unconditioned only in content. Its form will be determined by the first and second principles.

Fichte indicates in very broad terms the sense in which the third principle is unconditioned in content and conditioned in form: "The *task* [= the form] which it poses *for action* is determinately given by the two propositions preceding, but not the resolution of the same [= content]" (FW I, 105–6, SK 106). So the form is conditioned by the other two principles in the sense that they determine the task expressed in the third principle. That task will be one of synthesis—at least up to the most extreme point, where the full accomplishment of the task can occur only through "a decree of reason." (We will have more to say about this later.)

The first step is to let the opposition between the first and second principles come into play. Here the opposition is between the two positings expressed in these principles; that is, the opposition is between the self-positing I and the (counter-)positing of the not-I. The question is: If the I absolutely posits itself (if it has only itself as its object and thus has as its object only what lies within its own sphere), then how can a not-I be (counter-)posited over against it? In other words, how can a not-I be posited as the object of the I, despite not belonging to its sphere—that is, as a thing in itself?

It seems that each side would simply eliminate or cancel the other: the essential alterity of the not-I would seem to violate the self-sufficient interiority, the pure self-relation of the I. Thus the task is one of synthesis—specifically, a synthesis by which the I would be joined to the not-I without mutual elimination. The third principle expresses this task and the manner in which it must be carried out, namely, by mutual limitation. The synthesis must be such that the opposed terms (I and not-I) come to limit one another, to eliminate one another *only in part*. Such limitation (in part) is possible only if the terms have parts and can be partitioned—that is, only if the terms are *divisible*. Hence Fichte formulates the third principle in this way: "I posit in the I a divisible not-I counter [opposed] to the divisible I" (FW I, 110; SK 110). He then says: "No philosophy goes further in knowledge than this" (FW I, 110; SK 110). Shortly after this, he adds that, from this point on, "every proposition will contain a synthesis" (FW I, 114; SK 113)—and all these syntheses must be grounded in the synthesis expressed in the third principle.

The synthesis expressed in the third principle would allow the opposites to remain without mutual elimination: the not-I would be what the (limited) I is not. That is, each would be posited to the extent that (in the same measure as) the other is not posited. And yet this also compounds the task by reopening the circle (opposition) in another direction. For the limited I that the synthesis would join to the limited not-I is, by its very limitation, opposed to the absolute I as expressed in the first principle. In other words, the circle between the I and the not-I is simply replaced by a circle between the limited I and the absolute I, between finite and infinite. The synthesis, the deduction that is to be carried through must attend to both oppositions, both circles.

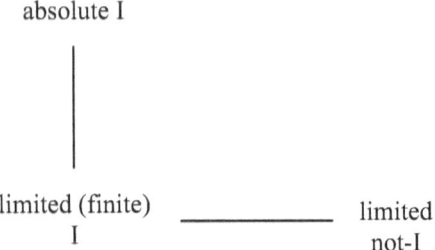

The third principle expresses an all-inclusive synthesis by which the opposition between the I (as self-positing) and the not-I (as counterposited to the I) would be resolved. However, it expresses this synthesis only in general—as mutual limitation. The task is to work out (deduce, exhibit) the full structure of this synthesis. This will be done by analyzing the concept of synthesis given in the third principle so as to expose oppositions contained in it. Then Fichte will seek out specific syntheses to resolve such oppositions.

Let us consider now in detail the deduction that leads to the determination of the task that is posed. This deduction involves three stages (A, B, C).

A. (1) Insofar as the not-I is posited in the I, the I is not posited in the I. (This is because the not-I nullifies the I or is its negation.) (2) Insofar as the not-I is posited in the I, the I must be posited in the I. (This is because the not-I can be posited only if there is posited the I to which it can be opposed.) (3) These two conclusions are opposed. But they are both derived from the second principle, hence implicit in it. So the second principle is opposed to itself and nullifies itself. (4) But the second principle nullifies itself only because what is counterposited nullifies what is posited—that is, only because the second principle is valid. So if it nullifies itself, then it is valid and hence does not nullify itself. Thus the second principle nullifies itself and also does not nullify itself. (5) The same conclusion applies to the first principle. What is posited in the I is posited. But the second principle is posited in the I but then is not posited in the I (since it nullifies itself). So the first principle nullifies itself and also does not nullify itself.

B. (1) Now it can be seen what the *task* is: these conclusions (by destroying the first principle) entail the elimination of the *identity* of consciousness or the I, which is the foundation of all knowledge. It is therefore necessary to discover some X by means of which these conclusions can be granted without doing away with the identity of the I. Specifically, one must find some act of the mind = Y, whose product is X. (2) The form of this act is determined by the task: it must be such as to unify the I and the not-I without mutual elimination. (3) But the content (the how) is not determined by the task. So we must ask: How can the I and the not-I be thought together without mutual elimination? The answer: only if they mutually *limit* one another. The act Y will therefore be a limiting of each opposite by the other, and X will denote the limits. (4) To limit something means to abolish its reality, not wholly but *in part* only, by negation. But to abolish part of something requires that that thing have parts; that is, it requires that it be *divisible*. So by the act Y, both the I and the not-I must be absolutely posited *as* divisible (as having the capacity for quantity). (Note that Y is not an act that follows the act of opposition, since it first makes opposition possible. It occurs *with* the act of opposition. The two acts are one and the same—distinguished only in reflection.)

C. (1) This act allows the opposites to remain without mutual elimination: the not-I *is* what the (limited) I is not—each is posited to the extent that (in the same measure as) the other is not posited. (2) However, this limited (divisible) I is now to be contrasted with the absolute I (of the first principle), which is indivisible: insofar as there is a not-I opposed to the I, this (limited) I is in opposition to the absolute I. These are the two fundamental oppositions in the *Wissenschaftslehre*: on the one hand, the I versus the not-I; on the other hand, the limited I versus the absolute I. The problem is to work out the syntheses that bridge these oppositions.

Thus we come finally to the third principle (which expresses this synthesis): "In the I, I oppose a divisible not-I to the divisible I." Fichte then says: "No philosophy goes further in knowledge than this. . . . Everything that is to emerge hereafter in the system of the human mind must be derivable from what we have established here" (FW I, 110; SK 110).

4. Additional Points concerning the Three Principles

Fichte proceeds to derive a logical principle from the third principle of the *Wissenschaftslehre*. If we abstract from the content (the I and the not-I), we get the mere *form* of the union of opposites through the concept of divisibility. The expression of this form is the logical principle called the "grounding principle" (*der Satz des Grundes*): "A in part = ~A." Further abstraction yields the category of determination or limitation—hence, one of the Kantian categories. The grounding principle says, in more expanded form: (a) Every opposite is like its opponent in one respect (= X). (b) Every like is opposite to its like in one respect (= X). X is, then, the *ground* of (a) conjunction and (b) distinction.

Corresponding to the two sides of the grounding principle, Fichte defines two procedures: (1) an antithetic procedure (antithesis), which involves seeking in things equated the respect in which they are *opposed*—that is, seeking the ground of distinction; and (2) a synthetic procedure (synthesis), which involves seeking in opposites the respect in which they are *alike*—that is, seeking the ground of conjunction. The point is, then, that antithesis and synthesis are governed by the grounding principle, which, in turn, was derived from the third principle of the *Wissenschaftslehre*. Furthermore, we saw that the act expressed in the third principle is inseparable (except in reflection) from that expressed in the second principle. However, if they are inseparable, then whatever is governed by one will also be governed by the other—hence, antithesis and synthesis are governed (ultimately) by *both* the second and third principles. In fact, the very distinction between antithesis and synthesis corresponds to the distinction between the second and third principles. Accordingly, just as the separation between the two principles occurs only in reflection, so the separation between antithesis and synthesis is always the result of abstraction. In other words, there can be no antithesis without a synthesis, and no synthesis without an antithesis.

We noted that antithesis and synthesis are derived from the second and third principles. But antithesis and synthesis are the procedures of the *Wissenschaftslehre* itself: they constitute its general form. Thus the form of the *Wissenschaftslehre* is determined by the second and third principles. This means that the *Wissenschaftslehre* supplies its own form (rather than merely imposing on the matter some form foreign to it).

Furthermore, the third principle expresses the all-inclusive synthesis in which all other, specific syntheses must be contained. The task is to exhibit the full structure of this synthesis—the totality of syntheses in their interconnection. Specifically, the procedure will involve first seeking out oppositions that still remain in the synthesis expressed in the third principle; Fichte will then proceed to unite them through a new ground of conjunction. In the opposites thus united, he then seeks out new oppositions and again unites them through a new ground of conjunction. So, beginning with the synthesis expressed in the third principle, the procedure will involve a movement from antithesis to synthesis, to a new antithesis and a new synthesis, and so on. Fichte adds that he must continue this as far as possible. He notes (by way of anticipation) that one eventually arrives at opposites that cannot be synthesized and that one is thereby transported into the practical part of the *Wissenschaftslehre* (FW I, 115; SK 113).

Whereas the second and third principles determine the course of the system (at least of its theoretical part), the first principle is what prescribes *that* there should be a system at all. Fichte writes: "The *form* of the system is based on the highest synthesis; *that* there should be a system at all, on the absolute thesis" (FW I, 115; SK 114). Specifically, since the first principle expresses an absolute positing in which the I is not opposed to any opposite but just absolutely posited in its unlimited identity with itself, it prescribes that opposition must be resolved until such absolute unity is effected. That is, it prescribes that a synthesis be carried out in such a way as to unite opposites within a whole, a one, a system. We should note Fichte's remark that within the theoretical part of the *Wissenschaftslehre*, the first principle is involved only in a regulative function. It is in the practical part that its role will be decisive. Here we may recall the Kantian concept of pure reason: with theoretical knowing it is merely regulative; it becomes constitutive only as pure *practical* reason.

Finally, in the discussion of all three principles, Fichte indicates the two-fold derivation that can be carried out on the basis of the respective principle. This derivation corresponds to two successive acts of abstraction: (1) from the specific content (I and not-I), which yields a logical principle; and (2) from the specific activity of judging (i.e., from the determinate form of judgment) so as to be left only with the general type of the mind's action—which yields a category.

Principle of WL	Logical Principle	Category
1st	Law of Identity $(A = A)$	Reality
2nd	Principle of Opposition $(\sim A \neq A)$	Negation
3rd	Grounding Principle (A in part $= \sim A$)	Determination (limitation)

Note that Fichte has deduced the Kantian categories of quality. Also, in a sense, he has—in arriving at the third principle—deduced the category of quantity.

5. The Foundations of Theoretical and Practical Knowledge
(Fichte's Grundlage, *Parts II–III)*

THE THIRD PRINCIPLE expresses the all-inclusive synthesis of the I and the not-I. However, it expresses this synthesis only in general—as mutual limitation. The task is to exhibit the full structure of this synthesis. This will be done by analyzing the concept of synthesis given in the third principle so as to exhibit oppositions contained in it. Then Fichte will proceed to seek out the synthesis that resolves this opposition.

1. The Initial Syntheses (Sections A–D of Part II)

A. Determination of the Synthetic Proposition to Be Analyzed

In the third principle, two propositions are contained:

1. The I posits the not-I as limited by the I.
2. The I posits itself as limited by the not-I.

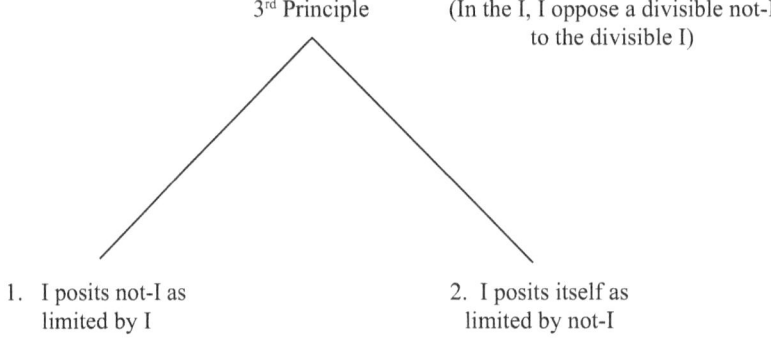

About these propositions Fichte makes the following observations:

(1) Proposition 2 is the basis of the theoretical part of the *Wissenschaftslehre* (though this can be evident only after its completion). All subsequent deductions in part II derive from it.

(2) Proposition 1 will turn out to underlie the practical part. However, at this point it is problematic, because thus far the not-I is simply nothing, sheer

negation, having no reality. This is because the not-I is absolutely opposed to that which underlies all reality (the I), in relation to which the very category of reality is established. Thus it is inconceivable how the I could limit the not-I (i.e., deprive it of reality), since it possesses no reality. Furthermore, because this proposition is problematic, the possibility of the practical part remains problematic.

(3) Thus reflection must begin from the theoretical part—and, more generally, the *thinkability* of the practical principle depends on the theoretical. Yet it will eventually become apparent that theoretical reason does not make practical reason possible; it is the other way around: "Reason in itself is purely practical" (FW I, 126; SK 123).

(4) At this point, however, even the division between theoretical and practical remains problematic.

B. Interdetermination

We come to the first full step in the deduction—that is, an *analysis* that draws out opposites and a *synthesis* that then unites them. The analysis can be presented as follows:

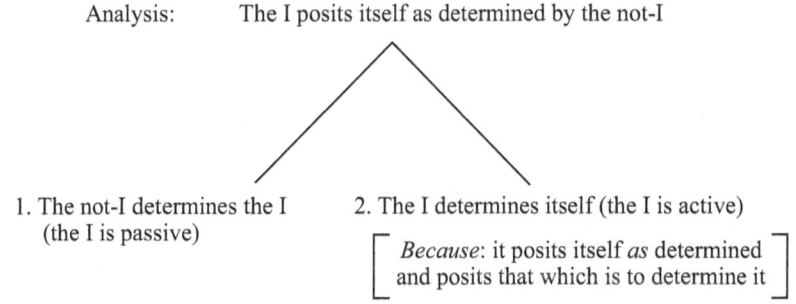

Why does the I determine itself (proposition 2)? Because it posits itself *as* determined and posits that which is to determine it.

Before we follow the development that stems from this division (analysis), let us take a long-range view of what lies ahead. This will help us to recognize the significance of the intricate development that is to come.[1]

Proposition 1 expresses the direction taken by the "synthesis of efficacy" or of causality. To say that "the not-I determines the I" entails that the limitation or passivity in the I is caused by the not-I, by its affecting the I. The problem is that being passively acted on is at variance with the nature of the I (as act, as self-positing). Here the I would be determined by the not-I, but it would not posit itself as so determined. The synthesis of efficacy is aimed at resolving this problem.

---

1. See appendix 1 for a diagram of the initial syntheses in part II of the *Grundlage*.

Proposition 2 expresses the direction taken by the "synthesis of substantiality." To say that "the I determines itself" entails that the limitation or passivity in the I is posited by the I itself. In other words, the I posits the limitation in itself. The problem is that such a limitation would have no relation to the not-I. Here the I would posit itself as determined but not as determined by the not-I. The synthesis of substantiality is aimed at resolving this problem.

And yet, Fichte concludes: "Thus, both syntheses, employed in isolation, fail to explain what they should, and we still have the contradiction complained of above: if the I posits itself as determined, it is not determined by the not-I; if it is determined by the not-I, it does not posit itself as determined" (FW I, 148; SK 140). Thus what is needed is for *both* syntheses to operate together—that is, a kind of synthesis of syntheses.

Now what the two directions (efficacy and substantiality) represent are forms of realism and idealism. Realism, corresponding to the concept of efficacy, finds the sufficient ground in the not-I. Thus it takes account of the finite I's relation to the not-I (its dependence on something *other*) but not of its character as an I (as self-positing). Idealism, corresponding to the concept of substantiality, finds the sufficient ground in the I as such. Thus it takes account of the finite I's character as an I (that it posits itself) but not of its finitude (its submission to otherness).

What is required, then, is a mediation between realism and idealism, corresponding to the synthesis of syntheses mentioned above. In fact, this is how the theoretical *Wissenschaftslehre* proceeds. There is a series of stages. At each stage, an idealism (which takes account of the I-character) and a realism (which takes account of finitude) are exhibited in their opposition. The progression through the successive stages mediates the opposition. This means that as the *Wissenschaftslehre* proceeds through the stages, it arrives at progressively more adequate, less one-sided types of idealism and realism.

Let us now follow the detailed development that leads to and fills out these general conclusions. Resuming the analysis, we saw that it began as follows:

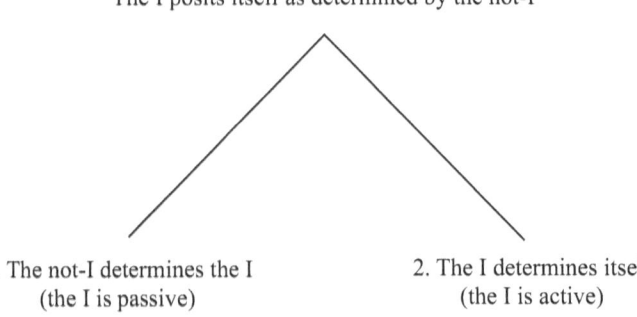

The I posits itself as determined by the not-I

1. The not-I determines the I
(the I is passive)

2. The I determines itself
(the I is active)

These two propositions contradict one another. But they are both contained in the proposition: "The I posits itself as determined by the not-I." Hence this proposition annuls itself. But this proposition is itself contained in the third fundamental principle—which thus annuls itself as well. And yet the third principle cannot annul itself if the unity of consciousness (i.e., the foundation of all knowledge, expressed in the first principle) is to be maintained. Thus it must be possible to unify the opposites—that is, to reconcile the opposition between the derived propositions. The problem is to determine the relevant synthesis.

Let us turn now to that synthesis. According to the third principle, the opposition between the I and the not-I is, in general, to be resolved by limitation (determination), in which the opposites are posited as divisible (as having quantity). The question is: What specific form must this determination (limitation) take to resolve the opposition between the two propositions? To state the matter more precisely: the opposition between these propositions can be resolved only if it can be shown that the I determines itself *in part* and is *in part* determined. In fact, such partition is precisely the kind of resolution prescribed by the concept of limitation (in connection to the third principle). But if there is to be a genuine synthesis (unity), then the I's determining of itself and its being-determined (by the not-I) cannot be separated occurrences but must be "one and the same"—that is, "in the very respect in which the I is determined, it must be self-determining" (FW I, 129; SK 125). The specific form of determination that is sought must be such as to bring this about.

To understand the precise character of the requisite determination, there are two preliminary points that we need to develop. First, Fichte makes use here of the concept of reality (*Realität*). This is to be understood in the same sense that it has in Kant. It does not mean existence (*Dasein*) or actuality (*Wirklichkeit*). Rather, "the real" is that which belongs to *what* something is, to its *essence*. The reality of something means the totality of elements that constitute the essence of that thing. For Kant, the absolute totality of "reals" is the transcendental ideal. And to determine something (in its essence, its reality) means to determine it with respect to this totality. For example, suppose that the totality of reals consists of: E = extended, T = thinking, W = willing, C = colored. To determine the essence of something means to determine it with respect to each of these. Thus the essence of body would be: E, ~T, ~W, C. (Determination therefore involves negation.[2])

The second preliminary point has to do with the relation between reality and the absolute I of the first principle. Fichte expresses this relation by saying that all reality is posited in the I. At the simplest level, this is merely a result of the fact that the category of reality is grounded on the I. As in Kant, the category extends

---

2. [Editor's note: Cf. Spinoza's famous line: *omnis determinatio est negatio*.]

only to what is *for* the I—that is, in Fichte's terms, posited in the I. But there is a deeper sense also involved here. We can see it in another formulation: the absolute totality of the real (i.e., of reals) is posited in the I by the I. But the I simply posits itself. So this amounts to saying: the absolute totality of reals is posited in the I's positing of itself—that is, the I posits itself as the totality of reals.

On what basis does Fichte maintain this? The I's positing of itself involves no negation, which enters only in the second principle. There is no real (= A) such that the I posits itself as not-A. In different terms, the I's positing of itself involves no determination (limitation), which enters only in the third principle. So the I (of the first principle) is absolutely everything (all reals), yet it is absolutely no determinate thing—"not something." In other words, the I posits itself as everything but does not determine itself as anything. We might say: in the absolute I, Kant's transcendental ideal is unified with transcendental apperception.

Now let us consider the synthesis. It must be shown how the I both determines itself and is determined by the not-I (and how these are one and the same). Suppose that the I determines itself. This means that the I posits within itself only *part* of the absolute totality of reals and thereby negates the remainder of this totality within itself—that is, excludes them from itself. But to exclude them from itself is to posit them in the not-I. Thus however many portions of negation the I posits in itself, it posits the same number of portions of reality (i.e., reals) in the not-I. That is, for every negation posited in itself, a corresponding real is posited in the not-I. However, since the not-I is the negation of the I, the reality in the not-I *negates* the corresponding reality in the I (so that there is negation rather than reality in the I). As a consequence, the I is determined by the not-I. Therefore, insofar as the I determines itself, it is determined by the not-I, and vice versa.

The concept of synthesis established here is a more specific form of the determination or limitation expressed in the third principle. Whereas the concept of determination merely indicated that for the I and the not-I to subsist together, they must be capable of quantity (have parts), the present concept specifies the quantity of one in terms of its opposite. The quantity of reality in the I is the same as the quantity of negation in the not-I (and hence determines the quantity of reality in the not-I)—and conversely. This more specific concept of determination is interdetermination (*Wechselbestimmung*) (FW I, 131; SK 127). Fichte identifies it with what Kant calls "relation" (thus we arrive at the third set of Kantian categories).

We should observe, however, that a fundamental question is left unanswered—namely, how the I could posit negation in itself or reality in the not-I, since it posits itself (by the first principle) as the absolute totality of the real, and since the not-I is the sheer negation of the real. All Fichte has established here is the reciprocity between the I's positing negation in itself and its positing reality in the not-I. In this fundamental question, here left unanswered, there is contained the kernel of the entire development to come.

C. Efficacy

The problem now is to determine the concept of interdetermination more specifically in order to discover how negation can be posited in the I and reality in the not-I. A further opposition must therefore be drawn out to determine the synthesis more specifically:

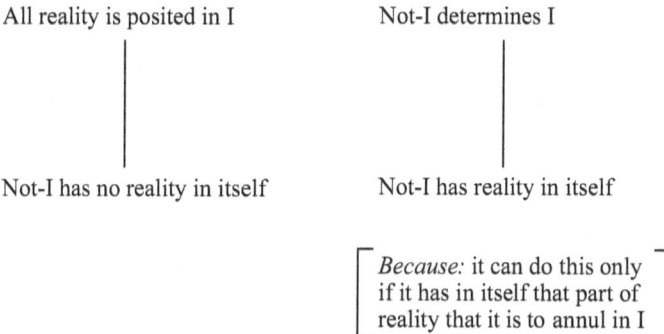

On the one hand, if all reality is posited in the I, then *the not-I has no reality in itself*. On the other hand, if the not-I determines the I, then *the not-I has reality in itself*. This is because the not-I can determine the I only if it has in itself that part of reality that it is to annul in the I.

The two propositions contradict one another. However, both are contained in higher principles that must be maintained to preserve the unity of consciousness. So the opposition must be resolved. What kind of interdetermination does this require?

We can formulate Fichte's answer in three steps. (1) He replaces the concept of reality (which easily falls into relativity) with a more adequate concept. We can see the replacement in these terms: The I is (posits itself as) reality (the totality of the reals). Moreover, the I is self-positing. So reality and self-positing are identical. But self-positing is identical with activity (*Tätigkeit*). Thus reality = activity. He thus replaces the concepts of reality and negation with those of activity (*Tätigkeit*) and passivity (*Leiden*). He also stresses that the concept of activity is to be framed in an absolutely pure fashion: "It can designate nothing but what is contained in the I's own absolute assertion of itself; nothing but what is immediately implicit in the proposition 'I am.' Hence it is clearly necessary to abstract completely, not only from all *temporal conditions* but also from every *object* of activity" (FW I, 134; SK 129).

(2) So now, to say that the I is determined means that activity is annulled in it, or there is passivity in the I. That is, there is something in the I that is not immediately contained in the 'I am,' in the I's positing of itself. Such passivity in the I is *affection*.

(3) We come to the synthesis. When there is passivity in the I, then (by the law of interdetermination) the same degree of activity must be carried over to the not-I. Thus we have the concept of a synthesis in which activity is posited on the basis of passivity—that is, one-directional interdetermination, from passivity (negation) to activity (reality). Such a synthesis resolves the contradiction: the not-I has no reality of its own (hence the first of the opposed propositions is granted), but it has reality insofar as the I is passive or is affected (hence the other opposed proposition is granted). This synthesis is the synthesis of efficacy (*Wirksamkeit*) or of causality (*Kausalität*). That which is active is the cause; that which is passive is the product (*das Bewirkte*) or effect (FW I, 136; SK 131).

D. Substantiality

A problem is carried over from the previous synthesis: How can passivity be posited in the I? This would seem to be impossible. The I is activity, and the I posits itself. So the I posits activity, not passivity. Fichte poses this problem by drawing out the opposites contained in the previous proposition.

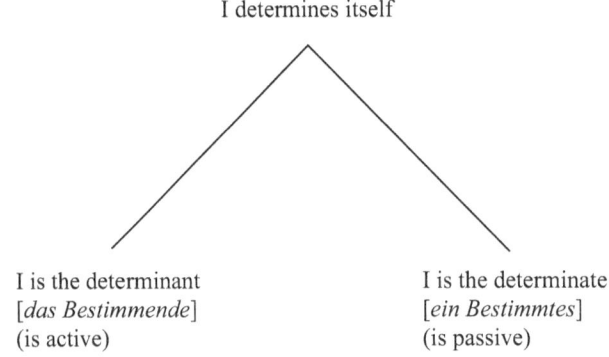

If the I determines itself, then the I is the determinant (*das Bestimmende*) and is active. But since the I determines *itself*, the I is also the determinate (*ein Bestimmtes*) and is passive. So the I is both active and passive—a contradiction. But again, these propositions are contained in the higher propositions so that, if the contradiction is not removed, the unity of consciousness is destroyed. So what is the synthesis by which these opposites can be resolved? In other words, how can the I be both active and passive?

In the I, the whole of activity (i.e., the totality of reals) is posited. Suppose, then, that a quantum of activity not equal to the whole is posited in the I. Then this quantum of activity is *not* the whole of activity—and to this extent, it is passivity. In other words, it is opposed to activity, not to activity as such but to the whole of activity. The quantum that is posited is an activity when considered in relation to the not-I (because it is posited in the I), but it is a passivity insofar as it is related to the totality of activity—it is *not* this totality.

Now this quantum of activity is not activity in general but a *determinate* activity. For example, "I think" expresses such an activity. But as a determinate activity, it excludes all other modes of being of the I (e.g., desiring and willing), and hence it is opposed to the whole of activity.

So how is the I both activity and passivity? By a positing of passivity by means of a positing of activity. This is the synthetic act needed to resolve the contradiction. Note that the order of interchange is the opposite of that involved in the synthesis of efficacy.

This synthesis is the synthesis of substantiality. It is in reference to it that Fichte defines substance and accident. Substance is the I regarded as containing all realities, as the whole of activity. To the extent that the I is posited within a determinate area of this whole (i.e., as a quantum of activity), it is accidental or has an accident within it (FW I, 142; SK 136).

Finally, note that one question remains unanswered: How can the I posit a lower degree of activity in itself? In fact, this is the same question that has repeatedly been left open in various forms: How can the I posit negation in itself? How can the I posit passivity in itself? How can the I posit a lower degree of activity in itself? (See appendix 1.)

2. Fichte and Spinoza

Fichte's introduction of the concept of substance provokes us to ask about his relation to the modern philosophical tradition—especially to Spinoza. By looking at this relation, we can prepare ourselves for the overall view of the *Wissenschaftslehre* that he is about to present.

The concept of substance figures very prominently in the history of modern philosophy before Kant. We see this already in Descartes. The problem that emerges from Descartes's work is the problem regarding substance. Specifically, it is the problem of the communication of substances—that is, of thinking substance (mind) and extended substance (body). But why is there a problem here? To answer this question, we must see what Descartes means by substance.

In part I of the *Principles of Philosophy*, Descartes writes: "By *substance* we can understand nothing other than a thing which exists in such a way as to depend on no other thing for its existence."[3] Substance, therefore, does not mean something unchanging beneath change (*substratum*), nor does it mean (as in

---

3. Part I, §51. René Descartes, *The Philosophical Writings of Descartes*, trans. John Cottingham, Robert Stoothoff, and Dugald Murdoch, vol. 1 (Cambridge: Cambridge University Press, 1985), 210.

Locke) some underlying *x* in which accidents inhere. Rather, substance is that which is *absolutely independent*. This is why there is a problem of communication between substances. The problem is: How can things that are absolutely independent affect one another, since any such affection would negate their independence? In the same passage, Descartes goes on to say: "And in fact only one single substance can be understood which clearly needs nothing else, namely God. We perceive that all other things can exist only by the help of the concourse of God. That is why substance does not pertain univocally to God and to other things."[4] So for Descartes, there are not two types of substances but three ("Cartesian dualism" is a misnomer). But in another sense, there is only one substance: God. Thus the concept of substance in Descartes is equivocal.

Spinoza is to be understood in relation to this equivocation. At the beginning of the *Ethics*, he defines substance in almost the same terms as Descartes: "By substance I understand what is in itself and is conceived through itself."[5] But, confronted with the problem of communication of substances, he eliminates the equivocation that persisted in Descartes. That is, he argues that if a substance is absolutely independent (not limited or determined by anything else), then there can be only one substance—namely, God. If there were two different substances, then each would limit the other in that it would have certain attributes that the other would not have. So there is only one substance, and it is infinite (unlimited). This means that everything must be conceived as somehow inherent in this single substance: "Whatever is, is in God, and nothing can be or be conceived without God."[6]

What happens, then, to the problem of communication? It is eliminated in its extreme form, since there is only one substance. For Spinoza, thought and extension are *attributes* of the infinite substance, and particular things (e.g., minds and bodies) are simply *modes* of substance. Thus Spinoza's famous statement: "The order and connection of ideas is the same as the order and connection of things."[7] This is so not because there is communication between two different kinds of substance but because ideas and things are just modes of one and the same substance.

How is this related to Fichte? Fichte says that the theoretical part of the *Wissenschaftslehre* is "Spinozism made systematic" (FW I, 122; SK 119). The connection is especially clear in Fichte's remark immediately following his definition of substance: "There is initially only one substance, the I; within this one substance, all possible accidents, and so all possible realities, are posited" (FW I, 142; SK 136). This means that the I of the first principle corresponds to Spinoza's substance. However, in this correspondence there is also a crucial difference: "Any given I

---

4. Ibid.
5. *Ethics*, part I, definition 3; Benedict de Spinoza, *A Spinoza Reader: The Ethics and Other Works*, trans. Edwin Curley (Princeton, NJ: Princeton University Press, 1994), 85.
6. *Ethics*, part I, proposition 15; Spinoza, *A Spinoza Reader*, 94.
7. *Ethics*, part II, proposition 7; Spinoza, *A Spinoza Reader*, 119.

is itself the one ultimate substance" (FW I, 122; SK 119). Whereas Spinoza goes beyond the I to some (presumably) more ultimate substance (unity), Fichte insists that one cannot transcend the I (the one thing from which you cannot abstract is yourself). Hence Fichte poses against Spinoza the crucial question: "What right did he have to go beyond the pure consciousness given in empirical consciousness?" (FW I, 101; SK 101).

Now, if the ultimate substance is the I, then it is no longer possible simply to include thought and extension (i.e., finite subject and object) in it as attributes or modes. This is because there is an opposition (1) between the absolute I and the finite subject—and especially (2) between the absolute I and objects (not-I). So the opposition between subject and object that Spinoza resolved breaks out again in Fichte. It is even, in a sense, his supreme problem.

In the problem's sharpest form, Fichte puts it thus: How can the not-I operate directly on the I, and vice versa? Since, by their very nature, one cannot operate directly on the other, what is required is a mediation between them by which they can operate indirectly on one another. That is, what is required is a synthesis by means of a third thing inscribed between them.

> The genuine highest task that embraces all others is: how can the I have a direct effect on the not-I, or the not-I on the I, since both are to be utterly opposed to each other? One interposes some X in between them, on which both may act, so that they also work indirectly upon one another. But one soon discovers that there must again be some point in this X at which I and not-I directly meet. To prevent this, one interposes between them and replaces the sharp boundary by a new term Y. But it soon appears that here too, as in X, there must be a point at which the two opponents directly touch one another. And so it would go on *ad infinitum*, if the knot were not cut, rather than loosed, by an absolute decree [*Machtspruch*] of reason, which the philosopher does not make but merely exhibits: since there is no way of unifying the not-I with the I, *let there be* no not-I at all. (FW I, 143–44; SK 137)

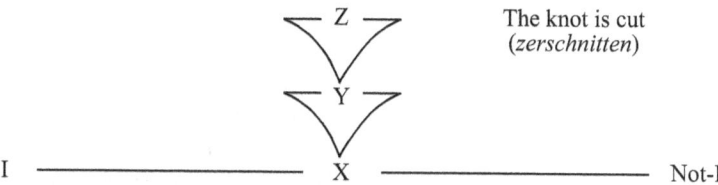

The knot is cut (*zerschnitten*)

The question is: What is this "absolute decree of reason," and what authorizes the philosopher even to exhibit it? What are we to make of a decree that simply abolishes the not-I?

We have seen that the opposition between the I and the not-I (i.e., the synthesis that makes this opposition possible) generates another essential opposition—between the limited I and the absolute I. Hence we encounter another problem of synthesis. Fichte formulates this as the problem of synthesizing the finite and the infinite:

> One can regard the matter from still another side.—Insofar as the I is limited by the not-I, it is finite; in itself, however, as posited through its own absolute activity, it is infinite. These two, its infinity and its finitude, are to be unified. But such a unification is in itself impossible. For a time, indeed, the conflict is settled by mediation; the infinite delimits the finite. But finally, once the utter impossibility of the attempted unification becomes manifest, finitude as such must be superseded [*aufgehoben*]; all limits must disappear, and the infinite I must alone remain, as one and as all. (FW I, 144; SK 137–38)

So the synthesis fails—but the very failure somehow leads to a further result in which only the infinite I remains. In this way, the outcome is analogous to Spinoza's solution to the Cartesian problem: the resolving of all oppositions into an infinite substance.

But what is the character of this resolution? For now, suffice it to say that it is a *practical* solution. This means that the infinite in which oppositions would be resolved is not put forth (as in Spinoza) as something that *is* but as something that *ought* to be. Fichte says: "Our idealism is not dogmatic but practical; [it] does not determine what *is*, but what *ought* to be" (FW I, 156; SK 147).

3. Introducing Section E of Part II

We can understand the task of section E (and its importance for the entire *Wissenschaftslehre*) in terms of our preliminary formulation of the task of the *Wissenschaftslehre*, drawn from the *First Introduction*. The task of the *Wissenschaftslehre* is to exhibit the I as the ground of those presentations that are accompanied by the feeling of necessity—presentations in which things are presented as existing outside us and independently of us. In other words, the task is to show that what exists for the I is brought forth by the I. Now, that power by which the I brings something forth is what Fichte calls *imagination* (*Einbildungskraft*). And so it is evident that the problem of imagination is at the center of his problematic. The importance of section E lies in the fact that it is the deduction of imagination.

In each of the first three syntheses there was a question left open. More precisely, what was left open were successive forms of the same question: How can the I posit negation in itself? How can the I posit passivity in itself? How can the I posit a lower degree of activity in itself?

At the beginning of section E, this question is reformulated as a circularity. Fichte says that all that has preceded moves in a circle: (1) For activity to be posited in the not-I, passivity must be posited in the I (the concept of efficacy). (2) For passivity to be posited in the I, a lower degree of activity must be posited in the I (the concept of substantiality). (3) But the I cannot posit absolutely a lower degree of activity in itself, for it posits the whole of activity (the totality of the real) in itself. (4) So for a lower degree of activity to be posited in the I, there must be a prior activity of the not-I that abolishes part of the I's activity. (5) But this is impossible, since (by the concept of efficacy) the not-I can be credited with activity only to the extent that passivity is posited in the I.

Activity in not-I	→	Passivity in I	→	Lower degree of activity in I	→	Activity in not-I

The same issue can be formulated in terms of the two specific concepts of synthesis that have been derived. The question is: How can limitation (i.e., negation, passivity, or a lower degree of activity) arise in the I? There are two alternatives, corresponding to the two concepts of synthesis.

First, in terms of the concept of efficacy, it might be supposed that the passivity of the I arises from the activity of the not-I—that is, the activity of the not-I is the cause of affection in the I. In this case, the I would be limited by the not-I, but it would not be aware of its limitation. It would merely be passively acted on and thus would be acted on in a way inappropriate for an I. In other words, the I would be determined by the not-I, but it would not posit itself as determined. The leading proposition, however, says that the I *posits itself* as limited by the not-I.

Second, in terms of the concept of substantiality, it might be supposed that the I has the power, independently of any influence of the not-I, of positing a lesser degree of activity in itself. But then the difficulty is that this limitation would have no relation to anything in the not-I as its cause: the I would simply be the "cause." So the I would posit itself as determined—but *not* as determined by the not-I. The leading proposition, however, says that the I posits itself as determined by the not-I. And so Fichte writes (in a passage cited in the synopsis above): "Thus both syntheses, employed in isolation, fail to explain what they should, and we still have the contradiction complained of above: if the I posits itself as determined, it is not determined by the not-I; if it is determined by the not-I, it does not posit itself as determined" (FW I, 148; SK 140).

As noted earlier, these two alternatives represent the most extreme forms of realism and idealism. (1) Realism, corresponding to the concept of efficacy, finds the sufficient ground in the not-I. Thus it takes account of the finite I's relation to the not-I (i.e., its finitude in the sense of dependence on something external) but not of its character as an I. (2) Idealism, corresponding to the concept of substantiality, finds the sufficient ground in the absolute I. Thus it takes account of the finite I's character as an I (its I-hood) but not of its finitude (in the sense of dependence on something external). What is required, then, is a synthesis of the two concepts of synthesis—that is, a synthesis of realism and idealism. This requirement determines the underlying movement in section E: the movement back and forth between various forms of realism and corresponding forms of idealism.

But before this synthesis is undertaken, the basic contradiction needs to be formulated in still more precise terms—hence, in a third formulation. The circle in its simplest form is:

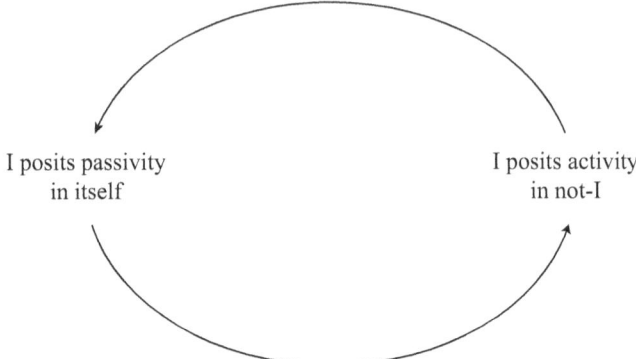

Now, each presupposes the other. Hence the I can do neither of the two positings without already having done the other. This means that the I can do neither.

Accordingly, there is a twofold result. First, it is not the case that the I posits passivity in itself by positing activity in the not-I. This is because it would already have to have posited passivity in the I in order to posit activity in the not-I. Second, it is not the case that the I posits activity in the not-I by positing passivity in itself. This is because it would already have to have posited activity in the not-I in order to posit passivity in the I. However, this result contradicts what was already established in the previous synthesis—and established precisely as the necessary condition for maintaining the fundamental principles. If the third principle is to hold, if there is to be a limited I over against the not-I, then the I must posit passivity in itself by positing activity in the not-I, and vice versa.

So the contradiction must be resolved. Fichte says that the two results are related as reality and negation (the first negates what the second affirms). But reality and negation are, in general, united by quantity (by partition). What is required, then, is that both results hold but only *in part*. Thus (1) the I *in part* posits passivity in itself insofar as it posits activity in the not-I—but *in part* it does not posit passivity in itself insofar as it posits activity in the not-I. This means that there is an activity posited in the not-I that does not lead to the positing of passivity in the I, and that is not opposed (by interdetermination) to a passivity in the I. This activity is an *independent activity* in the not-I. (2) By the same argument, there must be an activity in the I that does not lead to the positing of passivity in the not-I—that is, there must also be an independent activity in the I.

Now the difficulty is that this independent activity is not subject to the law of interdetermination. However, according to the earlier principle, all activity must be subject to this law (that is, all activity must lead to the positing of passivity in the opposite). What is therefore required is for the independent activity to be *and* not be subject to the law of interdetermination. That is, it must be subject to it only in a certain sense. But in what sense?

Consider that in the I there are two kinds of activity: A_1 and A_2. A_1 is linked to passivity (P) by interdetermination (i.e., it is subject to the law of interdetermination). A_2 is not linked to passivity (it is an independent activity). Now, how is A_2 subject to the law of interdetermination? By being linked not to a passivity but to the interplay of A_1 and P.

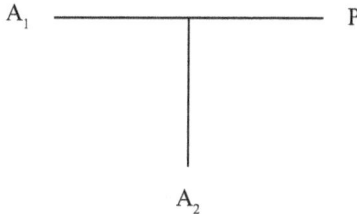

So Fichte formulates the matter thus: "Independent activity is determined by interaction and passion (action and passion determining one another by interdetermination); and, conversely, interaction and passion are determined by independent activity" (FW I, 150; SK 142). In general:

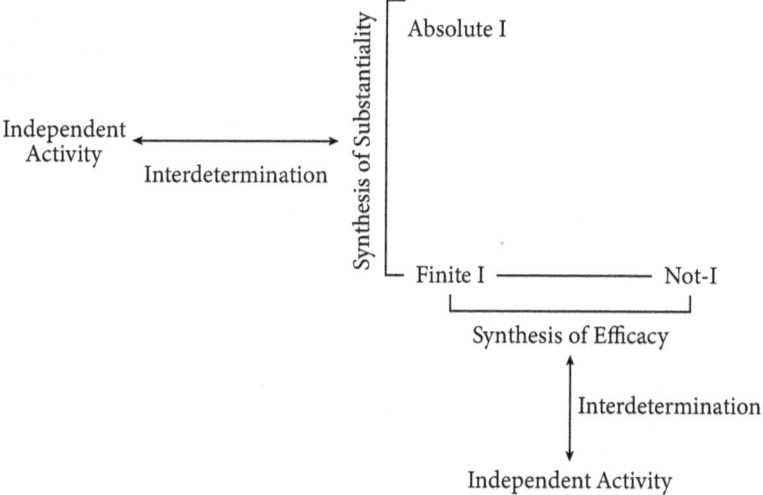

These connections determine the formal structure of section E.

4. The Problem of Finitude and the Stages of Idealism-Realism (Section E, continued)

Fichte's philosophy, like Kant's, takes with utmost seriousness the problem of human finitude. However, to take finitude seriously does not mean simply to take up the question "What is finitude?" along with the other questions considered. Rather, to take finitude seriously requires that one also take seriously the finitude of the philosopher himself—the finitude of the finite being who questions about finitude. In other words, for a philosophy to take finitude seriously, it must take seriously the fact that philosophy itself is a finite affair.

Most generally, this means that philosophy must take account of the fact that human knowing (hence, philosophical knowing) is not immediate comprehension: it is not a knowing in which what is known is simply laid out before us so that all we need to do is gaze at it. Rather, philosophy must proceed by mediation, by a progression through which access is gradually gained to what is to be known—that is, it must proceed *methodically*. Thus any philosophy that takes finitude seriously must also take methodology seriously: "In uttering the word *explain* we are already in the realm of finitude; for all *explanation*, that is, not immediate comprehension, but a progression from one thing to the next, is a finite affair" (FW I, 281; SK 248). Philosophy is not a mere seeing, a mere grasping (not even in reflection). It has rather to concern itself with the way in which what is to be known can be made accessible for a knowing. It is in this connection that we are to understand the need for the complex syntheses through which Fichte works in section E.

The formal structure of this system of syntheses is generated by the basic distinction drawn in the introductory part of section E—the distinction between syntheses or interplays (of efficacy and substantiality, respectively) and independent activities that stand in a relation of interdetermination with them. In effect, the system of syntheses (1) elaborates these distinctions (i.e., draws out further distinctions within them) and (2) brings the distinguished items to synthetic unity. (See appendices 2–4.) There is, however, another kind of structure, a dynamic structure within this formal structure. By thematizing it, we can get an overview of what is happening with respect to the fundamental issue of the theoretical *Wissenschaftslehre*.

Let me begin by trying to formulate the fundamental issue of the theoretical *Wissenschaftslehre*. We can take our clue from the proposition that stands at the beginning of the entire theoretical part: the I posits itself as determined by the not-I. This contains two propositions:

1. The I posits itself.
2. The I (as so posited) is determined by the not-I.

The problem in section E is the synthesis of these two propositions: How can the I (1) posit itself—which it must do by its very concept (according to the first principle)—and yet (2) be determined (limited) by something other than itself (i.e., be finite)? In other words, it is the *problem of the finite I*, the problem of reconciling I-hood and finitude.

Suppose, now, that we consider the system of syntheses (= section E) from the perspective of this problem. We can see several major stages. At each such stage, there are two positions described: a realism and an idealism. These positions correspond to the two sides of the problem. On the one side, idealism takes account of I-hood but not of finitude. On the other side, realism takes account of finitude but not of I-hood. Also, there is at each stage some consideration of a third position, which would synthesize idealism and realism—and thus take account of both sides of the problem.

As we proceed through the stages, we get progressively more adequate (less one-sided) versions of idealism and realism. The end is reached when the most adequate synthesis of realism and idealism is obtained—at least the most adequate that can be obtained within the sphere of theoretical knowledge. We will deal with the four most important stages in this dialectic of realism and idealism.

A. The First Stage

The first stage is discussed, parenthetically, in (I) (under efficacy, where an independent activity in the not-I is established as the activity that makes possible the matter of the interplay of efficacy). In *dogmatic idealism*, the I is simply the cause (substance) of presentations. The not-I has no sort of reality apart from presentation; it is nothing self-subsistent but merely an accident of the I. The difficulty of this position is that it can give no account of how the I is limited. It must simply— *dogmatically*—cut off questioning regarding affection and limitation—that is, finitude (FW I, 155; SK 147).

In *dogmatic realism* (= Spinozism), the not-I is regarded as the cause of presentations—as real ground of everything. The I is a mere accident of the not-I. The difficulty of this position has already been indicated in the criticism of Spinoza: it claims to go beyond the I to something more ultimate. But one cannot transcend the I—and, in fact, when one claims to do so, it is because one has not really reached the standpoint of the I. As a result, this position involves the most extreme failure to account for the I-hood of the I (FW I, 155; SK 146–47).

The question thus arises regarding the synthesis of these two positions. However, Fichte does not actually develop the synthesis—perhaps because these forms of idealism and realism are too gross to permit any such development. Rather, he uses the question as a means for presenting "a view of the whole system" (FW I, 154; SK 146)—to anticipate the course that is about to be followed through:

> Hence the real question at issue between realism and idealism is as to which road is to be taken in explaining presentation. It will become evident that in the theoretical part of our *Wissenschaftslehre* this question remains completely unanswered; that is, it is answered by saying: Both roads are correct; under a certain condition we are obliged to take the one, and under the opposite condition we must take the other; and by this, then, all human, that is, all finite reason is thrown into conflict with itself, and embroiled in a circle. A system in which this is demonstrated is a critical idealism, of the kind most fully and coherently set forth by Kant. This conflict of reason with itself must be resolved, even if it should not prove possible within the theoretical *Wissenschaftslehre*; and since the absolute existence of the I cannot be given up, the issue must be decided in favor of the second line of argument, just as in dogmatic idealism (but with this difference, that our idealism is not dogmatic but practical; does not determine what *is*, but what *ought* to be). (FW I, 155–56; SK 147)

So what is to be established within the theoretical sphere is a critical idealism, which, rather than resolving the circling between realism and idealism, demonstrates the circle as belonging to *finite* reason. But, beyond the theoretical sphere, what is to be established is something similar to dogmatic idealism—except that it is *practical*.

B. The Second Stage

The second stage occurs in the α-stage of the synthesis dealing with efficacy (FW I, 171–78; SK 159–64). The items involved are:

A (f) = transference (positing by means of non-positing).[8] This is the activity of the I by which it posits reality in the not-I by not positing reality in itself.

A (m) = activity in the not-I.[9] This is the activity by which the not-I would affect the I and cause passivity in it.

In the position of *qualitative idealism*, A (f) → A (m). It says: transference determines the activity in the not-I. This means that the not-I has no reality in itself. Its reality is simply the result of the transference of reality to it. In other words, the activity in the not-I is simply a result of the I's positing of passivity in itself. The one-sidedness here is evident: it is not explained how the I could posit passivity in itself (for the I posits only activity, reality in itself). More specifically, this position takes no account of any affection of the not-I on the I by which the I might be limited or come to have passivity in itself. Thus this position does not take account of finitude.

In the position of *qualitative realism*, A (m) → A (f). It says: the activity in the not-I determines transference. This means that the not-I is the ground of

---

8. [Editor's note: "A (f)" stands for "activity of the form." Cf. FW I, 171; SK 159.]
9. [Editor's note: "A (m)" stands for "activity of the matter." Cf. FW I, 171; SK 159.]

the passivity in the I (from which transference proceeds). Thus the not-I has an independent reality and operates on the I, causing passivity in the I. The not-I is therefore a thing in itself. But here, too, there is a one-sidedness: it is not (and cannot) be explained how such a not-I could operate on the I. Since the I is what it posits itself to be, it could be limited by the not-I *only if* it posited itself as so limited. Thus this position fails to take the I-hood of the I into account.

Finally, in the position of *critical idealism*, A (f) ↔ A (m). This says: transference and the activity of the not-I are mutually determining. In effect, it just reinstates that circle that arose earlier (in the introductory part of section E): activity can be posited in the not-I only by the positing of passivity in the I (i.e., through transference) *and* there can be passivity in the I only if there is a prior activity in the not-I that causes it.

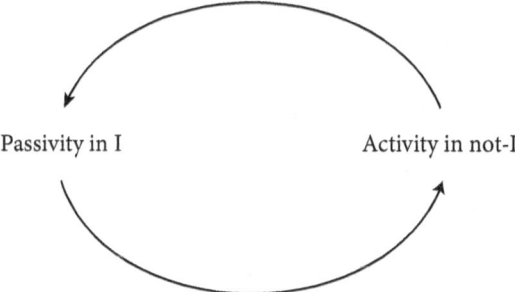

Passivity in I   Activity in not-I

The synthesis amounts to retaining the circle. The resultant synthetic unity (= A) is called "mediate positing," a positing of reality by way of a non-positing (FW I, 181; SK 167). More specifically, the mediacy of positing means: (1) the I can be posited only through the non-positing of the not-I, corresponding to A (f), and (2) the not-I can be posited only through the non-positing of the I, corresponding to A (m). In other words, each is posited through the non-positing of the other (cf. FW I, 181–83; SK 167–68).

But then the question arises: What grounds the circle itself? One cannot say that the circle is absolutely posited—for the only thing that is absolutely posited is the I, and in the I as such, there is no such circle with a not-I. Furthermore, Fichte says, the ground of the circle (whatever it may be) is already presupposed by the principle at the head of the theoretical *Wissenschaftslehre* (the I posits itself as determined by the not-I) and so is not within the scope of the theoretical *Wissenschaftslehre*. This means that the ground of the circle must lie outside the boundaries of the theoretical *Wissenschaftslehre* (FW I, 177; SK 164).

C. The Third Stage

The third stage occurs in the γ-stage of syntheses dealing with efficacy. The items involved are:

A = mediate positing
I = opposition (essential and real) between the I and the not-I.[10]

In the position of *quantitative idealism*, A → I. It says: mediate positing determines (grounds) the opposition between the I and the not-I. This means that the opposition between the I and the not-I is not something existing prior to positing but is founded on a positing. In simpler terms: it is a law of the I to posit mediately—to posit in such a way as to institute the opposition between itself and the not-I (i.e., in such a way as to institute finitude). The I simply posits itself as finite; the I is absolutely finite. So, unlike earlier forms of idealism, this form takes some account of finitude. But it simply tries to incorporate it into I-hood, thereby making it absolute. But "absolute finitude" is a self-contradiction.

In the position of *quantitative realism*, I → A. It says: the opposition between the I and the not-I grounds the mediacy of positing. So opposition is fundamental. However, this position understands this opposition in a more subtle way than did qualitative realism (which supposed a thing in itself). This position does not assume that the not-I has independent reality. Rather, it maintains merely that there is a *real limitation* present in the I *without* any contribution on the part of the I (i.e., there is a limitation whose ground does not lie in the I). This position does not make the further inference to an independently existing not-I as the real cause of this limitation. This realism still fails to take sufficient account of I-hood: it cannot explain how a *real* determination can become a determination *for* the I. In other words, it cannot show how the I's absolute positing of itself could be determined by something extrinsic to that positing.

The question thus arises as to the synthesis of these two positions (A ↔ I). To see what form the synthesis needs to take, we need to note that the basic difference between the two positions concerns the *ground* of the mediacy of positing. According to quantitative idealism, the mediacy of positing is simply grounded in positing as such: it is the character of positing as such. This means that mediacy has its ground *in the I*. According to quantitative realism, however, the ground is located in the passivity of the I (the presence in the I of a determination independent of the I). This means that the ground is *not in the I*. The synthesis would thus require that this ground lie in *both* the I and the not-I. But Fichte says that there is no way of seeing how it could lie in both. So, he concludes: "We confess our ignorance on this topic." This position of established ignorance is called "critical quantitative idealism" (FW I, 190; SK 174). Thus, once again, the attempt at a direct, final synthesis has broken down.

---

10. [Editor's note: When used as a symbol, "I" stands for "interplay" (*Wechsel*), just as "A" stands for "activity" (*Tätigkeit*).]

D. The Fourth Stage

The final stage coincides with the γ-stage of the synthesis of substantiality. The items involved are:

A = the absolute conjoining and holding fast of opposites. The opposites involved here are the I and the not-I. So this activity is a conjoining (*Zusammenfassen*) of the I and the not-I in their opposition. The power that is operative in this activity is the imagination.

I = the sheer clash (*Zusammentreffen*) of the opposites, the incursion of each on the other.

On the one hand, A → I. Here this means that the activity by which the I conjoins opposites determines the clash of the components. In other words, the I and the not-I become components only by virtue of the activity of the I. The opposition between the I and the not-I (hence presentation, "experience") is grounded in an act of the I. This is an *idealism*. It is the same as quantitative idealism except that it replaces the concept of the mediacy of positing (the positing of the I by the non-positing of the not-I and the positing of the not-I by the non-positing of the I) with a single act in which both the I and the not-I are posited. However, it still fails to explain how the I (which posits only itself) could posit the opposition between itself and the not-I. In other words, it does justice to I-hood but not to finitude.

On the other hand, I → A. This means that the I's activity of conjoining opposites is determined by the mere clash of opposites. In other words, the sheer encounter between the I and the not-I is the ground of the possibility of that activity of the I (= imagination) by which the subjective and the objective are conjoined in their opposition. What is most important is the way Fichte elaborates this alternative: he regards the clash (encounter) as the presence of a "check" (*Anstoß*) on the I. This means that, for some reason (not grounded in the I), the subjective sphere (posited by the I) proves not to be indefinitely extensible—that is, the I's positing of the subjective (i.e., of itself) is restrained or checked. This does *not* mean that a bound is set to the I's activity but rather that the I is given the task of setting bounds to itself. In other words, the check merely indicates that bounds must be set, but it is not itself a definite bound. Then, to set these bounds, the I must oppose something objective to the subjective and conjoin them (hence the activity).

This position is a *realism*. But it is even more abstract than quantitative realism. It does not presuppose a not-I existing independently of the I (qualitative realism). Nor does it even presuppose a determination (bound) present in the I but not derived from the I (quantitative idealism). It assumes merely that there occurs a check to the I's activity (of positing itself), a check that indicates the necessity for a determination to be made. However, even this realism is inadequate.

Like every realism, it fails to explain the transition from the not-I to the I—that is, it fails to do justice to I-hood. Specifically, it explains the requirement that the I be bounded and determined (i.e., the check) as something involving no assistance from the I. But it does not explain how the check could be something *for* the I.

So we come to the final synthesis of section E: A ↔ I. This means: the occurrence of the clash and the I's activity of conjoining the subjective and the objective are mutually determining. Here I will touch only on the most important points. (More detailed analysis is given in appendix 4.)

This synthesis overcomes the one-sidedness of the previous two syntheses. It poses a more genuine synthesis of I-hood and finitude. On the one hand, it overcomes abstract realism: rather than regarding the check as something that occurs independently of the I's activity, this synthesis maintains that there can be a check *only* insofar as the I is active. The check's possibility depends on the activity of the I. On the other hand, this synthesis overcomes abstract idealism: the I's activity is also conditioned by the check.

This activity is a conjoining of the subjective and the objective in their opposition—that is, it is an activity in which the I *bounds* or limits itself (over against the objective). The question is: What must be the character of the activity for it to be conditioned by the check? What is required is this: the activity must be such that, if the check did not occur, the activity would not bound itself—it would be unbounded, infinite. So, in itself (considered independently of the check), the activity must be *infinite*.

Now the synthesis says that the activity is conditioned by the check. This means: if the check occurs, then this infinite activity posits the boundary between the subjective and the objective—that is, it bounds and determines itself. But to determine itself is to posit itself *as finite*. So the I posits itself as *both finite and infinite*.

The interplay in which the I posits itself as both finite and infinite, in which the I endeavors to unite the irreconcilable, is the power of imagination (*das Vermögen der Einbildungskraft*). The imagination is the power of holding together, in their interplay, the infinite and the finite—that is, I-hood and finitude. So it is the imagination that makes it possible for the I to bound itself, to oppose an object to itself and yet still remain an I. In other words, the imagination is the *productive* power that brings forth the object: "The not-I is itself a product of the self-determining I, and nothing at all absolute or posited outside the I" (FW I, 218; SK 195). "Our doctrine here is therefore that all reality—*for us* being understood, as it cannot be otherwise understood in a system of transcendental philosophy—is brought forth solely by the imagination" (FW I, 227; SK 202).

But the imagination does this only on the condition that the check occur (even though the check, in turn, cannot occur without the concurrence of the I).

Here we have the residual aporia of the theoretical *Wissenschaftslehre*: the possibility of the check remains unexplained. "As to the question how and by what means there occurs that check to the I that is prerequisite for explaining presentation, this alone is not to be answered here: for it lies beyond the bounds of the theoretical part of the *Wissenschaftslehre*" (FW I, 218; SK 195).

5. On Imagination

At this point, let us briefly interrupt the systematic development in order to regard the outcome in a broader perspective and to introduce more completely Fichte's concept of imagination. One of the most significant achievements of the *Wissenschaftslehre* lies in showing the role of imagination. Already in Kant's first *Critique*, imagination is the operation of synthesis, which is required for even the possibility of knowledge. Thus already in Kant, imagination has become essential to knowledge. This way of conceiving imagination goes beyond the traditional understanding of imagination as φαντασία—the conjuring up of images. Fichte goes still further in giving importance to the imagination.[11]

We have seen that there are four successive stages such that at each stage there is a reduction of the opposition between idealism and realism. Each becomes less one-sided, and so they come closer together and converge. At the final stage, all that still separates them is a *check*, which gives the I the task of setting bounds to itself by opposing a not-I to itself. So the not-I is neither a thing in itself nor a mere affection but an object that, as the check occurs, is posited by the I.

Now, if the check could be derived (explained), then a convergence of idealism and realism, of the I and the not-I, would be demonstrated. However, the check cannot be deduced. It remains an inexplicable residue and prevents the syntheses from being carried through to the end (where all opposition would be dissolved). Instead, there remains a certain opposition between the I-character of the I (its positing itself, its infinitude) and its being limited by the not-I (its finitude).

However, the synthesis must in some sense be possible. Otherwise, the principle of the theoretical *Wissenschaftslehre*, which expresses precisely this synthesis, cannot hold. And if it cannot hold, then the third principle would collapse. The point, then, is this: if there cannot be a synthesis in the sense of a resolution (dissolution) of all opposition, there must be a synthesis in another sense—namely, in the sense of *holding together* the opposed terms. The movement or interplay in which such a synthesis would occur Fichte calls the power of *imagination*.

---

11. [Editor's note: this paragraph includes material from the Fall 2010 lecture course.]

> This interplay of the I in and with itself, whereby it posits itself at once as finite and infinite—an interplay that consists, as it were, in self-conflict and is self-reproducing in that the I endeavors to unify what is not unifiable, now attempting to bring the infinite into the form of the finite, now, driven back, positing it again outside the latter, and in that very moment seeking once more to bring it into the form of finitude—this is the power of imagination [*das Vermögen der Einbildungskraft*]. (FW I, 215; SK 193)

> The imagination posits no sort of fixed limits; for it has itself no fixed standpoint; reason alone posits anything fixed, in that it first gives fixity to the imagination itself. Imagination is a power that hovers [*schwebt*] in the middle between determination and nondetermination, between finite and infinite. (FW I, 216; SK 194)

So the imagination has no fixed standpoint but is the movement of displacement as such. It posits no fixed limits but circulates among the opposites so as to hold them together (finite and infinite, self-positing and relation to the not-I). The imagination hovers in between opposites so as to hold them together *in their opposition*. This is a unique kind of relatedness or connectivity. It is not a simple, undifferentiated unity or a unity produced by synthesis. Nor is it a superseding (*Aufheben*) as in Hegel, where the opposites are retained in their opposition but submitted to a higher unity. This kind of relatedness, this connectivity, I have taken over in *Force of Imagination* and have undertaken to rethink within a contemporary, phenomenological context.[12]

Finally, in turn, the critical investigation of the foundations of theoretical knowledge (i.e., theoretical philosophy) must reflect on this opposition—that is, this oppositional space composed by the imagination. And so this opposition, that is, "something contradictory . . . must be laid at the ground of all our philosophizing" (FW I, 283; SK 249). At the level of philosophical reflection, as we have seen, this opposition takes the form of the opposition between idealism and realism. Fichte says regarding these two courses: "One ought to follow neither of these courses: one ought to reflect neither on the one alone nor on the other alone but on both together, to hover in between the two opposed determinations of this idea. This is the business of the *creative imagination*. . . . It is this power that determines whether one philosophizes with, or without, spirit" (FW I, 284; SK 250). So the theoretical *Wissenschaftslehre* converges on imagination (this hovering between opposites). And from what is thus disclosed, the philosophical reflection is reflected back to itself, disclosed to itself, as an enactment of creative imagination.[13]

---

12. See John Sallis, *Force of Imagination: The Sense of the Elemental* (Bloomington: Indiana University Press, 2000).

13. [Editor's note: for a fuller discussion of the place of imagination in Fichte, see John Sallis, *Spacings—Of Reason and Imagination in Texts of Kant, Fichte, Hegel* (Chicago: University of Chicago Press, 1987), ch. 2.]

6. The Deduction of Presentation

What do these results entail with respect to the theoretical *Wissenschaftslehre* as a whole? In effect, they provide an explanation for the proposition that stands at the beginning of the entire theoretical *Wissenschaftslehre*: "The I posits itself as determined by the not-I." Specifically, it has been shown that "the I cannot posit itself otherwise than as determined by the not-I (no object, no subject)" (FW I, 218; SK 195). That is, the I must posit itself as determined by the not-I in order to posit itself *as* determinate at all (as a subject). Fichte says: "The determination of the I, its reflection upon itself as something determinate, is possible only on the condition that it bounds itself by an opposite" (FW I, 218; SK 195). But it has also been shown how the I is able to posit itself as so determined (despite its character as an I, i.e., its character as self-enclosed self-positing, immune to externality). It is able to do this because that which determines it (the not-I) is not a thing in itself but its own product (brought forth by the imagination).

Thus the principle with which the theoretical *Wissenschaftslehre* began has been completely exhausted: all the contradictions involved in it have been overcome, and it has thus been exhibited in its basic possibility. So, in a sense, the theoretical *Wissenschaftslehre* is completed. All the elements necessary to explain presentation (*Vorstellung*) must have been grounded. All that remains is simply to apply what has been established so as to provide this explanation. This is accomplished in the "Deduction of Presentation" (FW I, 227–46; SK 203–17).

But before proceeding to this, Fichte proposes to reflect on the course of the theoretical *Wissenschaftslehre* as a whole. He considers first the course already followed. This course began with the proposition "The I posits itself as determined by the not-I." The problem was to discover the conditions under which this proposition could hold. What Fichte has done is to consider all possible conditions—that is, he has enumerated systematically all possible determinations of the elements involved in the proposition—and then, by drawing out contradictions, he has gradually eliminated the inadequate determinations (such as those prescribed by the various kinds of idealism and realism). Thus he has finally discovered the only possible way of conceiving this proposition to be true—that is, the only possible determinations under which it can hold, and thus the only way in which it can be true.

Now, if the fundamental principles are true, then the proposition at the beginning of the theoretical *Wissenschaftslehre* must be true. But if it can be true only in the way established by the syntheses, then the result of the syntheses must be a *fact of consciousness*— "a primordial fact occurring in our mind" (FW I, 219; SK 196). Of course, all the possibilities considered in the syntheses are, in a sense, facts of consciousness—facts in the consciousness of the reflecting philosopher. But they are artificially brought forth by the spontaneity of reflection and do not necessarily correspond to anything present in the mind independently of the reflection. In fact, they cannot so correspond, since they are proved false. And yet the result of the syntheses must correspond to something in the mind independently of philosophical reflection—granted that the initial proposition is true and that it can be true *only* in that way established through the syntheses.

However, to say that it is a fact does not mean that it is something immediately evident. On the contrary, it is a fact that has to be explained—which the I must explain to itself. This is what is at issue in that section that, strictly speaking, forms the second half of the theoretical *Wissenschaftslehre*: "Deduction of Presentation." In precise terms, this is a (philosophical) reflection on that reflection in which the I explains this fact to itself.

Let us turn now to the "Deduction of Presentation" and—very briefly—mention only its general procedure. It begins with the result reached in the first half of the theoretical *Wissenschaftslehre*: the connectivity that is carried out by the imagination, since a final synthesis is not possible. Now Fichte reformulates this connectivity: he regards it as connecting (but without synthesis) the infinitely outreaching activity of the I and the occurrence of the check. This means that the activity of the I as purely self-positing is not impeded by anything outside itself—except the check. Fichte says that the condition of the I that results from this connectivity is *intuition*.

The deduction then proceeds in terms of what is required for intuition so regarded. To intuition (i.e., the activity of intuiting) there must be opposed something intuited. Here again the imagination comes into play by bringing forth an object of intuition. But then it is also required that the intuited be distinguished from the purely imaginary (pure phantasy). This requires that the intuited be stabilized, "brought to a stand" (FW I, 233; SK 207). And to satisfy this requirement, what is necessary is the understanding (*Verstand*). Thus Fichte has deduced what Kant considered to be the two stems of human knowledge, understanding and intuition, as well as imagination, which for Kant, connects these. Beyond this, Fichte proceeds similarly with respect to the other elements of presentation: reflection, judgment, reason, and so forth.

The most comprehensive and decisive result of this analysis, along with the account of the imagination as hovering between the I and the not-I, is the absolute centrality that Fichte accords to imagination: "It is therefore here taught that all reality—*for us* being understood, as it cannot be otherwise understood in a system of transcendental philosophy—is brought forth solely by the imagination." Thus he goes on to say: "On this activity of imagination is grounded the possibility of our consciousness, of our life, of our existence for ourselves" (FW I, 227; SK 202).

7. The Practical *Wissenschaftslehre*

Let us begin with a broad synopsis before considering the detailed development. We have seen that the opposition between the I and the not-I has the effect of generating an opposition of the I to itself—that is, the opposition between the absolute (self-positing, infinite) I and the limited I (the finite I opposed to the not-I).

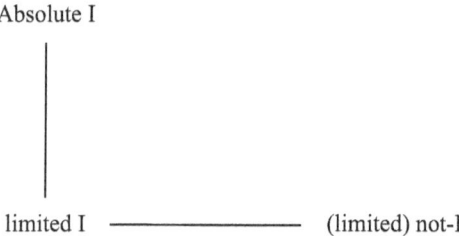

Now Fichte observes that the I (whether limited or not) must be one and the same I: the I is absolutely identical with itself. Thus this opposition must be resolved.

> Insofar as the I is limited by the not-I, it is finite; in itself, however, as posited through its own absolute activity, it is infinite. These two, its infinity and its finitude, are to be unified. But such a unification is in itself impossible. For a time, indeed, the conflict is settled by mediation; the infinite delimits the finite. But finally, once the utter impossibility of the attempted unification becomes manifest, finitude as such must be superseded [*aufgehoben*]; all limits must disappear, and the infinite I must alone remain, as one and as all. (FW I, 144; SK 137–38)

Here the transition is similar to that where it was a matter of opposition between the I and the not-I. There is a movement toward a synthesis that, if completed, would resolve the opposition. And yet no such synthesis can be reached. Whereas previously, this failure of synthesis led to the role of the imagination, as hovering between the opposites, here it broaches the transition to the practical. Specifically, the connection between the absolute I and the limited I is made possible by our *practical capacity*. This practical capacity has the character of striving (*Streben*).

Fichte says regarding the absolute I (with its activity of self-positing) and the limited I (whose activity also includes passivity, because of its opposition to the not-I): "We can only say that their likeness [*Gleichheit*] is absolutely demanded: they *ought* to be alike" (FW I, 260; SK 229). Thus the very identity of the I is grounded on the demand (imperative) that the limited I ought to be like the absolute I. This demand is the *categorical imperative*. The relation to (identity with) the Kantian conception of the categorical imperative can be seen in this statement from the *Critique of Practical Reason*: "The sole principle of morality consists in independence from all material of the law (i.e., from a desired object) and in the accompanying determination of choice by the mere form of giving universal law which a maxim must be capable of having" (AA 5, 33; CPrR 33). In Fichte's language: the moral law commands (1) independence from the not-I and (2) universality as represented by the absolute I. Fichte thus says: "Our idealism is not dogmatic but practical, does not determine what *is* but what *ought* to be" (FW I, 156; SK 147).

Let us turn now to the detailed analysis of the practical *Wissenschaftslehre*. We need to see (at least in general) what the main issues are here—and especially how the practical *Wissenschaftslehre* bears on the outcome of the theoretical *Wissenschaftslehre* and the character of the entire *Wissenschaftslehre*.

At the beginning of the theoretical *Wissenschaftslehre*, Fichte indicated that there are two propositions that follow directly from the third fundamental principle:

1. The I posits itself as determined by the not-I.
2. The I posits itself as determining the not-I.

The first proposition provided the basis from which the theoretical *Wissenschaftslehre* proceeded. The second proposition was initially problematic: there was no reason to assume the reality of the not-I, which, however, it must have in order to be limited by the I. However, the theoretical *Wissenschaftslehre* has now shown how the not-I has reality (*as* brought forth by the I)—and so this proposition can now be dealt with.

Fichte notes that it could be developed in the same way as in the theoretical *Wissenschaftslehre* (antithesis-synthesis). However, he proposes a shorter way: to focus on a single major antithesis within this proposition—specifically, the antithesis between:

1. the I as intelligence, as a presenting subject (hence, restricted) and
2. the I as absolutely posited (hence, unrestricted).

The task is to show that this antithesis can only be resolved by introducing a *practical capacity* of the I.

Fichte first proceeds to draw out the antithesis and exhibit it in its full range. On the one side of the antithesis, the I (as absolute) is what it posits itself to be (according to the first principle). It is wholly independent of everything external to itself, which means that the absolute I is wholly independent of the not-I. On the other side of the antithesis is the I as intelligence, which, though it brings forth the object, is dependent on the check. Specifically, the I can be a subject (an intelligent I) only by virtue of the check—that is, only by virtue of something external to the I (an indeterminate not-I). To this extent, the intelligent I is not absolute and thus is opposed to the absolute I.

But the I must be one and the same: the I is absolutely identical with itself. Hence this opposition must be removed. So Fichte now makes a first attempt to resolve the antithesis. In fact, however, this attempt only serves to exhibit the full range of the antithesis. Here is how he proceeds. The antithesis can be resolved only if the dependence of the intelligent I on the not-I is eliminated. How is this possible? It is possible only if the not-I (i.e., the check) can be regarded as itself determined by the I—that is, only if the absolute I is the *cause* of the not-I. This would then mean that the I determines itself to be intelligence (and the positing of the not-I is just the means by which it does this). In other words, the intelligent I's dependence on the not-I would ultimately be a dependence of the I on itself. However, such a resolution involves a contradiction. The absolute I cannot posit the not-I, because (as the theoretical *Wissenschaftslehre* has shown) positing the not-I amounts to restricting the I, whereas the absolute I cannot restrict (not-posit) itself.

Fichte notes that a point has now been reached from which the true meaning of the second fundamental principle can be seen:

> In the second principle, only some part is absolute; part, on the contrary, presupposes a fact that cannot in any way be proved a priori, but only from the experience of a given individual.
>
> In addition to the self-positing of the I, there is also to be another positing. A priori, this is a mere hypothesis; *that* such a positing occurs, can be demonstrated by nothing other than a fact of consciousness, and everyone must demonstrate it for himself by this fact; nobody can prove it to another on rational grounds. (FW I, 252; SK 223)

He is saying that it cannot be proved *that there is* another positing besides the I's positing of itself, but only that if there is such a positing, it must be a counterpositing (i.e., what is posited must be the not-I). That there is such an additional positing can be demonstrated only by reference to one's experience. In other words, finitude (subjection to externality) cannot be derived from I-hood. Finitude is a fact that the I can only explain to itself. Without being entirely explicit, Fichte indicates that precisely such an explanation is what was really taking place in the consideration of the second principle in part I.

In the first attempt to resolve the conflict between the I as absolute and the I as intelligence, it was necessary to suppose that the I (as absolute) is the cause of the not-I. But this causality turned out to involve a contradiction. Nevertheless, it is the only way to resolve the antithesis between the absolute I and the intelligent I. So the contradiction involved in the concept of such causality (of the I on the not-I) must be resolved. As preparation for this, Fichte proceeds to reformulate more precisely the contradiction at issue. It is between two different aspects of the I. The first aspect is the I as absolute. It posits whatever is—and whatever it posits (hence, whatever is) is posited *as* the I (that is, all its positing belongs to its positing of itself). In this respect, the I is infinite and unbounded; it cannot posit a not-I, for whatever it posits is just itself. The other aspect is the I as opposing to itself a not-I, positing a not-I and thereby limiting itself—hence, positing itself as finite.

The conflict can also be regarded as a conflict between two kinds of activity in the I. Hence Fichte gives yet another formulation of the contradiction. On the one hand, there is the activity in which the I posits itself as infinite. This is an activity that relates only to the I (that is, what is posited is only the I, nothing else). It is an activity that returns on itself, a self-reverting activity. Fichte calls this "pure activity." The I so regarded is the "pure I" (FW I, 256; SK 226). On the other hand, there is the activity in which the I posits itself as finite. This is an activity in which it opposes a not-I to itself (and thus causes the not-I). This activity is not related immediately to the I but to the not-I. Fichte calls this "objective activity" (FW I, 256–57; SK 227). It is especially important to note that "pure activity" is just the positing described in the first principle. "Objective activity" is just the positing described in the second and third principles (taken together, as they must be). Accordingly, the conflict at issue is simply the conflict between the first principle on the one hand and the second and third principles on the other.

Now, both activities must belong to one and the same I. There must therefore be a bond between them. What is the bond? The most obvious answer would be *causality*—that is, that pure activity is the cause of objective activity (hence, mediately the cause of the not-I).

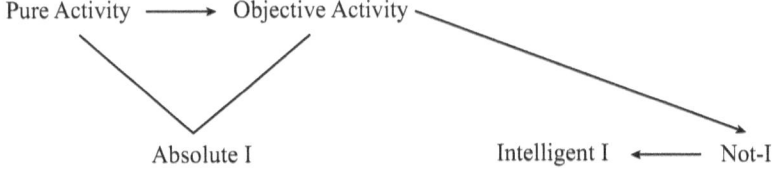

This would mean that the act by which the I posits itself absolutely (the first principle) would be the cause of the act by which the I posits the not-I (the second principle). In other words, the second principle would be derivable from the first. But it is precisely this connection that is denied by what was said earlier about the second principle: *that* counterpositing occurs cannot be proved a priori but is established only by appeal to experience.

Thus another kind of bond between the two activities is required. This bond, this mediation is precisely the practical capacity that Fichte indicated would need to be introduced. The name for this practical capacity is "striving" (*Streben*) (FW I, 261; SK 231). Fichte's derivation of this striving and related matters is extremely complex, and we cannot treat it in detail. Let me merely indicate the most general lines of the deduction.

The source of the conflict between pure activity and objective activity is this: For the I to posit the not-I, it must negate (not posit) itself—whereas pure activity can involve no negation (it is simply the I's positing of itself). So if the conflict is to be overcome, the activity (= reality) posited in the not-I must somehow *not* require negation of pure activity in the I. In other words, the pure activity of the I must persist independently of the activity posited in the not-I. This is what is required if the I is to posit the not-I without negating its own character as an I.

However, although the pure activity and activity in the not-I must be independent (neither negates the other), in another respect they must be connected. More specifically, they must be absolutely alike, because both are related to one and the same I: the pure activity is the activity of that I; the activity in the not-I is posited by that I—and what the I posits is just itself. So the two activities must be absolutely alike. But insofar as they must be entirely independent and insofar as the opposition between the I and the not-I is to remain, they *cannot be alike*. Thus Fichte says: "We can only say that their likeness is absolutely demanded: they *ought* to be alike" (FW I, 260; SK 229). In other words, the condition of the possibility of the unity of pure activity and objective activity (of the I's self-identity) is a demand for this likeness—a demand that the not-I conform to the I. This demand is the *categorical imperative*. It is the demand of practical reason.

Let me mention only one of the many consequences of this. Fichte has shown that the possibility of the intelligent (i.e., theoretical) I presupposes the objective activity of the I. And, in turn, the objective activity (as activity *of* the I) is possible only on the basis of the demand for conformity of the not-I to the I—that is, only on the basis of practical reason. Thus practical reason is the condition of the possibility of theoretical reason.

8. Conclusion

To conclude our study of Fichte, let me mention two ways that the *Wissenschaftslehre*, near its end, turns back on itself. First, the significance of the first fundamental principle gets determined only at the end, within the framework of *practical reason*. This principle expresses the concept of the infinite I (of the I as self-positing), and it is only at the end that this I is really identified. The identification comes *after* the basic developments in the practical *Wissenschaftslehre*:

> Here the meaning of the principle, *the I posits itself absolutely*, first becomes wholly clear. Therein there is no reference at all to the I given in actual consciousness; for the latter is never absolute, but its state [*Zustand*] is always grounded either immediately or mediately, on something outside the I; the reference is rather to an idea of the I that must necessarily lie at the ground of its infinite practical demand, which, however, is unattainable for our

consciousness and so can never appear immediately therein (though it may, of course, mediately, in philosophical reflection). (FW I, 277; SK 244)

Thus we might say: the absolute I is not what I am (I am the finite I); it is instead what I am bound to strive for (as the very condition of my being an I at all).

Here one can also grasp the significance of the initial theoretical act. That is, the significance of setting up the absolutely first fundamental principle (the expression of the absolute I) at the beginning (*as* the beginning) of the *Wissenschaftslehre*. The significance lies in the character of that act as being ultimately not theoretical but practical—a response to the infinite practical demand and hence a matter of duty. Thus it is that (in the *Second Introduction*) Fichte calls the *Wissenschaftslehre* a product of practical necessity—and continues: "Transcendental idealism thus appears at the same time as the only dutiful mode of thought in philosophy, as that mode of thought in which speculation and the moral law are most intimately united. I *ought* in my thinking to set out from the pure I, and to think of the latter as absolutely self-active; not as determined by things, but as determining them" (FW I, 467; SK 41).

Finally, since the entire deduction of the conditions of the possibility of *theoretical* knowledge depends on the first fundamental principle, and since this principle proves to be a (the) practical principle, it follows that theoretical knowledge is grounded in the practical. There is a primacy of practical reason.

6. The Early Development of Schelling's Thought

LET ME BEGIN with a passage from Schelling's *Ideen zu einer Philosophie der Natur* (1797). Schelling writes: "Philosophy is not something which originally and by nature is present in our spirit without its cooperation. It is thoroughly a work of freedom. It is to each only that which he himself has made it; and thus even the idea of philosophy is only the result of philosophy itself, which, as an infinite science, is at the same time the science of itself" (SW II, 11; PGI 167). This statement touches the center of Schelling's thought. It says that philosophy as a science is also a science of itself. This means that philosophy is a problem for itself—continual self-reflection belongs to the essence of philosophy. Indeed, we find this principle exemplified in Schelling's work: what is at issue in his work is not only a philosophy but also the very idea of philosophy.

This reflexivity is most directly (and most profoundly) exemplified with respect to freedom. Philosophy is "a work of freedom," and, in turn, freedom is a problem for philosophy—in fact, *the* problem for Schelling's philosophy. Thus, insofar as philosophy makes freedom problematic, it calls itself into question, makes a problem of itself. Here we have a first—very preliminary—indication of the issue of Schelling's treatise on human freedom: through what it accomplishes with respect to the question of human freedom, it brings about a radical transformation of the idea of philosophy. This is what Heidegger has in mind when he says of Schelling that "from within German Idealism he forces it beyond its own fundamental position."[1] And this is why Heidegger says that Schelling is "the genuinely creative and farthest-reaching thinker of this whole age of German philosophy."[2]

Heidegger's assessment of Schelling's thought can, of course, be contested; it should indeed be contested. For one can offer support for the more common view that it is Hegel who brings German Idealism to its genuine fulfillment while also providing—even if not always deliberately—openings beyond it, which most

---

1. Martin Heidegger, *Schellings Abhandlung Über das Wesen der menschlichen Freiheit (1809)*, ed. Hildegard Feick, 2nd ed. (Tübingen: Niemeyer, 1995), 4; Martin Heidegger, *Schelling's Treatise on the Essence of Human Freedom*, trans. Joan Stambaugh (Athens: Ohio University Press, 1985), 4.
2. Heidegger, *Schellings Abhandlung Über das Wesen der menschlichen Freiheit (1809)*, 4; Heidegger, *Schelling's Treatise on the Essence of Human Freedom*, 4.

certainly are to be found in his *Aesthetics*.³ As regards Schelling himself, the question can be raised as to whether his achievement in the ways that Heidegger mentions can be fully discerned by considering—as Heidegger does—only the 1809 treatise on human freedom.

1. Philosophical Beginnings

In 1790, at the age of fifteen, Schelling entered the famous seminary in Tübingen, the *Tübinger Stift*. For five years he studied in the *Stift* and at the university. During much of this period, he was closely associated with fellow students Hölderlin and Hegel. There was continual exchange among these three for at least a decade.

Two things especially united them during the Tübingen period. The first was their allegiance to the Kantian philosophy and especially to the central place it accorded to freedom. Writing to Hegel from Tübingen in 1795, Schelling says: "The last time Fichte was here, he said that one must have the genius of Socrates in order to enter into Kant. I find this truer every day."⁴ He goes on to criticize the "Kantians" for sticking to the letter of Kant's work.

The second thing that united Schelling, Hölderlin, and Hegel was their enthusiasm for Spinoza and his idea of an absolute that would encompass all things. This they expressed in the slogan:"Ἐν καὶ πᾶν. In another letter to Hegel in 1795, Schelling responds to a question his friend had posed to him. The question was (in Schelling's words) "whether by means of the moral proof we reach a personal being."⁵ Dismissing "the orthodox concepts of God," Schelling answers: "We reach still farther than a personal being. Meanwhile I have become a Spinozist. Don't be astonished. Soon you will hear how. For Spinoza the world (the object in distinction from the subject) was everything; for me it is the I."⁶

In this double allegiance there was a tension. For Spinoza, all finite things are merely modes of the one infinite substance or nature. They have no freedom but simply belong to the occurrence of nature, *natura naturans*. So in this respect it is precisely the opposite of the critical philosophy, for which freedom is central. The tension is expressed in the phrases "Spinozism of freedom" and "system of freedom," as well as in the opposition between freedom and nature. This tension—though it evolves and becomes more developed—runs throughout Schelling's work from his earliest works (1794–95) up through his great treatise on human freedom (1809). But already in the letter to Hegel, Schelling indicates

---

3. See my discussion in chapter 5 of *Transfigurements: On the True Sense of Art* (Chicago: University of Chicago, 2008).
4. Schelling to Hegel, January 6, 1795, in *Aus Schellings Leben: In Briefen*, ed. G. L. Plitt (Leipzig: Hirzel, 1869), 73.
5. Cf. §87 of Kant's *Critique of Judgment*, titled "On the Moral Proof of the Existence of God."
6. Schelling to Hegel, February 4, 1795, in *Aus Schellings Leben*, 76.

how these two sides will be brought together: the substance of Spinoza, which encompasses everything, will be thought now as the I.

Yet the initial impetus for Schelling's work came primarily from Fichte. In the 1795 letter to Hegel, he writes: "Fichte will elevate philosophy to a new height, before which most of the Kantians up to now will disappear."[7] Already in 1794 (while still in Tübingen), Schelling read "Concerning the Concept of the *Wissenschaftslehre*." A few months later—he was only nineteen—he published his first philosophical work, a short text titled *On the Possibility of a Form of Philosophy in General*.

At the outset of this work Schelling refers to Kant. He observes that the problem with the *Critique of Pure Reason* is that it attempts to lay the ground that would determine the form of all philosophy, and yet it failed to establish an "original form" (*Urform*) (SW I, 87; UHK 38). By this, Schelling means that the first *Critique* lacked a fundamental principle on which the entirety of the philosophical system would be based and that would give a form to that system. (This is essentially the same criticism that Fichte levels at Kant.) Schelling regards all the attacks on critical philosophy to have resulted from this lack of an original form. He mentions the critical attack by *Aenesidemus*, Fichte's review of *Aenesidemus*, and Reinhold's *Elementarphilosophie* (based on his theory of representation).

Schelling then proceeds in a way that parallels very closely Fichte's text "On the Concept of the *Wissenschaftslehre*" (as it already sketches the *Grundlage*). Schelling states: "Philosophy is a science, that is, it presents a specific content in a specific form" (SW I, 89; UHK 40). He adds that the content determines the form, and the form determines the content: they are mutually determining. He goes on to introduce the self-positing I as the ground expressed in the first principle, then introduces the not-I as what is expressed in the second principle. The third principle in itself combines both I and not-I—that is, it expresses the mediation of the two.

When the work appeared, Schelling sent a copy to Fichte along with a letter (September 26, 1794) in which he expressed his deep admiration for Fichte and requested Fichte's response to his work. Fichte sent an encouraging reply along with the first two parts of the *Grundlage*. A few months later (April 1795), Schelling published a much longer work, *On the I as Principle of Philosophy*. This work parallels the *Grundlage* very closely. Like Fichte, Schelling says that he will give "an exposition of Kant's philosophy based on higher principles" (SW I, 154; UHK 66). Regarding Kant, Schelling's goal is to "assert the still more original sense of his thoughts" (SW I, 155; UHK 66). This is a variation of the old interpretive strategy that Kant himself employs: to understand an author better than

---

7. Schelling to Hegel, January 6, 1795, in *Aus Schellings Leben*, 73.

he understood himself.[8] The parallel to the *Grundlage* is nowhere more striking than in Schelling's discussion of the moral law. He says that the moral law presents an *ought*, and then he continues: "Since the supreme law by which the being of the infinite I is determined is the law of its identity, the moral law in the finite being must present the identity not as existing but as demanded. Therefore, the supreme law for the finite being is: *Be absolutely identical with yourself*" (SW I, 199; UHK 98).

Fichte himself enthusiastically endorsed Schelling's book. In a letter to Reinhold (July 2, 1795) Fichte wrote:

> Judging by what I have been able to read of it, Schelling's entire essay is a commentary on my writings. But he has grasped the matter splendidly, and several people who did not understand me have found his essay very clear. Why he does not say so [i.e., that his essay is a commentary on the *Wissenschaftslehre*] I do not quite understand.[9] He will not wish to deny this, nor could he do so. I believe I may conclude that he did not want to have his errors attributed to me, should he not have understood me correctly.... I am particularly fond of his references to Spinoza, on the basis of whose system mine can most properly be explained. (EPW 401)

Yet even in this very first phase, while Schelling was still a student in Tübingen, we can see the tension foreshadowed in his thought. More precisely, we see that Schelling's thought was rooted not only in Fichte—nor even in Fichte along with Spinoza—but that it had its roots also in ancient thought. A few years ago, a set of Schelling manuscripts from 1792–94 were published that consist primarily of studies of Plato's *Timaeus*.[10] We should note two things about these Plato studies. First, Schelling in general construes Plato's thought in Kantian terms. Thus he quotes (in Greek) the passage (27d–28a) in which Timaeus distinguishes between being (τὸ ὄν) and becoming (or the generated: τὸ γιγνόμενον)—and then Schelling continues: "Thus here Plato himself explains ὄν as something that is the object of pure understanding." In turn, Schelling calls becoming "the empirical, that which has arisen through experience."[11]

Second and more significantly, Schelling stresses the passage at *Timaeus* 48a: "For this cosmos in its origin was generated as a compound, from the combination

---

8. [Editor's note: Cf. Kant's comments in reference to Plato: "I need only remark that it is by no means unusual, upon comparing the thoughts which an author has expressed in regard to his subject, whether in ordinary conversation or in writing, to find that we understand him better than he has understood himself" (A 314/B 370).]

9. Schelling never mentions Fichte's name in *On the I*.

10. Friedrich Wilhelm Joseph Schelling, *"Timaeus" (1794)*, ed. Hartmut Buchner (Stuttgart-Bad Cannstatt: Frommann-Holzboog, 1994). See the discussion in chapter 5 of John Sallis, *Chorology: On Beginning in Plato's "Timaeus"* (Bloomington: Indiana University Press, 1999).

11. Schelling, *"Timaeus" (1794)*, 23. Cf. Sallis, *Chorology*, 159.

[σύστασις, standing-together] of ἀνάγκη and νοῦς."[12] The entire second half of Schelling's *Timaeus* essay focuses on this ἀνάγκη (translated as *Notwendigkeit*). Specifically, Schelling focuses on ἀνάγκη as the receptacle of all generation—that is, as a third kind along with the rational (νοῦς = the intelligible paradigm) and the empirical (= the sensible images of the paradigm). He also refers to it as the "nature [φύσις] that receives all bodies" (*Timaeus* 50b). Schelling thus marks in the Timaeus the tension between (1) the rational/intelligible and (2) receptive nature/necessity. Here already there is the tension that runs throughout his work. We are especially reminded of this in his 1809 treatise where he poses as primary the tension between the divine understanding and "Platonic matter" (SW VII, 360, 374; PI 30, 41).[13]

2. Introduction to the *System of Transcendental Idealism*

Published in 1800, the *System of Transcendental Idealism* was Schelling's most comprehensive work up to that time—though, as we will see, it still does not present the whole of philosophy. It was with this work that Schelling first attained broad recognition as an original philosopher. Nonetheless, in the preface he refers (though not by name) to Fichte: "In regard to basic inquiries, nothing can be found herein that has not already been said long since, either in the writings of the originator of the *Wissenschaftslehre* or in those of the present author" (SW III, 330–31; STI 2). We should note one other point in the preface: he speaks of presenting the whole of philosophy "as what in fact it is, namely a progressive history of self-consciousness" (SW III, 331; STI 2). Now, though *System* does not present the whole of philosophy, this description applies to what it does present: it is a progressive history of self-consciousness. It can thus be regarded as an earlier version of Hegel's *Phenomenology of Spirit*.

In the introduction, Schelling begins with the concept of truth: truth means agreement of representations with their objects. Accordingly, since knowing is a knowing of the true, "all knowledge is founded upon the agreement of something objective with something subjective" (SW III, 339; STI 5). The sum of what is objective in our knowledge is nature. The sum of what is subjective is the I or intelligence. The problem of philosophy, then, is to explain the agreement between the subjective and objective—that is, between the I and nature.

There has been much discussion about the so-called subject-object distinction. Sometimes it is simply asserted that this is a presupposition that runs throughout modern philosophy (including German Idealism)—even that it is a presupposition that a more rigorous philosophy would need to eliminate. Yet

---

12. Cited in Schelling, *"Timaeus" (1794)*, 50.
13. [Editor's note: See Sallis, *Chorology*, 164–65.]

here one needs to be more precise. In fact, Schelling does not presuppose that this distinction (separation) is operative in knowledge. When I am actually knowing, the subjective and the objective (representation and object) are not distinguished. They are "simultaneous and one" (SW III, 339; STI 5).

It is only when I set about to *explain* knowledge that this distinction is drawn. More generally, it is only with the onset of philosophy that separation and the reflection that introduces separation enter in. In the introduction to *Ideas on the Philosophy of Nature*, Schelling writes: "As soon as man sets himself in opposition to the external world . . . he takes the first step toward philosophy. For with this separation reflection begins. Henceforth he separates what nature had forever united: objects from intuition, concept from image, and finally, by becoming his *own object*, he separates himself from himself" (SW II, 13; PGI 168–69). But Schelling goes on to say that reflection (and thus separation) is only a means, not an end. In the end (as the aim of reflection), the two sides that it separates are to be reunited—yet in such a way that their unity is made intelligible. Thus, ultimately, reflection moves toward its own annihilation. As Schelling writes:

> Opposite reflection stands true philosophy, which views reflection simply as a means. Philosophy *must* presuppose that original separation, because without it there would be no need to philosophize. For this reason, philosophy assigns reflection only a *negative* value. It takes that original separation as a point of departure in order to reunite through *freedom* what was originally and *necessarily* united in the human spirit, i.e., in order to annul that separation forever. And insofar as philosophy itself was made necessary by that separation, was itself only a necessary evil, a corrective of reason gone astray, it works in this sense towards its own annihilation. (SW II, 14; PGI 169–70)

Let us return to the introduction to the *System of Transcendental Idealism*. As we have seen, the problem of philosophy is to explain the agreement between the subjective and the objective, between the I and nature. To do this, we must begin with one side and move from it to the other. Thus there are two possible ways in which philosophy may proceed. First, one can begin with the subjective and move to the objective—that is, show how the objective is added onto (joined to) the subjective. This is transcendental philosophy, Schelling's version of the *Wissenschaftslehre*. Second, one can begin with the objective and move to the subjective—that is, show how the subjective is added onto (joined to) the objective. This is the philosophy of nature. These are, then, the two parts that together comprise the whole of philosophy—"the entire system of philosophy" (SW III, 342; STI 7). In the preface, Schelling says that these two sciences "must forever be opposed to one another and can never merge into one" (SW III, 331; STI 2). On the other hand, they "reciprocally seek and complement each other" (SW III, 342; STI 7). This issue will be decisive in (1) Schelling's debate and eventual break with Fichte, and (2) the development that his work will undergo immediately after the *System*.

Let us look at these two parts of philosophy more closely. The philosophy of nature begins with the objective (nature) and undertakes to move from nature to intelligence. It carries this out by bringing theory into the phenomena of nature—that is, by eliciting theoretical (intelligible) structures (concepts) from nature. Then natural phenomena appear, not merely as the opposite of intelligence but as structured by concepts (belonging to, deriving from intelligence). Stated differently, in brute nature, there are no concepts. There are concepts in nature (that is, it appears as embodying concepts, as intelligible) only insofar as these concepts are drawn out of nature by intelligence. But then nature no longer appears as brute phenomena but as embodying something (concepts) that falls on the side of intelligence. Schelling says: "Hence it is that the more the lawful element emerges in nature itself, the more the husk disappears" (SW III, 340–41; STI 6). When this process has been completely carried through, nature will have been resolved into intelligence. Then it will become evident that in brute nature there are "only unsuccessful attempts of nature to reflect itself"—that it is "unripe intelligence" (SW III, 341; STI 6). Nature becomes finally objective to itself only in man, in reason.

By contrast, transcendental philosophy begins with the subjective. The problem, then, is to explain "how an objective factor [*ein Objektives*] that agrees with it can be added [*hinzukommen*] to it" (SW III, 341; STI 6). In other words, transcendental philosophy starts with the subjective and shows how something objective arises out of it—that is, how something objective is already contained in the subjective. So transcendental philosophy begins with universal doubt regarding the reality of the objective: it suspends the basic, natural prejudice that there exist things outside us. Schelling says that the only thing certain is the proposition "I am." Transcendental philosophy will show that the proposition "There is something objective" is identical with the proposition "I am."

In ordinary consciousness, these two propositions are fused. That is, in ordinary consciousness, "the intuiting itself [grounded in 'I am'] loses itself in the object" (SW III, 345; STI 9). Transcendental philosophy separates these. It focuses on the intuition of knowing and so becomes a knowing of knowing. That is, it apprehends the concept as concept, arrives at the concept of concept. Thus transcendental contemplation is "a continual becoming-object for itself of the subjective" (SW III, 345; STI 9). Transcendental reflection, therefore, discovers in the subjective something objective—precisely in that the subject becomes objective for itself. And so the transition is made from the subjective to something objective.

Note that Schelling presents the character of these two transitions in two different ways. Initially, the transition is presented as a matter of one side (subjective, objective) being *added* to the other (objective, subjective). In other words, it is to be shown how, beginning with the subjective, the objective comes to be added on to it—and conversely. However, the transitions are also characterized as a matter of one being already contained in the other; for example, in the subjective the objective is already contained, and transcendental philosophy has only to draw it out. The second of these forms of transition is what Schelling actually demonstrates: each is already contained in the other, and philosophy simply draws it out.

Also note that in this sketch of transcendental philosophy (which corresponds to the *Wissenschaftslehre*), Schelling lays out a course quite different from that of Fichte. We can see this at two points. First, Schelling begins with universal doubt regarding the reality of the objective. Then his analysis is based on the certainty of the proposition "I am." On the other hand, Fichte begins with the certainty of the proposition "I am I"—that is, the proposition that the I is identical with itself. Fichte makes a point of saying that in this beginning the proposition "I am" is *not* proven. We see, then, that, in contrast to Fichte, Schelling's way of beginning is basically Cartesian. It involves universal doubt (which plays no role for Fichte) and the "I am" or *cogito ergo sum* as the sole certainty.

Second, Schelling's way of moving from the subjective to the objective is different from Fichte's way. For Schelling, the objective is revealed in the subjective, in the capacity of the subjective to become objective (to itself). For Fichte, the objective (not-I) is shown to be necessary for the I to be itself (for I = I). Without the object, there can be no subject.

In the remainder of the introduction, Schelling lays out the various divisions (parts) of transcendental philosophy. He contrasts the first part (theoretical philosophy) with the second part (practical philosophy): in the theoretical sphere, the subject is bound (determined) by the object; in the practical sphere, however, the subject (through freedom) can determine the object. He then goes on to show how this contradiction is resolved by the concept of preestablished harmony (his version of Leibniz's doctrine), which is, in turn, based on teleology. Finally, he shows how the identity of knowing and practice (ideal and real) is established in aesthetic activity. Thus "the objective world is only the original, as yet unconscious, poetry of the spirit . . . and the keystone of the entire arch—*the philosophy of art*" (SW III, 349; STI 12).

Note, finally, how Schelling has reconstituted the Kantian *Critiques*:

1. theoretical philosophy—*Critique of Pure Reason*
2. practical philosophy—*Critique of Practical Reason*
3. teleology and philosophy of art—the two parts of the *Critique of Judgment*

We are now in a position to look more closely at the structure of the project carried out in the *System of Transcendental Idealism*, going beyond the material in the introduction. As we have seen, transcendental philosophy begins with the subjective and shows how the objective arises out of it—that is, it shows how the objective is already in the subjective and emerges in a series of phases: theoretical knowledge, practical knowledge, teleology, and art. And yet, transcendental philosophy *only shows how* this emergence of the objective occurs. So the activity carried out by transcendental philosophy must be distinguished from the emergence itself—from the *original* evolution or original activity through which the object emerges. The transcendental philosopher merely reenacts this original activity, undertaking a "free imitation" of it.

> As long as the I is considered in the original evolution of the absolute synthesis, there is only one series of acts, that of the original and necessary acts; as soon as I interrupt this evolution and freely project myself back to its starting point, there arises for me a new series in which what was *necessary* in the first series is now *free*. The former is the original, the latter the copy or imitation [*Nachahmung*]. If the second series contains no more and no less than the first, the imitation is perfect, and a true and complete philosophy is engendered.... Philosophy as such is therefore nothing else but the free imitation, the free repetition [*freie Wiederholung*] of the original series of acts in which the one act of self-consciousness evolves. (SW III, 397; STI, 49)

Now this says that there are two series. On the one hand, there is the original and necessary series in which, from the subjective as such (hence from every subject), the objective evolves. On the other hand, there is the series enacted by the philosopher. The philosopher interrupts (breaks with) the first series and returns to the starting point (where the objective is completely within the subjective). Then the philosopher reenacts freely the first, necessary series—"imitates" it. Thus transcendental philosophy is the free imitation or the free repetition of the original series of acts.

In the cited passage, there is a phrase that requires further explication. At the end, Schelling refers to the original series as that "in which the one act of self-consciousness evolves." The question is: How is it that in the original series (in which the object emerges) there is also an evolution of self-consciousness? The decisive point is that the object is not something other than the subject. Rather, the object is already contained in the subject and arises from it. Or, more precisely, there is an identity of subject and object. So when, in the original series, the subject comes to know the object (at various levels), this knowing is ultimately a knowing of itself—that is, self-consciousness. In other words, what is apprehended by the subject is just itself objectified. So the different levels at which the object appears are merely different levels of self-consciousness; that is, they are different epochs in the history of self-consciousness. Schelling writes: "Transcendental philosophy is nothing other than a constant raising of the I to a higher power [*Potenzieren*]; its whole method consists in leading the I from one level of self-intuition to another, until it is posited with all the determinations that are contained in the free and conscious act of self-consciousness" (SW III, 450; STI 90). And earlier in the text he notes: "Philosophy is thus a history of self-consciousness, having various epochs, through which that one absolute synthesis is successively put together" (SW III, 399; STI 50). The "absolute synthesis" mentioned here is the synthesis in which the identity of subject and object is established and revealed by philosophical repetition.

3. Imagination and Art

In the *System of Transcendental Idealism*, there are three expressions regarding the character of the imagination. Though they are related, they are not identical. There is a progression toward more radical conceptions.

The first occurs in Schelling's analysis of art, to which we will return below. Schelling characterizes imagination as "that alone by which we are capable of thinking and of holding together even what is contradictory" (SW III, 626; STI 230). This description closely parallels Fichte's: the imagination hovers between opposites so as to hold them together in their opposition.

The second description of imagination occurs in the course of Schelling's account of willing. He observes that willing requires the presentation of a determinate object to which the willing can be directed. In being thus bound to an object, the willing subject is finite. However, willing is an act of freedom: I freely choose to will the object presented. A free act is one that is not determined by (not dependent on) anything beyond itself. It is absolute (absolved). As not limited or bound by anything, it is infinite. "Thus, through willing there immediately arises an opposition, in that through it I am conscious, on the one hand, of freedom, and thus also of infinity, while, on the other hand, I am constantly drawn back into finitude by the compulsion to present. Hence, with this contradiction, there must arise an activity that hovers [*schwebt*] in the middle between infinity and finitude" (SW III, 558; STI 176). Schelling identifies this activity as imagination.

The third description also occurs in the section devoted to practical philosophy. Schelling observes that, in and through its hovering, imagination will also *produce* something that hovers between the infinite and the finite. He identifies such a product as an *idea*, in distinction from a concept (following the Kantian distinction). In the conclusion that he then draws, Schelling employs the Kantian distinction between the understanding (which relates to concepts) and reason (which relates to ideas): "In this hovering, imagination is not understanding but rather reason; and, conversely, what is commonly called theoretical reason is nothing other than imagination in the service of freedom" (SW III, 559; STI 176).

Turning now to art, we can note that there are three stages in Schelling's account: (1) the deduction of art, (2) the account of artwork, and (3) the account of the role of art with respect to philosophy. The section on art is the final section of the *System of Transcendental Idealism*, and so it presupposes some of the earlier accounts.

This is especially the case in the "Deduction of the Art Product in General" (Section VI, §1). We must therefore begin with the last paragraphs of the previous account. Schelling observes that the aim of transcendental philosophy is to explain how the harmony between the subjective and the objective becomes an object to the I itself. Thus it must be possible to point out an intuition in which this harmony appears. Schelling says that in this way—by disclosing such an intuition—it becomes possible to resolve the supreme problem of transcendental philosophy: to explain the accord between the subjective and the objective. Such an intuition will prove to be the intuition of art (SW III, 610–11; STI 217–18).

Schelling focuses on the *product* of the intuition. The product involves two different components: "The product will have in common with the product of freedom the fact that it is produced with consciousness, and with the product of nature that it is produced unconsciously" (SW III, 612; STI, 219). These two components are conjoined to form the product when the objective is added to the conscious without the cooperation of freedom.

Think of it this way: in the production of an artwork, the artist sets out with a certain intention or conception (usually vague and indeterminate). But then, when the artist creates the work, the intention gets embodied (in fully determinate form) in the object, in the artwork. And yet this embodying (the addition of the objective to the conscious) is not simply achieved through the freedom (free, independent activity) of the artist. Alluding to the idea of inspiration, Schelling says: "So the objective element [i.e., what overflows or exceeds the intent] is added to his production as though without his cooperation" (SW III, 617; STI 223).

This unaccountable achievement (outside the control of the artist) can only have come about by what is called *genius*: "Just as the man of fate does not accomplish what he wills or has in view but rather what he must, by an incomprehensible destiny under whose influence he stands, so the artist, however deliberate he may be, nevertheless, in regard to what is truly objective in his creation, seems to stand under the influence of a power that sets him apart from all other men and compels him to express or represent things he does not himself fully see through and whose meaning is infinite" (SW III, 617; STI 223). Schelling calls genius something "inborn by the free gift of nature" (SW III, 618; STI 223–24). Here he is simply reformulating Kant's definition of genius in §46 of the *Critique of Judgment*: "Genius is the innate mental predisposition through which nature gives the rule to art" (AA 5, 307; CJ 174). Schelling goes on to discuss, in words only slightly different from Kant's, the distinction between what comes through genius and what can be taught, learned, and attained through practice.

In the next section, "Character of the Art Product" (§2), Schelling notes three characteristics:

(1) In the artwork there come together *conscious activity* (the intention and conscious activity of the artist) and *unconscious activity* (which comes about through genius). Schelling says that the opposition between these is infinite—that is, it is not mediated or limited by anything else, and thus is absolute. He concludes that the basic character of the artwork is an *unconscious infinity*. This means that in the artwork these infinitely opposed components are brought together in a way of which the artist is not conscious. From this, he draws the further conclusion: in the artwork there is an infinity that no finite understanding can unfold. For this reason, a genuine artwork is susceptible of infinite interpretation.

(2) If the artwork has this infinite character, then what is its character in more concrete terms? "Every aesthetic production starts from the feeling of an infinite contradiction. Hence also the feeling that accompanies the completion of the art product must be the feeling of such a satisfaction, and this feeling must in turn go over into the work of art itself. The outward expression of the work of art is therefore the expression of repose and of quiet grandeur, even where the greatest tension of pain or of joy is to be expressed" (SW III, 620; STI 225). Artistic creation issues in the feeling of satisfaction. This is reflected in the work itself as its "expression of repose and quiet grandeur."

(3) Granted that art has this infinite character, then in the artwork "an infinite will be finitely presented." But, says Schelling, "the infinite finitely presented is beauty" (SW III, 620; STI 225).

The third stage in Schelling's account of art concerns the role of art in relation to philosophy. Philosophy begins with intellectual intuition, which Schelling distinguishes from sensory intuition. Whereas in sensory intuition the intuiting is distinct from the intuited object, in intellectual intuition the object is not independent. Here there is "a knowing that is simultaneously a producing of its object—an intuition freely productive in itself, and in which producer and product are one and the same" (SW III, 369; STI 27). The I not only carries out such intuition but is nothing other than this: "The I is such an intuition, since it is through the I's own knowledge of itself that the very I (the object) first comes into being. . . . The I itself is thus a knowing that simultaneously produces itself (as object)" (SW III, 369; STI 27). In other words, intellectual intuition is just an enacting of the self-positing I.

Though philosophy begins with intellectual intuition, intellectual intuition is completely nonobjective. It is confined to the subjectivity of the one who enacts it. The question is, then: How can it be established as objective so that we could be assured that it is not merely a subjective illusion? Schelling answers: the intuition by which this is established is that of *art*. "For aesthetic intuition is precisely intellectual intuition become objective. The work of art merely reflects to me what is otherwise reflected by nothing" (SW III, 625; STI, 229–30). In other words, intellectual intuition shines back to us from the art product, the artwork. But, in turn, if art confers objectivity on the intellectual intuition with which philosophy begins, then it also confers objectivity on all that is deduced from this first principle—that is, the entire system of philosophy.

But how is it that art is intellectual intuition become objective? Schelling does not develop an explicit account of this connection, but he does indicate that its primary sense has to do with infinity. Consider that in intellectual intuition, in the I's productive intuition of itself, the connection between the I (as subject) and the I (as object) is not limited by anything else and is not determined by anything outside the I. This means that it is absolved from all alterity and thus is absolute—that is, it is infinite.

The same holds for the artwork. Schelling has already shown that the artwork is infinite but that it also involves finitude, since it is a concrete, limited object. In other words, the artwork is a finite presentation of infinity—that is, it is beautiful. Therefore, whereas intellectual intuition is infinite (though merely subjective), aesthetic intuition involves an infinity that is finitely presented—that is, it is presented in an object and hence *objectively*. Thus art is intellectual intuition become objective.

Schelling says: "A system is completed when it has returned to its starting point" (SW III, 628; STI 232). In other words, a system comes to its end when it returns to its beginning. This has to be understood by reference to the double series: that of the original, necessary I *and* that of the philosophical I that observes or reenacts the original I. Schelling says that by rendering intellectual intuition objective, "we have conducted our object, the I itself, gradually to the point at which we ourselves stood when we began to philosophize" (SW III, 628–29; STI 232). What Schelling does not say explicitly is that the objectivation of intellectual intuition demonstrates the validity of this beginning: it shows that it is not just a subjective illusion. It thus grants to philosophy its beginning.

Finally, since art grants to philosophy its beginning and its standpoint, it surpasses philosophy. Thus Schelling draws a final, prophetic conclusion: "But now, if it is art alone that can succeed in making objective with universal validity what the philosopher can only represent subjectively, then it is to be expected (to draw this further inference) that as philosophy, and with it all the sciences that were brought to perfection by it, was born from and nurtured by poetry in the childhood of science, so now after their completion they will return as just so many individual streams to the universal ocean of poetry from which they started out" (SW III, 629; STI 232). Schelling concludes with a reference to a "new mythology." Here we touch on the "Oldest Systematic Program of German Idealism," which declares that "philosophy must become mythological" (PGI 162–63).

4. The Break with Fichte and Collaboration with Hegel

In May 1800, Schelling sent Fichte a copy of the *System of Transcendental Idealism* along with some shorter texts on the philosophy of nature. In the accompanying letter, he wrote that he would be very thankful if Fichte would reply and give him his assessment, especially of the *System*. Fichte did not answer right away. In the following months, there was some malicious gossip stemming from Friedrich Schlegel: he spread the rumor that Fichte had expressed grave reservations about Schelling. Schlegel regarded Schelling as his competitor with respect to the Kantian-Fichtean legacy. Also, there was intrigue because at the time Schelling had formed a liaison with Caroline Schlegel, the wife of Friedrich's brother, A. W. Schlegel. There were several letters back and forth between Schelling and Fichte, with Fichte trying to undo the damage that Schlegel's gossip had done. Schelling referred to Fichte as his "most sincerely honored friend."[14] Fichte in turn referred to Schelling as his "true, dear friend."[15]

In any case, Fichte finally read the *System of Transcendental Idealism*, and then on November 15, 1800 he wrote to Schelling about it. He begins with praise: "It is everything that is to be expected from your genial presentation."[16] But then Fichte continues: "I still do not agree with your opposition between transcendental philosophy and the philosophy of nature. Everything seems to rest on a confusion between *ideal* and *real* activity. . . . In my view the thing is not added to consciousness nor consciousness to the thing, but rather both are immediately unified in the I, [which is] idealreal, realideal."[17]

Schelling's letter of November 19, 1800 is a direct response. Schelling is somewhat conciliatory, saying that it is "of the highest importance" that they reach an agreement on the points Fichte had raised in his letter. He continues: "The primary point is the opposition between transcendental philosophy and the philosophy of nature. I can assure you that I do not set up this opposition because of the difference between ideal and real activity. About the thing added to consciousness and consciousness added to the thing, I speak only in the introduction, where I undertake to ascend from the common [i.e., ordinary] standpoint to the philosophical standpoint. To the common standpoint that unity [of ideal and real] appears as an adding-on."[18] Schelling goes on to say that in the *System* itself it is a matter of the unity of ideal (= subjective) and real (= objective). This is, in fact, what we have already discerned in the introduction.

---

14. Schelling to Fichte, August 18, 1800, in *Fichte-Schelling Briefwechsel*, ed. Walter Schulz (Frankfurt: Suhrkamp, 1968), 77.
15. Fichte to Schelling, end of October 1800, in *Fichte-Schelling: Briefwechsel*, 97.
16. Fichte to Schelling, November 15, 1800, in *Fichte-Schelling: Briefwechsel*, 105.
17. Fichte to Schelling, November 15, 1800, in *Fichte-Schelling: Briefwechsel*, 105.
18. Schelling to Fichte, November 19, 1800, in *Fichte-Schelling: Briefwechsel*, 107.

However, Schelling then goes on to insist: "But the *Wissenschaftslehre* (as you have established it) is still not philosophy itself."[19] "What I call philosophy of nature is, as I maintain [in the *System*], a completely different science from the *Wissenschaftslehre*."[20] Then Schelling goes on in a way that anticipates the move beyond the *System* in which at this very time he is engaged: "Now, however, as you can see, I no longer consider the philosophy of nature and transcendental philosophy as opposed sciences but rather only as opposed parts of one and the same whole, namely of the system of philosophy."[21] This points to Schelling's work of 1801: *Darstellung meines Systems der Philosophie* (*Presentation of My System of Philosophy*), the first work in which he presents philosophy as a whole. It is also the first work in which, though opposition remains, the unity of transcendental philosophy and the philosophy of nature is developed.

Fichte's response in his letter of December 27, 1800 is conciliatory: "I had written you concerning some differences in our views, not as though they represented an obstacle to our association in working together but in order to give you proof of my attentive reading of your texts."[22] Then Fichte goes on to say that, while certain principles put forth by Schelling do not follow from the principle of transcendental philosophy as thus far developed (and so fall outside such transcendental philosophy), "they can be grounded through a broader extension of transcendental philosophy, indeed in its principles."[23] Fichte refers to his own further developments of the *Wissenschaftslehre*. Indeed, during this period, from 1796 on, Fichte presented in his lectures in Jena a new, very different formulation of the *Wissenschaftslehre* under the title *Foundations of Transcendental Philosophy: The Wissenschaftslehre Nova Methodo*. Fichte did not publish this, and it only survived in the form of two student transcripts, which form the basis of the text we have.

Fichte's conciliatory letter served for a while to prevent a real break between him and Schelling. And yet, though Fichte did not say so directly, he saw the philosophy of nature as a mere relapse into dogmatism. In Fichte's view, what was needed was an extension of the *Wissenschaftslehre*, not a second philosophical science (the philosophy of nature) added to it.

Toward the end of 1800, at about the time when Fichte and Schelling had reached a somewhat precarious reconciliation, Schelling received a letter from Hegel. Though they had been close friends in Tübingen, they had not had much contact since leaving in 1796. Hegel had been employed as a private tutor in

---

19. Schelling to Fichte, November 19, 1800, in *Fichte-Schelling: Briefwechsel*, 108.
20. Schelling to Fichte, November 19, 1800, in *Fichte-Schelling: Briefwechsel*, 109.
21. Schelling to Fichte, November 19, 1800, in *Fichte-Schelling: Briefwechsel*, 109.
22. Fichte to Schelling, December 27, 1800, in *Fichte-Schelling: Briefwechsel*, 115.
23. Fichte to Schelling, December 27, 1800, in *Fichte-Schelling: Briefwechsel*, 116.

Frankfurt. During this time, he was much closer to Hölderlin. Especially after being called to Jena in 1798, Schelling rapidly became very famous, whereas Hegel at this time had published nothing and was completely unknown. In his letter, Hegel wrote: "I have watched your great public career with admiration and joy." Then he went on: "I hope we rediscover each other as friends."[24] He asked Schelling whether he could recommend some place where he could go to prepare himself for a year or two before coming to Jena, then the philosophical capital of Germany. Schelling urged him to come directly to Jena. This he did—settling into a residence next door to Schelling.

Thus began the great period of their collaboration. Schelling founded the *Critical Journal of Philosophy*. He first invited Fichte to join him in this undertaking. But when Fichte declined (perhaps even before), Schelling invited Hegel to be his collaborator. During the relatively short period when the journal was published (1802–3), Schelling and Hegel published several very important works. They were unsigned—but in most cases the author can be determined. For instance, in 1802 Schelling and Hegel cowrote the introduction to the *Critical Journal*, "On the Essence of Philosophical Criticism" (Hegel was the primary author). This passage offers a sample: "Philosophy is, by its very nature, something esoteric, neither made for the vulgar nor capable of being got up to suit the vulgar taste; it is only philosophy in virtue of being directly opposed to the understanding [*Verstand*][25] and hence even more opposed to healthy common sense [*gesunder Menschenverstand*] . . . in its relationship to common sense the world of philosophy is in and for itself an inverted world" (HW 2, 182; BKH 282–83). We have seen a particular case of this in the introduction to the *System of Transcendental Idealism*: for ordinary experience, the subjective and the objective are completely unified; for philosophical reflection, they are separated.

Another key text is "Relationship of Skepticism to Philosophy," written by Hegel. This is a critical discussion—not to say refutation—of the skeptical position of Schulze (*Aenesidemus*), as he had directed it at Kant and Reinhold in 1792—and now had expressed it again in a work of nearly two thousand pages, the *Critique of Theoretical Philosophy*. Hegel's criticism is relentless. Here is a sample:

> Without the determination of the true relationship of skepticism to philosophy, and without the insight that skepticism itself is in its innermost heart at one with every true philosophy, and hence that there is a philosophy which is neither skepticism nor dogmatism, and is thus both at once—without this, all

---

24. Hegel to Schelling, November 2, 1800, in *Hegel: The Letters*, trans. Clark Butler and Christiane Seiler (Bloomington: Indiana University Press, 1984), 64.
25. That is, philosophy is on the side of "reason" (*Vernunft*) as opposed to "understanding" (*Verstand*).

the histories, and reports, and new editions of skepticism lead to a dead end. This *sine qua non* for the cognition of skepticism, this relationship of skepticism to philosophy . . . therefore, the concept of a philosophy as such, this it is that has escaped Mr. Schulze. (HW 2, 227; BKH 322–23)

After Hegel's critical attack, little or nothing was heard again from or about Mr. Schulze. But more significant than his banishing Schulze from the philosophical scene was Hegel's contention that skepticism, rather than being opposed to philosophy, actually belongs integrally to it. This will have enormous consequences for Hegel, especially in the *Phenomenology of Spirit*. Skepticism is an expression of negativity, of the power of the negative, which turns out to be what drives (in Schelling's phrase) "the progressive history of self-consciousness."

Not long after Hegel arrived in Jena—in fact, before the collaboration with Schelling on the *Critical Journal* began—Hegel published his first book: *The Difference between Fichte's and Schelling's System of Philosophy* (1801), commonly known in German as the *Differenzschrift*. In the preface, Hegel begins by declaring that Kant has discovered "the principle of speculation," which Hegel identifies as "the identity of subject and object" (HW 2, 10).[26] This is what is articulated in Kant's transcendental deduction of the categories. Fichte establishes this identity more rigorously in the form I = I—that is, pure thinking that thinks itself (and so is both subject and object of the thinking). Yet for Fichte, this identity is fully established only on the side of the subject, not on the side of the object (nature). In other words, for Fichte, this identity is fully established only as a subjective subject-object. So what is required is to establish the identity also on the side of the object—and this is what Schelling's philosophy of nature would carry out: "In the philosophy of nature Schelling sets the objective subject-object beside the subjective subject-object and presents both as united in something higher than the subject" (HW 2, 12).[27] The "something higher" to which Hegel refers is Schelling's "absolute identity."

Finally, to complete our survey of Hegel's works during this period of collaboration with Schelling, we should mention another text from the *Critical Journal* published in 1802: *Faith and Knowledge*. This is a critical engagement with Kant, Jacobi, and Fichte. The crux of Hegel's criticism is given in a passage from the introduction: "The fundamental principle common to the philosophies of Kant, Jacobi, and Fichte is . . . the absoluteness of finitude and, resulting from it, the absolute antithesis of finitude and infinity, reality and ideality, the sensuous and the supersensuous, and the beyondness of what is truly real and absolute"

---

26. Georg Wilhelm Friedrich Hegel, *The Difference between Fichte's and Schelling's System of Philosophy*, trans. H. S. Harris and Walter Cerf (Albany: SUNY Press, 1977), 80.
27. Hegel, *Difference*, 82.

(HW 2, 295–96).[28] Here we can think of the Kantian subject, which is dependent on receptivity, affection, and intuition. Kant contrasts this finite subject with originary intuition—unlimited (hence infinite) intuition, which gives itself its object.[29] We can think also of Fichte: the difference between the finite I and the absolute (infinite) I cannot be overcome—the finite can only strive for the infinite. Finally, we can think of Jacobi, who dismisses reason, which is linked to the finite, for the sake of faith in the infinite divine.

Hegel's criticism is aimed at the very distinction or separation of the finite and the infinite. He says: "They understood the sphere of this antithesis, a finite and an infinite, to be absolute: but if infinity is thus set up against finitude, each is as finite as the other" (HW 2, 297).[30] The point is: if the finite is set over against the infinite, then it limits the infinite, which therefore is not infinite. In other words, if the finite is set over against the infinite (= the absolute), then the absolute is not absolved from everything beyond itself—hence it is not absolute, not infinite. This point is crucial to Hegel's determination of the infinite in the *Science of Logic*, which he will publish a decade later in 1812. As he says in that text, if the finite is set over against the infinite, then "the infinite is only the limit of the finite and is thus only a determinate infinite, an infinite that is itself finite" (HW 5, 152).[31]

Let us return now to Schelling's increasingly strained relationship with Fichte. In January 1801, Fichte published a public announcement about the forthcoming publication of his new exposition of the *Wissenschaftslehre—Darstellung der Wissenschaftslehre*. In this announcement he mentioned Schelling, but in a way that was less than complimentary: he suggested that Schelling was merely his disciple and that Schelling had perhaps not fully understood the *Wissenschaftslehre*.

Schelling was annoyed, and he broke off his correspondence with Fichte for several months. During this time, he set about writing his *Darstellung meines Systems* (*Presentation of My System*), indicating in the title that he wanted to distinguish himself from Fichte.[32] This is clear also from the outset of the book. For example, he writes: "Fichte could think idealism in a completely subjective sense, whereas I have thought it in an objective sense" (SW IV, 109). In his *Darstellung*, Schelling thinks the two sides together. On the one side, the subject is thought

---

28. Georg Wilhelm Friedrich Hegel, *Faith and Knowledge*, trans. Walter Cerf and H. S. Harris (Albany: SUNY Press, 1977), 62.

29. [Editor's note: for a discussion of the contrast between the finite subject and intellectual intuition in Kant, see John Sallis, *The Gathering of Reason*, 2nd ed. (Albany: SUNY Press, 2005), chapter 1.]

30. Hegel, *Faith and Knowledge*, 63

31. Georg Wilhelm Friedrich Hegel, *The Science of Logic*, trans. A. V. Miller (London: Allen & Unwin, 1969), 140.

32. [Editor's note: for a parallel discussion of the break with Fichte, see John Sallis, *Elemental Discourses* (Bloomington: Indiana University Press, 2018), 71–74.]

Early Development of Schelling's Thought | 113

as containing the object in itself—such that through reflection, the object can be drawn out, or shown to be contained in, the subject. This is the side of transcendental philosophy. On the other side, the object is thought as containing the subject. This is the side of the philosophy of nature. Now Schelling thinks the identity of subject and object without giving priority to either side—that is, he thinks this identity as absolute. This requires putting reflection aside. Schelling identifies this absolute identity as what is thought in/as philosophy as a whole, as "the system of absolute identity" (SW IV, 113).

When Fichte read Schelling's *Darstellung*, he was completely repelled. The letter that he sent in response is dated May 31, 1801, though it was not sent to Schelling until August. It was extremely critical. Though Fichte begins by addressing Schelling as his dear friend who has given him hopes for science, he then goes on to say regarding Schelling's philosophy of nature: "In this I saw again the old error [*den alten Irrtum*]. But I hoped that in your scientific labors you would find the right way."[33] He proceeds to condemn Schelling's idea of a derivation of intelligence from nature—the central project of the philosophy of nature. After mentioning he has received Schelling's *Darstellung*, he objects: "In the introduction you say some problematic things about my idealism."[34] A little later he adds: "The questions whether the *Wissenschaftslehre* takes knowing subjectively or objectively, [and] whether it is idealism or realism, make no sense; for these distinctions are first made within the *Wissenschaftslehre*, not outside it and prior to it."[35]

Schelling replied on October 3, 1801. Now he is open about his differences, criticizing Fichte's concept of nature as reductive. He also says regarding the concept of Being (*Sein*): "For you, Being means the same thing as reality, even as actuality. But Being in the most eminent sense has no opposite, for it is the absolute unity of the ideal and the real."[36] Then, near the end of the letter, Schelling writes: "Peaceful over the end and sure of my cause, I gladly leave everyone to find out for himself the truth of the affair. But I also cannot deprive someone of his own healthy sight and seek in any manner to hide something. Today a book appeared by a very superior head, which has as its title *Difference between the Fichtean and Schellingian Systems of Philosophy*; I had no part in it, but I also could not prevent it."[37]

Summing up, we can say that the main point of the contention between Fichte and Schelling concerns the philosophy of nature: Schelling maintains

---

33. Fichte to Schelling, May 31 / August 7, 1801, in *Fichte-Schelling: Briefwechsel*, 125.
34. Fichte to Schelling, May 31 / August 7, 1801, in *Fichte-Schelling: Briefwechsel*, 125.
35. Fichte to Schelling, May 31 / August 7, 1801, in *Fichte-Schelling: Briefwechsel*, 126.
36. Schelling to Fichte, October 3, 1801, in *Fichte-Schelling: Briefwechsel*, 133.
37. Ibid., 141. Translated in Frederick C. Beiser, *German Idealism: The Struggle Against Subjectivism, 1781–1801* (Cambridge: Harvard University Press, 2002), 505.

that a philosophy of nature had to be set up alongside transcendental philosophy (= *Wissenschaftslehre*) and that the two sciences together constitute the system of philosophy as a whole. Fichte maintains that there was no need for a philosophy of nature. More specifically, he regards Schelling's philosophy of nature as a relapse into dogmatism, because it begins with an object posited outside the sphere of consciousness—like those Kantians who posited the thing in itself. Fichte insists that the very distinction between subject and object is first opened up within the unfolding of the I (as traced in the *Wissenschaftslehre*). Thus the object cannot simply be taken as something outside (which could, then, serve as the starting point for a philosophy of nature).

The entire debate comes to a kind of climax when Hegel publishes the *Differenzschrift*, in which he puts forth vigorous arguments in defense of Schelling's position. Hegel's criticism of Fichte is that Fichte's system remains incomplete: in theoretical knowledge, there remains the *Anstoß*, which is entirely on the side of the object and which cannot be integrated with the subjective. Thus on the side of the object, there is a residue of pure objectivity, and therefore on this side, the identity of subject and object is not established. In practical knowledge, there is, to be sure, a striving by which the object would be assimilated and the finite would be raised to coincidence with the infinite. But this striving, as a mere striving, is never complete. So here, too, there remains a residue of the purely objective, and the identity of subject and object is not established.

7. Schelling's Treatise on Human Freedom

In 1809, nearly a decade after the *System of Transcendental Idealism*, Schelling published *Philosophical Investigations concerning the Essence of Human Freedom*. This is the last great work that Schelling himself published, even though he lived until 1854 and produced very extensive writings, published only after his death. There has been much debate as to why Schelling, who had previously been a prolific author, broke off his publications after the *Freiheitsschrift* (as it is known in German). Whether this had something to do with what he had ventured in this book remains, I believe, undecidable.

1. Beyond Absolute Identity: The *Freiheitsschrift* and the Progression of German Idealism

We can perhaps grasp most directly what is radical in this book by placing it within—or actually at the end of—the progression that we have begun to discern in German Idealism. We can distinguish five stages. The first stage is the subject-object relation as Kant formulated it, primarily in the *Critique of Pure Reason*. What is distinctive—in contrast to previous philosophy—is the turn that Kant expresses as a Copernican Revolution. The result of this turn is that the object is determined, in part, by the subject—specifically, by the forms of pure intuition and the twelve categories. Yet, except for these determinations, the object remains detached from (independent of) the subject. To this extent, it is a pure objectivity. This purely objective object is what was designated as a thing in itself.

The conservative Kantians (e.g., Johann Friedrich Herbart) continued to support the view that there are things in themselves; however, even some of these (e.g., Jacob Sigismund Beck) began to recognize that there are problems with this supposition. Others such as Jacobi and Schulze openly attacked this concept as inconsistent with the Kantian system. One such criticism was that, on the one hand, the categories apply only to phenomena (appearance) and thus cannot be extended to the things in themselves; on the other hand, the Kantians maintain that such things exist and cause our sensory affections—thereby applying to these things the categories of existence and causality.

In the second stage, these criticisms, along with the systematic developments by Reinhold, were brought together in Fichte's *Wissenschaftslehre*. Fichte regarded the *Wissenschaftslehre* as a systematic reformulation of the Kantian critique. With Fichte, the range of determination by the subject is greatly extended. Almost everything that had been taken to belong to the thing in itself is appropriated to the subject. There remains only the *Anstoß*, the impulse that prompts (stimulates) the subject to posit the object. Except for this residue of pure objectivity, there is a complete identity of subject and object. That is, everything about the object (except the *Anstoß*) is grounded in the subject. So, in the formulations of Schelling and Hegel, there is an identity of subject and object on the side of the subject (subjective subject-object). However, on the side of the object, there is not a complete identity, since the *Anstoß* remains as a pure objectivity outside the sphere of the subject.

In the third stage, this lack of identity on the side of the object is the focus of Schelling's criticism of Fichte. Along with the subjective subject-object, as established by transcendental idealism, it is also necessary to establish the identity of subject and object on the side of the object. This is the task of the philosophy of nature: it begins with the object and shows how it is permeated with subjectivity. In the *Freiheitsschrift*, Schelling's criticism of Fichte and his call for a philosophy of nature are deepened into an attack on idealism as such. In reference to idealism, he writes of "the abhorrence of everything real that finds the spiritual befouled through any contact with the latter." He continues: "Idealism, if it does not have as its basis a living realism, becomes just as empty and abstract a system as that of Leibniz, Spinoza, or any other dogmatist. The entire new European philosophy since its beginning (with Descartes) has the common defect that nature is not present for it and that it lacks a living ground" (SW VII, 356; PI 26).

In the fourth stage, once the objective subject-object (i.e., the identity on the side of nature) has been set beside the subjective subject-object, Schelling takes a further step. As Hegel describes it in the *Differenzschrift*, Schelling then "presents both as united in something higher than the subject" (HW 2, 12).[1] The name for this higher unity is *absolute identity* (of subject and object as such).

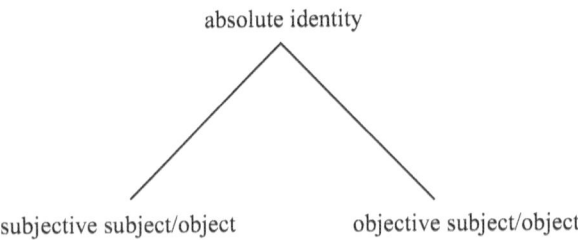

---

1. Georg Wilhelm Friedrich Hegel, *The Difference between Fichte's and Schelling's System of Philosophy*, trans. H. S. Harris and Walter Cerf (Albany: SUNY Press, 1977), 82.

This development constitutes what Schelling identifies as the first general presentation of his system as a whole. It is carried out in the 1801 *Darstellung meines Systems der Philosophie* (*Presentation of My System of Philosophy*), published just six months before Hegel's *Differenzschrift*. The system as a whole is presented as the system of absolute identity. At this higher level, there is "total indifference of the subjective and the objective" (SW IV, 114). In other words, the system is developed at "the indifference-point of the subjective and the objective" (SW IV, 115). Since, nonetheless, the system includes the subject and object in their absolute identity, Schelling can say that there is nothing outside absolute identity—that it is everything: "Absolute identity is absolute totality" (SW IV, 125).

We can note in passing that this is the point where Schelling—and Hegel, too, in complete solidarity—overcomes the subject-object distinction as an ultimate distinction. So the goal at which twentieth-century philosophy often aimed was already achieved by Schelling and Hegel. Furthermore, to confine Schelling and Hegel to a subjectivism that merely extends Cartesianism—a tendency sometimes in Heidegger—is to overlook this phase in Schelling's development. It is also to overlook the backdrop of the *Freiheitsschrift*, which Schelling says is to be read in relation to his system as a whole—that is, as developed in the *Darstellung*.

Finally, in the fifth stage, we arrive at the *Freiheitsschrift*. What is most remarkable is that in this text Schelling takes a step beyond absolute identity, beyond what it would seem has no "beyond." One of the names that Schelling gives to this "beyond" (uprooting it from its previous signification) is *nature*. He says: "Nature in general is everything that lies beyond the absolute Being of absolute identity" (SW VII, 358; PI 28). We might think of this as "radical alterity" beyond absolute identity.

Another name that Schelling gives to this "beyond" is *ground*. Yet, as ground, it is not simply beyond or outside of absolute identity but *before* it, antecedent to it. The entire *Freiheitsschrift* is based on a single fundamental distinction— that between a being insofar as it exists and the ground of its existence (SW VII, 357; PI 27). In passing, we should note that this is often formulated as a distinction between existence and ground. But this is not correct, except as a kind of shorthand. In an open letter to Eschenmayer from 1812, Schelling writes: "But I have not at all spoken of a distinction between *existence* and the ground for existence, but of a distinction between *that-which-exists* [*das Existierende*—"the existing"] and the ground for existence; this is a significant distinction" (SW VIII, 164).

Schelling's primary explication of this distinction is carried out in reference to God. This is because absolute identity can, in theological terms, be designated as God. However, Schelling's analysis is not primarily theological but ontological. Schelling distinguishes, then, between God as he exists (i.e., God regarded as absolute) and the ground of God's existence. The ground is inseparable from

God but is distinguished from him and (as ground) is prior to God. This ground Schelling designates as "the nature in God" (SW VII, 358; PI 27). It is that within God that is not God himself. It is not only the ground of God's existence but also the ground of the existence of (finite) things.

Schelling gives several descriptions of this ground. Among these descriptions, it is a "longing" (*Sehnsucht*)—specifically, "the longing the eternal One feels to give birth to itself" (SW VII, 359; PI 28). He continues: "This longing is not the One itself but is after all co-eternal with it. The longing wants to give birth to God, that is, unfathomable unity, but in this respect there is not yet unity in the longing itself" (SW VII, 359; PI 28). So the ground is a longing or a will. It is the will to give birth to God—and it does give birth to God. This longing can also be characterized as *darkness*, for all birth is from darkness into light: as man is born from his mother's womb, so from the darkness of longing is born the light of understanding (SW VII, 360; PI 29). Schelling also says that this "originary longing . . . moves, divining itself, like an undulating, surging sea, similar to Plato's matter" (SW VII, 360; PI 29–30). The reference is to the receptacle, χώρα.

Schelling also designates the ground as the *unruly* or *ruleless*. Especially significant in this regard is that he describes the ground *as it remains* after the birth of God and the becoming of the world of finite things: "After the eternal act of self-revelation, everything in the world, is, as we see it now, rule, order and form; but the ruleless still lies in the ground, as if it could break through once again, and nowhere does it appear as if order and form were what is original but rather as if something initially ruleless had been brought to order. This is the incomprehensible basis of reality in things, the irreducible remainder, that which with the greatest exertion cannot be resolved in understanding but rather remains eternally in the ground" (SW VII, 359–60; PI 29). Consider that the birth of God is his coming to himself, coming to self-consciousness, to absolute oneness with himself (= absolute identity, now thought in theological terms). The becoming of the world of finite things is the establishment of rule, order, and form. The point is that with respect to both of these processes of becoming, the ground (as unruly) has priority—a double priority. First, it is the unruly ground rather than rule and order that is originary. It is *from* the unruly ground that rule and order come to be. But also, even after rule and order have come to be, the unruly is not simply eliminated but *remains*. It is an irreducible remainder—irreducible to the divine understanding, to absolute unity and identity—and thus something beyond absolute identity. The unruly ground remains—as a force that could break through once again—like something suppressed that could eventually break through the forces of order that suppress it. This harks back to Alcibiades at the end of Plato's *Symposium*, but it also leaps ahead to the Dionysian in Nietzsche.

2. The First Introduction (SW VII, 336–38)

Let us now turn to a closer reading of the *Freiheitsschrift*. In addition to the foreword, there are also two introductions, though they are not labeled as such in the text. Let us consider the first introduction. According to Schelling, philosophical investigations of human freedom are concerned with two things: (1) the correct concept of human freedom (in contrast to the mere unexpressed feeling of freedom, ingrained in all men) and (2) the connection of this concept to the whole of a scientific worldview. What does "scientific worldview" mean? It means a philosophical system.

These two sides of the investigation coincide. Why? "No concept can be determined in isolation . . . and only the demonstration of its connection with the whole confers on it final scientific completeness" (SW VII, 336; PI 9). But why? Most generally, because all determination involves negation, since determination is always determination within an opposition (cf. Fichte). Schelling notes that such coincidence of the two sides of the investigation is especially the case with the concept of freedom, which must be "one of the dominant central points of the system" (SW VII, 336; PI 9).

However, there is an old opinion according to which the concept of freedom is entirely inconsistent with that of system. More specifically, the exclusion is mutual: (1) If philosophy lays claim to unity and completeness, it excludes freedom. (2) If freedom is maintained, then the concept of system is excluded. Schelling does not directly consider the problem in its first form—it would first need to be specified what system means. With respect to the second form of the problem, he says in effect: system cannot be denied, since it is itself necessarily posited with the positing of human freedom. Insofar as a free individual is posited, he is posited in contrast to others with whom, however, he exists together in the world. This "being-together-with" is already a system. So Schelling says that there must be a system at least in the ground of all beings—in the divine understanding. Such a system must coexist with freedom.

However, there are further difficulties. First, it can be maintained that the system in God is simply inaccessible to man. In effect, Schelling answers that this depends on how one defines the principle of knowledge. Then he goes on to repeat an old saying in which is indicated the principle that is to come into play in this work: "Holding his understanding clear and undimmed by malice, he alone [i.e., the philosopher] comprehends the god outside himself through the god within himself" (SW VII, 337; PI 10). Second, someone can—if he is sufficiently radical—go so far as to deny the system in God and "say that there are only individual wills of which each determines its own center for itself and is, according to Fichte's expression, the absolute substance of each and every 'I'" (SW VII, 337; PI 10). To this, Schelling answers only with a general reference to reason's striving toward unity.

In view of these difficulties, Schelling says finally: "Therefore, it seems that . . . the connection of the concept of freedom with the whole of a worldview will always remain the object of a necessary task without whose resolution the concept of freedom would teeter while philosophy would be fully without value. For this great task alone is the unconscious and invisible driving force of all striving for knowledge, from the lowest to the highest" (SW VII, 338; PI 10). Here we see that freedom is not just *one* of the main points of the system but *the* point—that the problem is that of a *system of freedom*. This is perhaps clearest in a statement in Schelling's later lectures on the history of modern philosophy: "A system of freedom—but in just such great lines, in equal simplicity, as the perfect counterpart of the Spinozistic system—this would be genuinely the highest" (SW X, 36).

3. Schelling's Opposition to Fichte

We have seen that Schelling adopts a critical stance toward Fichte in the *Freiheitsschrift* without, however, really developing his criticism. We might say that this divergence from Fichte is a further precondition for the *Freiheitsschrift*, and we need to consider it—though only briefly, since we have followed it closely above.

As we saw in chapter 6, Schelling's opposition to Fichte first becomes explicit and is to some degree elaborated in his *Darstellung meines Systems der Philosophie* (1801). In the *Freiheitsschrift*, Schelling refers to this work as the first general presentation of his system (SW VII, 333; PI 4). In the preface of the *Darstellung*, Schelling openly refers to his divergence from Fichte: he says that his system of absolute identity is completely removed from the standpoint of reflection (Fichte's standpoint). Also, he refers to Fichte's position as idealism in the subjective sense and to his own as idealism in the objective sense.

So Schelling breaks with the standpoint of reflection (i.e., of finite subjectivity). Expressed positively, he insists on the absolute standpoint as that which philosophy must "occupy." This is especially striking in light of the result that Fichte reached in the *Wissenschaftslehre* regarding the finitude of philosophical thought. Specifically, Fichte says: "The thing in itself is something for the I, and consequently in the I, though it ought *not* to be *in the I*" (FW I, 283; SK 249). In other words, when a finite I—in philosophizing—is compelled to suppose something beyond itself that would limit it, it *thereby* conceives it as something for itself and hence as *not* beyond itself. Thus for Fichte, philosophy remains within this circle of finite subjectivity.

In the 1804 *Würzburg Lectures* (titled *System der gesammten Philosophie*), Schelling explicitly discusses Fichte's position on this matter and opposes his own position to Fichte's:

If in our spirit itself there were not a knowledge which is completely independent of all subjectivity and is no longer a knowing of the subject as subject but rather a knowing of that which alone is as such and alone can be known, of that which is simply One, then we would in fact have to renounce all absolute philosophy; we would with our thought and knowledge be eternally enclosed in the sphere of subjectivity; and we would have to regard the results of the Kantian as well as the Fichtean philosophy as the only ones possible and immediately make them our own. (SW VI, 143)

But Schelling does not make these results his own. Rather, he writes immediately after this: "Here stands therefore the limit where our philosophy separates itself from both of these systems, according to which no knowledge of what is in itself is possible.... How such a knowledge is possible cannot be understood as long as all knowledge is regarded as something subjective" (SW VI, 143–44).

Even more directly, Schelling says that our finitude "must entirely disappear in philosophy" (SW VI, 140). In other words, the knowing that takes place in philosophy cannot be merely an activity of an individual subject that would be forever condemned to the sphere of subjectivity in the way described by Fichte. Still more to the point, Schelling writes: "That I say: I know or I am the one who knows, this is already the πρῶτον ψεῦδος. I know nothing, or my knowing, insofar as it really is *mine*, is no true knowing. Not I know, but rather only the All *knows* in me, if the knowing which I call mine is a real, a true knowing" (SW VI, 140). So the highest knowing is *not* my knowing of myself but reason's knowing of itself through me. Schelling says that the I is only the organ for the self-knowing of the absolute.

He says, finally: "This insight into the essence of reason and the possibility of absolute knowledge is the hinge of philosophy and the point in which it is grounded" (SW VI, 145). Similarly, in the 1803 *Lectures on the Method of Academic Study*, he writes: "All knowledge is absolute.... Our total system of knowledge can only be a copy of that eternal knowledge" (SW V, 216–17). This is indicated in the *Darstellung* when at the end of the preface, just before the series of definitions and propositions begins, Schelling writes: "Von jetzt an spreche nur die Sache selbst" (SW IV, 114). Not the finite philosopher, but "the thing itself" is to do the speaking.

4. The Second Introduction (SW VII, 338–57)

A. Pantheism and Freedom (SW VII, 338–48)

In the first introduction, Schelling had posed the general problem of a "system of freedom" (i.e., the problem of the compatibility of the concept of freedom with that of system). What is the precise sense of this problem? "System" has the same essential sense as in Fichte. It is not just a framework for ordering the material of knowledge. Rather, it is "the system of the world"—something to be discovered, not invented. In other words, the system is the inner structure of the knowable itself and not merely some copy of this structure invented by the philosopher. This means that the question of the system of freedom refers not merely to the insertion of the concept of freedom in a "system" of concepts but also (and primarily) to the possibility of accord between freedom and the structure of the totality of beings.

The second introduction begins by posing this same problem in a more definite form. Specifically, Schelling poses it in terms of the structure of the totality of beings. That is, he poses it in terms of the relation of all (πᾶν) beings to their ground, God (θεός)—in other words, in terms of *pantheism*. Thus the problem is whether accord is possible between freedom and pantheism, or whether pantheism necessarily involves the denial of freedom. It is the problem expressed in the assertion that "the only possible system of reason is pantheism, but this is inevitably fatalism" (SW VII, 338; PI 11).

Schelling's immediate response is to grant that indeed fatalism may be combined with pantheism. But he insists that fatalism is not essentially tied to it. As evidence, he offers the fact that many affirm pantheism precisely because of "the liveliest feeling of freedom" (SW VII, 339; PI 11). The point is that individual freedom is impossible *over against* divine omnipotence (they contradict one another). So the only way to save human freedom is by placing man (and his freedom) in God and by maintaining that man's activity belongs to God's life. This means that, far from requiring a denial of human freedom, pantheism is a way of saving human freedom.

However, Schelling insists that everything depends on determining the precise sense of pantheism: "For it should not be denied that, if pantheism denotes nothing more than the doctrine of the immanence of things in God, every rational viewpoint in some sense must be drawn to this doctrine" (SW VII, 339; PI 11). This means that every rational system involves the structure by which the totality of things are grounded on their ground. The question is: What is this grounding structure?

Schelling proceeds to consider three common interpretations of this structure (i.e., of pantheism)—all of them inadequate:

(1) All (= the totality of beings) is God, in the sense of a complete identification of God with things. God is the mere sum of things. Against this interpretation, Schelling offers Spinoza as a counterexample, the one who had commonly been charged with making such an identification. For Spinoza, God is "in himself" (*in sich*); that is, God is *original*—whereas finite things necessarily exist in another being; that is, they are *derivative*. And no combination can transform what is by nature derived into what is by nature original.

(2) Each individual thing is God. This is "still more fatuous" (SW VII, 341; PI 13). It says that each thing is a modified God. But a modified (derivative) God is no God at all—and so this interpretation collapses.

(3) Things are nothing. This is taken to follow from and express the real sense of "God is all." It means that all individuality is eliminated. But if this is so (if things are really nothing), then how can God be all things? So the entire conception seems to dissolve.

All these misinterpretations have a common source: a misunderstanding of the law of identity or the meaning of the copula in judgment. In other words, in the judgment "God is all," they misunderstand the "is." They mistake it to assert simple sameness, thereby betraying their "dialectical immaturity" (SW VII, 342; PI 14). On the positive side: the identity asserted in the "is" (and in the law of identity, understood dialectically) is actually "an immediately creative" unity (SW VII, 345; PI 17). Although God is the ground of things and things are thus dependent on God, such dependence does not exclude autonomy or even freedom. That is, the dependence of things on God need not determine *what* these things are—only that, whatever they are, they can be only as a consequence of God (SW VII, 346; PI 17). Schelling elaborates: "God is not a God of the dead but of the living. . . . The procession of things from God is God's self-revelation. But God can only reveal himself in that which is like him, in free beings acting on their own, for whose Being there is no ground other than God, but who are as God is" (SW VII, 346–47; PI 18). Note here how the concept of *spirit* enters in: the revelation of the self through an other that is nevertheless the same as the self.[2]

Schelling concludes that the concept of "derived absoluteness" is not contradictory (SW VII, 347; PI 18). In other words, there is no necessary contradiction between immanence in God and freedom. This means that the denial of freedom is not necessarily connected with pantheism.

B. From Spinozism to Idealism (SW VII, 349–52)

Granted that pantheism per se does not entail the denial of freedom, the question then arises: What is it that makes Spinoza's system end in fatalism? Spinoza's fatalism does not result from his pantheism—and so it must result from something else. From what? Schelling answers: "The error of his system lies by no means in his placing things *in God* but in the fact that they are *things*—in the abstract concept of beings in the world [*Weltwesen*], indeed of infinite substance itself, which for him is also a thing" (SW VII, 349; PI 20). In other words, Spinoza's arguments against freedom are deterministic rather than pantheistic: they result

---

2. Note also the remarkable lines about thoughts subjugating their mother and the role of the imagination (SW VII, 347; PI 18).

from making man (and all beings) into a *thing*. As Heidegger notes, Spinoza's basic error is not theological but ontological.[3]

Schelling proceeds to describe the transformation of Spinozism into idealism that he carried out (following Fichte) in his early writings. Over against the one-sidedly realistic system of Spinoza, Schelling sought a mutual interpenetration of realism and idealism—that is, the unity of transcendental philosophy and the philosophy of nature. Moreover, in transcendental philosophy (by which the whole is first raised into the genuine system of reason), he spiritualized Spinoza's fundamental concept by means of the principle of idealism. This involved replacing Spinoza's abstract concept of substance with the Fichtean concept of the I as self-positing. But such self-positing is precisely freedom in its Kantian-Fichtean sense—so that in such idealism "freedom rules" (SW VII, 350; PI 21). Furthermore, such self-positing is identical with willing in its most fundamental sense (cf. SW VII, 385; PI 50–51).[4] Thus Schelling says: "In the final and highest judgment, there is no other Being than willing [*Wollen*]. Willing is primordial Being [*Ursein*] to which alone all predicates of primordial Being apply: groundlessness, eternity, independence from time, self-affirmation. All of philosophy strives only to find this highest expression" (SW VII, 350; PI 21).

Genuine investigation of freedom can begin only at this point to which idealism has raised philosophy. A true concept of freedom (i.e., as self-determination) was simply lacking in all modern philosophy before idealism. Freedom was, at best, understood as mere mastery of intelligence over the senses and passions. However, idealism also has its inadequacy—if we want to enter more precisely into the question of freedom. It is not sufficient merely to prove that activity, life, and freedom are true actuality—rather, one must also prove the reverse: that all actuality (nature, the world of things) is grounded on activity, life, and freedom. In Fichte's terms, one must show not only that the I is all but also that all is the I. This amounts to saying that the philosophy of nature must be added to transcendental philosophy—that the idealism of Fichte must be accompanied by a "higher realism" (SW VII, 351; PI 22).

At the end of the second introduction, Schelling reiterates this critique of idealism (especially Fichte) much more strongly. In reference to idealism, he speaks of "the abhorrence of everything real that finds the spiritual befouled through any contact with it (SW VII, 356; PI 26). Schelling continues: "Idealism, if it does

---

3. Martin Heidegger, *Schellings Abhandlung Über das Wesen der menschlichen Freiheit (1809)*, ed. Hildegard Feick, 2nd ed. (Tübingen: Niemeyer, 1995), 107; Martin Heidegger, *Schelling's Treatise on the Essence of Human Freedom*, trans. Joan Stambaugh (Athens: Ohio University Press, 1985), 89.

4. Cf. Kant's account of the will as practical reason in the second *Critique* (AA 5, 29–30, 33; CPrR 28–29, 33–34).

not have as its basis a living realism, becomes just as empty and abstract a system as that of Leibniz, Spinoza, or any other dogmatist. The whole of modern European philosophy since its beginning (with Descartes) has the common defect that nature is not present for it and that it lacks a living ground" (SW VII, 356; PI 26).

More specifically, Schelling points out that such a "higher realism" would have been attained had Kant taken one additional step. Having arrived at freedom as the positive determination of the subject's being in itself, he should have gone on to extend this concept of being-in-itself (as freedom) to all things. In other words, in terms of Schelling's philosophy of nature, he should have gone on to exhibit nature as visible spirit. However, by doing this, he would have again opened up the problem of *human* freedom and made further inquiry necessary. Specifically, if freedom is a positive determination of *all* beings, then it becomes necessary to ask about the specific difference that delimits *human* freedom. In other words, one must ask: What is distinctive about human freedom? This is the question that idealism cannot answer.

C. The Problem of Evil (SW VII, 352–57)

Now Schelling states his answer to the question of human freedom: "But the real and living concept is that freedom is a capacity for good and for evil" (SW VII, 352; PI 23). What is problematic in this concept of freedom is: ". . . and for evil." Since the relation to evil is what is problematic, the *problem* of freedom is, in a sense, the problem of evil. But how is evil problematic? By the fact that it contradicts the concept of God. Specifically, if the reality of evil is admitted, then it is included in (i.e., grounded in) God. Hence the concept of God as an all-perfect being (absolutely excluding evil) is disrupted. On the other hand, if the reality of evil is denied, then the real concept of freedom must be given up.

Note that this is the point at which the genuine problem of uniting freedom and system becomes evident. The relation to evil is what generates the problem of the system of freedom in its genuine form (as contrasted with those sham forms that were mere results of dialectical immaturity). Specifically, that relation of all beings to their unitary ground (God) by which there is "a system of the world"— this is called into question by evil, which cannot be so grounded.

Schelling says that this dilemma—this conflict between God and evil—is the point of "most profound difficulty" (SW VII, 352; PI 23). He argues that the usual ways of attempting to resolve the difficulty fail. Specifically, he takes issue with that position that would regard evil not as a positive being for which God would be "responsible" (i.e., ground) but as a *mere privation* (which would be exempt from the demand for grounding in God). He insists that evil is no mere lack of good but rather something positive: "For the simple reflection that only man, the most complete of all visible creatures, is capable of evil, shows already that the ground of evil could not in any way lie in lack or deprivation.... The ground of evil must lie, therefore, not only in something generally positive but rather in that which is most positive in what nature contains" (SW VII, 368–69; PI 36–37).

In this same connection, Schelling denies that evil is simply derived from finitude. For example, he rejects the claim that evil is simply the failure of intelligence to master the senses and feelings (i.e., the bodily): "According to these notions, the sole ground of evil lies in sensuality or animality, or in the earthly principle, as they do not oppose heaven with hell, as is fitting, but with the earth" (SW VII, 371; PI 39). Let me mention, finally, that in the *Stuttgart Private Lectures*, Schelling elaborates this in a prophetic way: "Hence it is so important to recognize [1] that the body, too, in and of itself already contains a spiritual principle, and [2] that it is not the body which infects the spirit, but the spirit the body" (SW VII, 476).

Since evil can be neither denied a positive reality nor reconciled with God, the only solution is to pose a second ground (of evil) alongside God. But if this second power is separate from God, then dualism results. Schelling rejects any such dualism—because it is "only a system of the self-destruction and despair of reason" (SW VII, 354; PI 24). In other words, such a dualism would amount to the negation of unity and system—and of reason as the demand for unity and system. So the ground of evil, which is to be independent of God, must be in God himself. This means there must be in God something that is not God himself.

5. The Possibility of Evil (SW VII, 357–73)

Schelling introduces a distinction from the philosophy of nature: the existence (*Existenz*) of that which is versus the ground of existence (*Grund*—in the sense of "basis," not in the sense of *ratio*). In Schelling's formulation, it is "the distinction between a being [*Wesen*] insofar as it exists and a being insofar as it is merely the ground of existence" (SW VII, 357; PI 27). He proceeds to explicate this distinction by discussing its application to God. Since there is nothing outside God, he must contain within himself the ground of his existence. This merely says: God is *causa sui*. But what Schelling demands is that the ground in God not be treated as a mere concept but as something real and actual. This means that the ground is to be treated *as* grounding—*as* the basis from which God comes to exist. That is, the becoming of God's existence from the ground is to be dealt with.

Now this requires that the distinction between God as existing and the ground of his existence not be immediately collapsed (as in the traditional concept of God as *causa sui*). So one must maintain the distinction between: (1) God insofar as he exists (i.e., God viewed as absolute) and (2) the ground of his existence, which, though contained in God, is distinguishable from him. Schelling calls this ground the *nature* in God—and he adds that "nature in general is everything that lies beyond the absolute Being of absolute identity" (SW VII, 358; PI 28). Here we see clearly the connection of this problematic to earlier issues of the philosophy of nature and of the limitation of transcendental philosophy.

Schelling approaches the same distinction from another direction—from the consideration of things. The only concept that adequately expresses the nature of *things* is becoming (*Werden*). But things cannot become in God (considered absolutely, in his existence), for they are infinitely different from God. So they must become in a ground different from God. But since there can be nothing outside God, this ground can only be that within God that is not God himself—that is, the *ground* of God's existence (SW VII, 358–59; PI 28).

What is the character of this ground? And what is the character of that becoming (of God and of things) that arises from it? The ground is the longing (*Sehnsucht*) that the eternal one feels to give birth to itself—that is, it is the longing to give birth to God (a longing that is not yet God himself). So regarded, the ground is will—but a will in which there is no understanding, hence an incomplete will. This description applies to ground considered in itself; that is, independently of that becoming that proceeds from it. Indeed, there is reason to speak of the ground in this way: for though it is "submerged" by what arises from it, it is not eliminated.

This "endurance" of the ground is one of several issues in the first of a series of very important passages:

> After the eternal act of self-revelation, everything in the world is, as we see it now, rule, order, and form; but the unruly [*das Regellose*] still lies in the ground, as if it could break through once again, and nowhere does it appear as if order and form were what is original but rather as if what had been initially unruly had been brought to order. This is the incomprehensible basis of reality in things, the irreducible remainder, that which with the greatest exertion cannot be resolved in understanding [*Verstand*] but rather remains eternally in the ground. (SW VII 359–60; PI 29)

We should note several things here. First, Schelling here identifies the general character of that becoming that proceeds from the ground: it is the eternal act of self-revelation. God's becoming is his coming-to-himself, his being revealed to himself, his coming to self-consciousness. With respect to things, this becoming is an establishment of rule, order, and form—that is, creation. But rule, order, and form are not original. The original, the basis, is the unruly, "the irrational" (*das Verstandlose*)—and the rational is born from this. Schelling writes: "Only from the darkness of that which is without understanding (from feeling, longing, the sovereign mother of knowledge) grow luminous thoughts" (SW VII, 360; PI 29). Again: "All birth is birth from darkness into light" (SW VII, 360; PI 29). However, this birth of light out of darkness does not negate (eliminate) the darkness. The irreducible remainder cannot be resolved into understanding—the darkness of the ground remains![5]

This passage on the unruly is the first in a series of very important passages that, taken, together, give a basic sketch of Schelling's development of the problem of a system of freedom—at least at the level of the first half of the book. They are followed by a filling out of this sketch—and then by a highly problematic transposition of the entire development to a "higher" level. We need to consider the three additional passages. They deal with (1) divine becoming, (2) the becoming of things = creation, and (3) the created (and thus how evil is possible in man as something created).

> But, corresponding to the longing, which as the still dark ground is the first stirring of divine existence, an inner, reflexive representation is generated in God himself through which, since it can have no other object but God, God sees himself in an exact image of himself. This representation is the first in which God, considered as absolute, is actualized, although only in himself; this representation is with God in the beginning and is the God who was begotten *in* God himself. This representation is at the same time the understanding—the *Word*—of this longing, and the eternal spirit which, perceiving the word within itself and the same time the infinite longing, and impelled by the love that it itself is, proclaims the word so that the understanding together with longing becomes a freely creating and all-powerful will and builds in the initially unruly nature as in its own element or instrument. (SW VII, 360–61; PI 30)

Schelling speaks of the longing that is the first stirring of divine being. How is the longing (= ground) the divine being's first stirring? Schelling explains this in the immediately preceding sentence: the longing is turned toward the understanding (i.e., the divine). It involves a presentiment (*Ahnung*) of the divine. It is similar to the "matter" of Plato—he means the receptacle in the *Timaeus*.[6] However, the longing does not yet recognize what it is turned toward. It is a striving that does not have before it anything *definite* for which it strives. It is not able to *name* what it strives for—it lacks possession of words.

Corresponding to this longing there is born in (and *as*) God himself a presentation. What is this presentation a presentation *of*? Of God himself: "God sees himself in an image." This means that God sees an image of himself *in the ground.* Thereby, God's self-revelation (his coming to self-consciousness) is

---

5. [Editor's note: for a more extensive treatment of "ground" in the *Freiheitsschrift*, see ch. 18 of John Sallis, *Delimitations: Phenomenology and the End of Metaphysics*, 2nd ed. (Bloomington: Indiana University Press, 1995), 221–33.]

6. See Plato, Timaeus, 49a–b. [Editor's note: see John Sallis, *Chorology: On Beginning in Plato's "Timaeus"* (Bloomington: Indiana University Press, 1999), 158ff.]

initiated—and, as we saw, this self-revelation is precisely what constitutes the coming-forth (becoming) of God from his ground.

This presentation is the understanding—the *word* of that longing. It can name (set forth with definiteness) what the longing merely turned toward (God himself). But this presentation is also *spirit*, "which [perceives] the word within itself and at the same time the infinite longing" (SW VII, 361; PI 30). Here "spirit" signifies unity (unification) of word (i.e., of God himself, as existing, as understanding) and longing (i.e., the ground). So what is born is not just distinct from the ground out of which it arises but it unites that ground with itself. Note that because spirit is fundamentally unification, Schelling speaks of it as "moved by love" (i.e., by the most primordial force of unification).

Spirit utters the word—that is, it "speaks out" what previously remained within God. To what is the word addressed? To the ground, for the sake of God's apprehension of his image in the ground and the correlative unification of ground and existence. But in taking up the ground to himself, God (as spirit) becomes creative and omnipotent will *and* informs the ground—that is, brings order and form into disorderly, formless nature. God speaks out the word into nature. This is an act of *creation*.

> The first effect of the understanding in nature is the division of forces, since only thus can the understanding unfold the unity that is unconsciously but necessarily immanent in nature as in a seed, just as in man the light enters into the dark longing to create something so that in the chaotic jumble of thoughts, all hanging together, but each hindering the other from emerging, thoughts divide themselves from each other, and now the unity hidden in the ground and containing all raises itself up; or as in the plant the dark bond of gravity dissolves only in relation to the unfolding and expansion of forces, and as the unity hidden in divided material is developed. Because, namely, this being (of primordial nature) is nothing else than the eternal ground for the existence of God, it must contain within itself, although locked up, the essence of God as a resplendent glimpse of life in the darkness of the depths. However, longing aroused by the understanding strives from now on to retain the glimpse of life seized within itself and to close itself up in itself so that a ground may always remain. (SW VII, 361; PI 30–31)

Creation is God's informing of formless nature. What is the character of this informing? Schelling identifies it as "the division of forces." Further, he says that the division of forces is for the sake of unfolding the unity that is unconsciously in the ground (as in a seed). But why is division necessary to unfold unity? Because to unfold unity means to let it become manifest, not as an unarticulated one but as a one ruling over a many—as unifying unity, as the power of unification. In fact, the greater the division (articulation), the greater is the unfolding of the unity.

But what is this unity that gets unfolded through the division of forces? Before the unfolding, it is just the essence of God as a "resplendent glimpse of life in the darkness of the depths" (SW VII, 361; PI 30). In other words, it is God as he is in the ground (closed in, held in reserve, concealed) before his being born out of the ground. So, more generally, the unity that gets unfolded is ultimately just God himself—as existing, as absolute. Thus the unfolding of the unity is identical with God's self-becoming, his coming to be revealed to himself. Furthermore, God's self-becoming and creation of finite beings (= the division of forces and the unfolding of unity) are not two separate processes of becoming from the same ground. Rather, they are one and the same becoming: God's self-becoming and creation are identical.

The unfolding of unity from the ground is a revelation of the innermost center of the divine essence originally concealed in the ground. Over against this unfolding-revelation, there is a counterstriving back toward the ground: the ground, provoked by the lighting of understanding, strives to close itself up so as to maintain itself as ground. So there is a tension between lighting and darkening, closing-in and opening-out, revelation and concealment. Because of this tension, the unfolding of unity is not immediately accomplished—but takes place in stages. This means that in creation, there is brought forth a hierarchy of beings that are progressively more differentiated and, hence, more capable of revealing to God that unity which he is.

> The understanding as universal will stands against this self-will of creatures, using and subordinating the latter to itself as a mere instrument. But, if through advancing mutation and division of all forces, the deepest and most inner point of initial darkness in a being is finally transfigured wholly into the light, then the will of this same being is indeed, to the extent it is individual, also a truly particular will, yet, in itself or as the *centrum* of all other particular wills, one with the primordial will or the understanding, so that now from both a single whole comes into being. This raising of the deepest *centrum* into light occurs in none of the creatures visible to us other than man. In man there is the whole power of the dark principle and at the same time the whole strength of the light. In him there is the deepest abyss and the loftiest sky or both *centra*. The human will is the seed—hidden in eternal longing—of the God who is present still in the ground only; it is the divine panorama of life, locked up within the depths, which God beheld as he fashioned the will to nature. In him (in man) alone God loved the world, and precisely this likeness of God was possessed by yearning in the *centrum* as it came into opposition with the light. Because he emerges from the ground (is creaturely), man has in relation to God a relatively independent principle in himself; but because precisely this principle—without it ceasing for that reason to be dark in accordance with the ground—is transfigured in light, there arises in him something higher, *spirit*. For the eternal spirit proclaims unity or the word into nature. The proclaimed (real) word, however, is only in the unity of light and darkness

> (vowel and consonant). Now both principles are indeed in all things, yet they are without complete consonance due to the deficiency of that which has been raised out of the ground. Only in man, therefore, is the word fully proclaimed which in all other things is held back and incomplete. But spirit, that is, *God* as existing *actu*, reveals itself in the proclaimed word. Insofar as the soul is now the living identity of both principles, it is spirit; and spirit is in God. Were now the identity of both principles in the spirit of man exactly as indissoluble as in God, then there would be no distinction, that is, God as spirit would not be revealed. The same unity that is inseverable in God must therefore be severable in man—and this is the possibility of good and evil. (SW VII, 363–64; PI 32–33)

Everything that is created has a double principle. On the one hand, there is a principle by which things are divided from God himself—that is, by which they are in the ground. This is the willfulness of creatures, blind will. On the other hand, there is a principle by which they are identical with God—that is, the respect in which they are that unity (= God) at a certain stage of unfolding. This is the understanding, universal will. Now Schelling says that in creatures these two principles are, *to some degree*, one and the same. This is because the unity sealed away in the darkness of the ground is the same as the unity that is unfolded (= God). In fact, the unfolding is simply the transfiguring, the bringing into the light of what was originally closed up in the ground.

There is a point in the hierarchy of beings where the unity is completely unfolded, where "the deepest and most inner point of initial darkness in a being [a creature] is finally transfigured wholly into the light" (SW VII, 363; PI 32). Here the two principles come together entirely to form a unitary whole. The creature in whom this occurs is *man*: "In man there is the whole power of the dark principle and at the same time the whole strength of the light. In him there is the deepest abyss and the loftiest sky or both centra" (SW VII, 363; PI 32). Moreover, Schelling notes that in man alone has God *loved* the world. If we recall that love is the primordial force of unification, this means that only in man does God see the full image of himself in the world—so as to come to unification with himself (as self-consciousness).

Man as the unity of the two principles is *spirit*—and as spirit, he is in God. However, Schelling continues: "Were now the identity of both principles in the spirit of man exactly as indissoluble as in God, then there would be no distinction [*Unterschied*], that is, God as spirit would not be revealed" (SW VII, 364; PI 32–33). This says: if the unity of the two principles were indissoluble in man, then there would be no difference between man and God. Man would simply be God rather than being a perfected image in which God sees himself *as* the unity he is—and thus the revelation of God to himself would not come about. Schelling concludes: "The same unity that is inseverable in God must therefore be severable in man—and this is the possibility of good and evil" (SW VII, 364; PI 33).

Let me add two remarks to conclude our consideration of these passages. First, what is evil, considered in terms of its possibility? It is the dissolution of the unity of principles. Specifically, it is a dissolution that takes the form of exalting willfulness, a dissolution in which willfulness (the dark principle) seeks to be, as a particular will, what it can only be in its identity with the universal will (= the understanding).

Second, what about the question of system? God's revelation to himself (i.e., the final unfolding of unity) requires that evil be possible. But such an ultimate unfolding of the unity of God with himself (the full birth of God as absolute) is the condition for there being a system. Thus the possibility of evil—rather than excluding system—is required for the possibility of system in the sense that system takes on through Schelling's work on human freedom.

Conclusion

The Question of System

At the beginning of these lectures, I posed several questions. Most of them had to do with the outcome of German Idealism: What is that outcome? Was it a collapse (or fulfillment, etc.)? What is the import of this outcome for our present attempts to philosophize? We need, in conclusion, to return to these questions to see more clearly what the issues are in them.

In order to return to these questions, I must suppose something that we have not really shown: Schelling's work on human freedom is the primary locus where the outcome of German Idealism is to be discerned. But if we assume this, then we may say that what is fundamentally at issue in that outcome is the possibility and nature of *system*—system in that substantive sense developed by Fichte in connection with the first principle of the *Wissenschaftslehre* (the I as self-positing), system as the unity of all beings, as system of the world (not as a copy of this structure constructed merely in thought by philosophy).

Let me make three remarks regarding this issue. First, we have seen that, in a sense, Schelling's reflection on freedom (and evil) vindicates the concept of system: freedom and the possibility of evil are necessary for the ultimate unity of God with himself *as* imaged in nature—that is, they are necessary for that coming of God to himself that constitutes the system of the world. But we might ask: What is Schelling forced to relinquish for the sake of this vindication (this reconciliation of system and evil)? He relinquishes the character of God *as ground*—or, more precisely, the absolute identity of God with the ground. Now, this is not to say that there is a simple dualism. In fact, there is a unity of God with the ground, that is, with the image of himself in the ground. But this unity is subsequent, something accomplished and thus not already given in the concept of God himself. So the essence of God himself does not consist in his being ground. As Schelling had said earlier, the ground is that in God which is not God himself.

But then the question arises: What happens to the concept of God when the character of being ground is excluded from it? Should we even continue to speak of God if the God of whom we are speaking is neither ground nor creator in the strict sense? In other words, would it perhaps be appropriate to redetermine Schelling's duality of God and ground in a nontheological way? Let me suggest that Nietzsche's work might provide some means with which to begin such a redetermination—specifically, the duality involved in the image of the "music-practicing Socrates," which is the same duality that is at issue in the character Zarathustra.[1] We might also be able to contribute to such a redetermination by following a clue that Schelling gives when he identifies ground with Plato's receptacle. But here it is more difficult to remain outside theology, primarily because so much of the tradition has tended to conceal the genuine sense of the other "principle" that Plato opposes to the receptacle (εἴδη or, preeminently, τὸ ἀγαθόν).

Second, we need to ask: Is the question of system so completely settled in Schelling's work itself, as we have supposed? Schelling has reconciled freedom (the possibility of evil) with system *in that sense which system takes* through the development of the distinction between God and ground. But what about this sense of system?

At a later point in the *Freiheitsschrift*, Schelling writes: "In the divine understanding there is a system; yet God himself is not a system, but rather a life; and the answer to the question as to the possibility of evil in regard to God ... lies in this fact alone" (SW VII, 399; PI 62). This says: there is a system *only with respect to one moment* of the divine becoming—in the understanding (God as existing, as absolute) in contrast to the ground. But if there is system only in the understanding, then the ground is originally excluded from the system. Consequently, system is *not* system in the fundamental sense—as the totality of beings set back on their ground. We might say that the possibility of system reaches its limit—and breaks down—in the encounter with elusiveness, the self-maintaining darkness of ground. It is the reality of evil that compels us to that encounter.

Third, although Schelling says that there is a system only in the understanding, he nevertheless poses beyond the duality of system (understanding) and ground a still higher unity: "life." In the last major section of the book, which he calls the "highest point of the whole inquiry," he develops the concept of this higher unity. He calls it absolute indifference, nonground (*Ungrund*). He says:

> Since it precedes all opposites, these cannot be distinguishable in it nor can they be present in any way. Therefore, it cannot be called the identity of both [i.e., ground and existence], but only the absolute indifference of both. . . . Indifference is not a product of opposites, nor are they implicitly contained in it, but rather indifference is its own being separate from all opposition, a being against which all opposites ruin themselves, that is nothing else than their very not-Being and that, for this reason, also has no predicate, except as the very lacking of a predicate, without it being on that account a nothingness [*Nichts*] or non-thing [*Unding*]. (SW VII, 406; PI 68–69)

---

1. For Nietzsche's reference to the "music-practicing Socrates," see section 15 of *The Birth of Tragedy*. Friedrich Nietzsche, *"The Birth of Tragedy" and "The Case of Wagner,"* trans. Walter Kaufmann (New York: Random House, 1967), 98.

Conclusion: The Question of System

The question is: Could this higher unity as absolute indifference make possible a new idea of system—beyond the idea of system forged in Fichte's work? But what could be the character of a system by which beings would be set back in relation to a nonground rather than a ground?

We therefore see three possible outcomes that the outcome of German Idealism presents to our efforts to philosophize—that is, to our attempt to understand what philosophy can be today:

1. Relinquishing of God as ground for the sake of system—and, more generally, the detheologizing of philosophy.
2. Abandoning of the idea of system (in its Fichtean sense) in the face of the encounter with the self-maintaining (enduring) darkness of ground.
3. Questioning regarding a sense of system beyond that of modern metaphysics—correlative to nonground rather than ground.

Perhaps the most difficult thing of all is to understand whether and how these three "outcomes" belong together.

Editor's Afterword

THE FOREGOING TEXT is based on John Sallis's lecture course on German Idealism, held at Boston College during the 2016–17 academic year, with supplementary material from the lecture courses of spring 2006 and fall 2010 (also at Boston College). Although these lectures contain some discussions of Hegel's philosophy—particularly during his time in Jena—their focus is on Fichte and Schelling, in addition to the early reception of Kant's thought. Other volumes in the *Collected Writings* will contain Sallis's lectures on Hegel's aesthetics and mature philosophy.

In preparing the text, I have closely followed Sallis's handwritten manuscript, making only minor editorial interventions to shape the text into book form. In the fall of 2010, I had the good fortune to attend a previous iteration of Sallis's lecture course on German Idealism as well as a simultaneous seminar on Schelling. I consulted my notes from these courses when preparing the text, incorporating a small amount of material that offered helpful connections or elaborations in filling out the manuscript. Sallis himself has approved the final text.

Most of the footnotes in this volume are either purely bibliographical or contain material from the handwritten manuscript. When I have added additional notes—usually to indicate discussions of similar material in other works by Sallis—these are labeled "Editor's Note." The diagrams that appear throughout the text are designed by Sallis himself. The chapter and section divisions are largely based on section headings in the manuscript, though I have occasionally added more descriptive titles that reflect the content of the section.

As a graduate student hearing the lectures, I was struck by how clearly they gave a sense for the issues at the heart of German Idealism, despite the complexity of its development. It is an honor for me to play a part in making them available to the wider public.

Mark J. Thomas
Pella, IA
Winter 2023

Appendix 1

Structure of the Initial Syntheses in Fichte's Grundlage, *Part II*

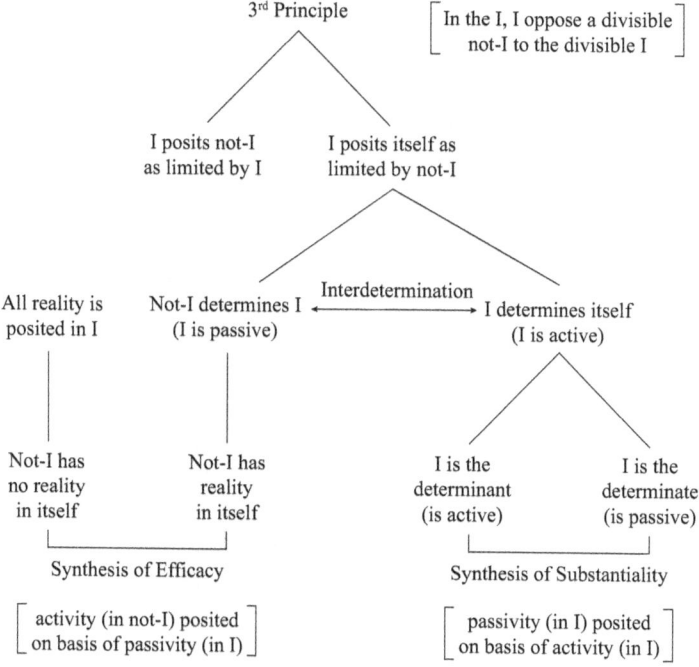

Appendix 2
Interplays and Independent Activities (Fichte's Grundlage, *§4, Section E)*

	Interplay		Independent Activity	
I: Identity of essential opposition and annihilation	I (m): Essential opposition (qualitative incompatibility) I (f): Mutual annihilation (coming-to-be through a passing-away)	Efficacy	A (m): Activity of not-I A (f): Transference (positing by means of non-positing) (activity of I)	A: Mediate positing
I: Clash (Incursion of each component upon the other)	I (m): Determinability of the totality I (f): Mutual exclusion of the components from the absolute totality	Substantiality	A (m): Positing of higher sphere incorporating both determinate and indeterminate A (f): Exclusion from a determinate sphere (alienation: non-positing by means of a positing)	Absolute conjoining and holding fast of opposites

Appendix 3

Formal Structure of Fichte's Grundlage, *§4, Section E*

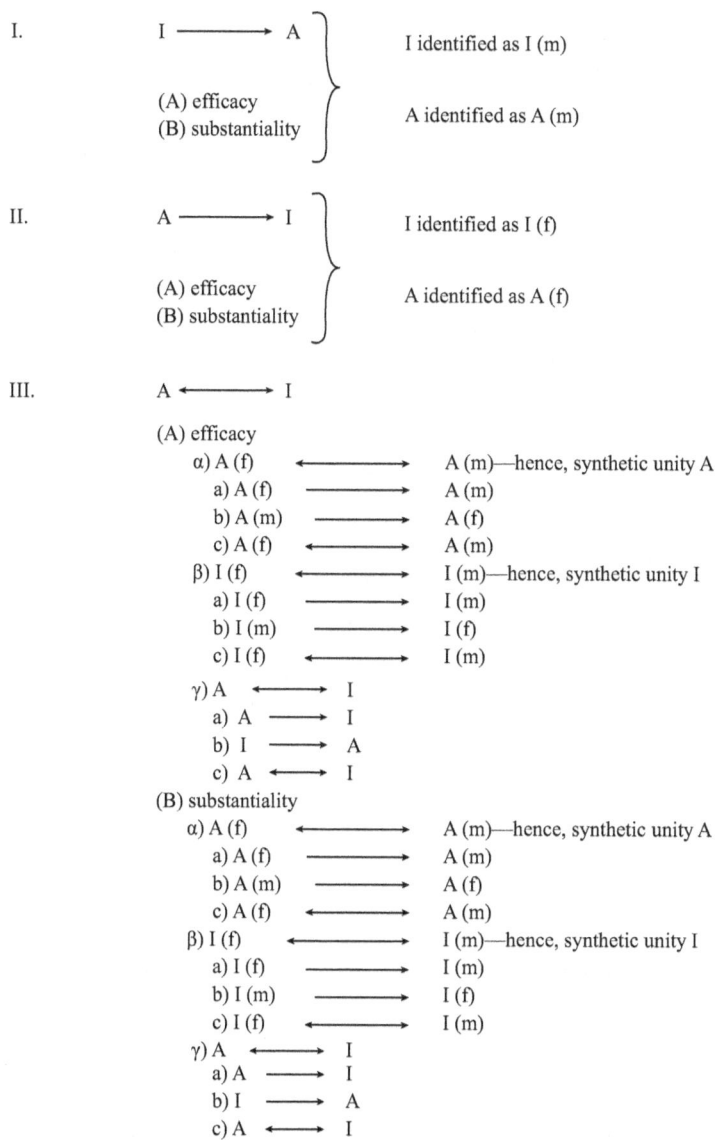

143

Appendix 4

Outline of Fichte's Grundlage, §4, Section E (FW I, 151–217)

The detailed considerations that make up most of section E proceed from the following proposition, which is itself the outcome of the series of syntheses in sections A–D: "Independent activity is determined by interaction and passion (action and passion determining one another by interdetermination); and, conversely, interaction and passion are determined by independent activity" (FW I, 150; SK 142). In this proposition, three propositions are contained:

(I) The independent activity is determined by interaction and passion—that is, by the interplay (I → A).
(II) The interplay is determined by the independent activity (A → I).
(III) Each is determined by the other (A ↔ I).

These three propositions determine the basic structure of section E. In dealing with each of these three propositions, Fichte proceeds through the following steps:

(I) He considers what the proposition means in general.
(II) He applies the proposition to
  (a) the interplay of efficacy
  (b) the interplay of substantiality.

(I)
The independent activity is determined by the interplay.
(I → A)

(1) General considerations. Here there are three questions:
  (a) What is the general character of the activity that is determined? According to the two concepts of synthesis established, there can be either a positing of activity by means of passivity (efficacy) or a positing of passivity by means of activity (substantiality). For such a transition between activity and passivity (which, as such, are opposed) to occur, there must be a third thing, a ground of conjunction, which makes the components fit for an interdetermination. This third thing is what is provided by the independent activity.
  (b) How is this independent activity determined? It is clear that the activity is not determined by the interplay in the sense of being made possible by it.

Rather, the contrary is the case: the activity makes possible the interplay. So what Fichte means is that the activity is determined by the interplay *only in reflection*. In other words, it is by reflection on the interplay that we are led to posit the independent activity as that which makes the interplay possible.

(c) What is the relation of this activity to the activity that, according to proposition II, determines the interplay? This relation is thematized in terms of the distinction between form and matter. Specifically, the first activity (proposition I) is determined simply as what is required for the possibility of the *components* of the interplay; thus, it is the ground of the *matter* of the interplay. The second activity (proposition II) is that which makes possible the *transition* from one component to the other; thus, it is the ground of the *form* of the interplay. Fichte refers to these as the activity of the matter, A (m), and the activity of the form, A (f).

(2) Application.

(a) Efficacy (A [m]). According to the previous considerations, in the synthesis of efficacy an activity of the not-I is posited through a passivity in the I—that is, the not-I has reality insofar as the I is affected or is passive. In other words, the passivity of the I is the ground of the activity of the not-I, an *ideal* ground. However, the question that has remained unanswered throughout the previous considerations of this synthesis is: How is there to be passivity in the I? This passivity can be regarded in two different ways:

(i) Quantitatively. In this case, the passivity appears only as a lesser degree of activity of the I. It is not something opposed to the I but only a diminished quantum of that activity that the I is. In this respect, the passivity could presumably have its ground in the I, since it is not opposed to the I; such a ground would be an ideal ground.

(ii) Qualitatively. In this case, the passivity appears as the opposite of activity; that is, it appears as something opposed to the nature of the I (which *is* activity). In other words, the passivity appears as something that could not have its ground in the I, since the I posits only activity in itself and not passivity. But if the passivity does not have its ground in the I, then it must have its ground in the not-I. Thus, the passivity in the I has *as its real ground* an activity in the not-I. This is the independent activity sought. It makes the synthesis of efficacy possible in that it makes possible a component of that synthesis (namely, the passivity in the I).

(b) Substantiality (A [m]). The previous consideration of the synthesis of substantiality was directed at the same question as the one just considered: How can passivity be posited in the I (which by nature is activity)? According to this synthesis, the passivity is posited by means of the positing of activity—specifically, by the positing of a lesser degree of activity, which, with respect to the whole of activity, is passivity. Thus, in the case of the synthesis of substantiality, the interplay is somewhat more complex. It is, first, an interplay between activity in the I and passivity in the I—that is, a positing of passivity by means of a positing of activity. But this is possible only if the activity is a diminished activity with respect to the totality of activity, which is to say that the relation to totality is essential. So the interplay can also be regarded as having for its components the totality of activity *and* diminished activity (= passivity).

Now consider the problem of the activity of the matter. Fichte wants to show that the possibility of the components in this interplay requires a certain independent activity. How is this requirement to be regarded? That is, what is it about the synthesis that leads us in reflection to posit an independent activity?

What do the two components of the synthesis (totality and diminished activity) have in common? What is the ground of their conjunction? It is simply *activity*. However, granted the synthesis of efficacy, this ground is also shared by the not-I; diminished activity is also posited in the not-I. The question is then: How is the diminished activity of the I to be distinguished from the diminished activity of the not-I? In other words, how are the I and the not-I to be distinguished, since the previous distinction (I: active; not-I: passive) has been abolished? Clearly, there must be some further property that characterizes the I but that could not possibly be attributed to the not-I; there must be some property by virtue of which there is a synthesis between totality and diminished activity but not between totality and the not-I. The only such property is: to posit and be posited absolutely (without any ground). So the diminished activity of the I must be *absolute*. But how is this possible? For to be absolute is to be unlimited, whereas this activity, by virtue of being a *diminished* activity, is limited. It is possible only if the activity is regarded from two different points of view:

 (i) Insofar as it is simply an activity, it is unlimited, absolute.
(ii) Insofar as it enters into the interplay (i.e., insofar as it is directed to an object), it is limited.

In the first respect, it is an independent activity that determines the interplay (by becoming a component of it); it is an "absolute activity that determines a reciprocity" (FW I, 160; SK 150).

It is important to note that, in a sense, the contradiction is not resolved but simply incorporated into this activity of the I (by considering the activity from two points of view). This is important because the name of this activity is "imagination." From its first appearance in the problematic, the imagination embodies a tension bordering on contradiction.

(II)
Interplay determined by independent activity.
(A → I)

(1) General considerations. The activity under consideration here (i.e., the activity that determines the interplay) is that which makes possible not the components involved in the interplay but rather the transition between these components. It is what Fichte calls the activity of the form (A [f]).

(2) Application.

(a) Efficacy. In the synthesis of efficacy, activity is posited in the not-I by means of passivity in the I—that is, a certain activity is *not* posited in the I (is removed from the I) and is posited instead in the not-I. If, in reference to this synthesis, we abstract from what is posited and from the components in which the positing occurs, we get the pure *form* involved in the synthesis. This form, which is called a "transference" (*Übertragen*), is: a positing by means of a non-positing. Since this is the formal character of the synthesis, it is the material character of the activity that brings about the interplay—that is, of the activity of the form. Thus, the independent activity (A [f]) is a transference, a positing by means of a non-positing. Since all positing is done by the I, this activity can be attributed to the I.

(b) Substantiality. In the interplay of substantiality, a quantum of activity is posited *as* limited (hence, as passivity) over against the absolute totality of activity. This means that a portion of the absolute totality is excluded from the limited activity that is posited—that is, a portion of the totality is posited *as not posited* in the positing of the limited activity (as excluded from it). In other words, the missing portion is posited in the totality but *not* posited in the limited activity—that is, it is posited *as* not posited. If, in this connection, we abstract from what is posited and from the components in which it is posited, we get the purely formal character of the interplay: a non-positing by way of a positing. Thus, the material character of the act that makes this possible is a non-positing by means of a positing. This independent activity is an activity of the I. Fichte calls it "alienation" (*Entäußern*); the term is meant to indicate that a portion of the totality is excluded, "alienated," from the diminished activity that is posited.

(III)
Each is determined by the other.
(A ↔ I)

The general structure of the subsection devoted to the third proposition is generated by the distinctions that have emerged in the consideration of the first two propositions. As previously, there are two interplays to be treated, that of efficacy and that of substantiality. But with respect to each of these, there are four elements to be distinguished:

(i) the form of the interplay: I (f)
(ii) the matter of the interplay: I (m)
(iii) the activity of the form: A (f)
(iv) the activity of the matter: A (m)

Schematically, these elements, as identified in the considerations of the first two propositions, may be represented as follows:

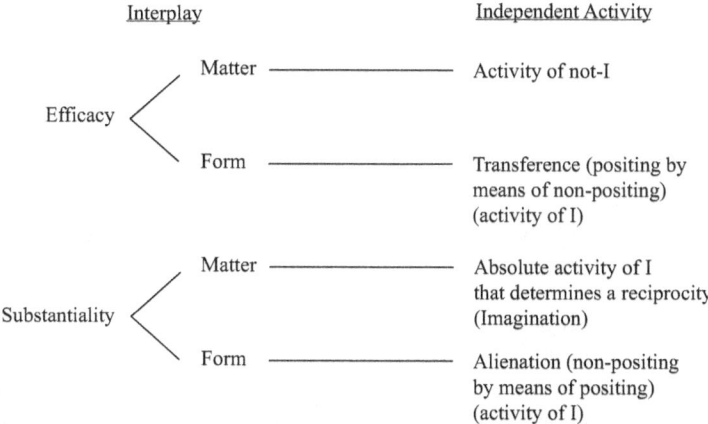

The third proposition asserts that the interplay and the independent activity determine one another. Taking account of the components, the synthesis prescribed by this proposition involves the following structure in the case of both efficacy and substantiality:

(α) A (f): hence, synthetic unity A
(β) I (f) ↔ A (m): hence, synthetic unity I
(γ) A ↔ I

(III, A). Efficacy

(α) A (f) ↔ A (m)

This proposition says: the I's activity of transference (i.e., positing by means of non-positing and thereby transferring reality from itself to the not-I) *and* the activity of the not-I determine one another and are synthetically united. Fichte's consideration of this synthesis proceeds in three steps:

(a) A (f) → A (m)

This means: transference by the I determines the activity of the not-I. In other words, the not-I is active only insofar as activity is transferred to it by the I;

that is, it is active only insofar as it is posited as active by the I (by means of a non-positing). Thus, according to this proposition, all reality of the not-I is simply transferred out of the I. Hence, the proposition leads to idealism (dogmatic idealism—or what Fichte later calls qualitative idealism).

(b) A (m) → A (f)

This means: the activity of the not-I determines the transference by the I (the positing by means of non-positing). More specifically, the not-I is ground of the non-positing, of the passivity in the I and, hence, determines the activity of transference (which proceeds from this non-positing). Thus, according to this proposition, an independent reality of the not-I must be assumed. Hence, the proposition leads to realism—or what Fichte later calls qualitative realism.

(c) A (f) ↔ A (m)

This means that both propositions are to be retained and synthetically united. What is the character of the synthesis?

(i) It is a synthesis of idealism and realism, a mediation between them. Fichte calls this position "critical idealism."

(ii) The two propositions that are to be synthetically united, regarded as one and the same, are:

(1) The activity of the not-I is transferred to it by the I (i.e., the I posits reality in the not-I).

(2) The not-I causes passivity in the I.

To see how these can be regarded as the same, the question needs to be asked: What would it mean for the not-I to operate on the I? (That is, what would it mean for the not-I to limit the I or annul something in it?) This could only mean: it annuls some positing in the I (since the I is nothing but a positing). In other words, it means that the not-I brings it about that the I does not posit something in itself. So the identity of the two propositions means: the I not positing something in itself is identical with its positing something in the not-I. In other words, neither of these grounds the other; they are one and the same act. So the result is that the I is capable of *not* positing something in itself only by positing it in the not-I, and conversely.

(iii) The synthesis can be considered in another way. The two propositions to be united express, in effect, that circle that was formulated at the very beginning of section E: activity can be posited in the not-I only by the positing of passivity in the I; but there can be passivity in the I only if there is a prior activity in the not-I that causes it. To retain both propositions means to retain this circle. Yet for it really to be a circle, that activity in the not-I that causes passivity in the I *must be the same as* that activity that is posited in the not-I by means of passivity in the I. However, the activity in the not-I that causes passivity is a *real ground*, whereas the other activity is something *posited as* the cause of passivity; that is, it is an *ideal ground*. To say that these are the same is to say that the ideal ground must become a real ground—that ideal and real ground are the same. Thus, Fichte writes: "Hence the deeper significance of the above synthesis is as follows: *In the concept of efficacy* (and so everywhere, since in this concept alone is a real ground present) *ideal and real ground are one and the same*" (FW I, 175; SK 162). This principle, he says, is the basis of critical idealism.

(iv) This synthesis shows, contrary to idealism, that the mere activity of the I does not ground the reality of the not-I (i.e., that the reality of the not-I is not simply posited by the I). And it shows, contrary to realism, that the mere activity of the not-I does not ground the passivity in the I. Rather, there is retained the interplay (circle) between these two. The question that then arises is: What is the ground of this interplay? What grounds the circle itself? Fichte says that this ground is incomprehensible within the framework of the theoretical *Wissenschaftslehre*—that at this point we are driven on to the practical part of the *Wissenschaftslehre*.

(β) I (f) $\leftrightarrow$ I (m)

(1) Identification of the items:

In general, the form of an interplay is the *mutual intrusion* of the components on each other. The matter is that feature of the components that makes them such that they can intrude. Applying this to the case of efficacy:

(a) It was found previously that the relevant form is a positing by means of a non-positing. If we now abstract from the activity (i.e., positing), we get as the form of the mere interplay: a coming-to-be through a passing-away—that is, a coming-to-be of one component through a passing-away of another. The form is: mutual (real) annihilation.

(b) The matter is that which makes the components fit for such an interplay. What does this is their incompatibility or inherent opposition to one another. Hence, the matter is: essential opposition or qualitative incompatibility.

(2) The synthesis:

According to the synthesis, each of the components determines the other; that is, they are one and the same. This means: real opposition (annihilation) is the same as essential or ideal opposition. Thus, as was the case previously (cf. α, 3), this synthesis prescribes the identity of ideal and real. In other words, it prescribes that what *is* opposed is the same as what *is posited as* opposed.

(γ) A $\leftrightarrow$ I

(1) Identification of the items:

The items to be synthesized are the results of the previous two syntheses:

(a) The activity as synthetic unity is: mediate positing. This means a positing in which the positing of one thing is identical with the non-positing of

something else. Specifically, what was shown earlier was that a positing of the activity of the not-I is a non-positing of the activity of the I.
(b) The interplay as synthetic unity is: the identity of essential opposition and real annihilation. In other words, the unity consists of ideal and real opposition in their identity.
(2) The synthesis:
(a) A → I
This means: the mediacy of positing is the ground of essential opposition, real annihilation, and their identity. This may be explained as follows: If A and B are the relevant components, then to say that they are mediately posited means that A is posited through the non-positing of B—that is, A is posited as not-B. In other words, A is posited as opposed to B (hence, essential opposition) *and* as a non-positing of B (hence, the annihilation of B). Thus, from the mediacy of positing, there follows essential opposition, real annihilation, and the identity of these. More generally, according to this proposition, the mediacy of positing is the ground of the interplay between the I and the not-I and, hence, is the ground of whatever reality is posited in them in the interplay. The question arises: What, then, is the ground of this mediacy of positing? It cannot be grounded in what it grounds, so it can be grounded neither in the not-I nor in the I *as* posited through the non-positing of the not-I (in distinction from the I as the one that posits). Thus, the ground of the mediacy of positing must lie in the absolute I (in the I that posits, not the I that is posited through the non-positing of the not-I). But since the absolute I *is* (simply) positing, it follows that the ground of the mediacy of positing is just positing as such—that is, positing is simply (absolutely) mediate. This means that the mediacy of positing has no ground: the absolute I posits mediately because it does so (on no further grounds).

Thus, this proposition leads to idealism, though to a more adequate idealism than the type considered earlier. According to the earlier form of idealism (qualitative idealism), a certain activity in the I is annulled and transferred to the not-I. But nothing was said as to how this happens, as to how the I (which simply posits itself absolutely) could come to annul reality in itself. According to the present version of idealism (quantitative idealism), there is not, first of all, the absolute self-positing and then, subsequently, a transfer of its activity to the not-I. Rather, according to quantitative idealism, it is a *law of the I* to posit mediately—that is, to posit itself only by the non-positing of the not-I, and conversely. Hence, the basic principle of this idealism is: the I is finite simply because it is finite; that is, the I is absolutely finite. However, the difficulty involved in this idealism is that absolute finitude is a self-contradiction; to be finite is to be limited, limited by something else, hence, not to be absolute.

(b) I → A

This means: the mediacy of positing is determined by the fact that the essence of the components consists of mere opposition. How this comes about is evident: if a component is nothing but opposition to the other, then the non-positing of one is the positing of the other, and conversely. So in the system prescribed by this proposition, the opposition is made the ground, and the mediacy of positing is founded on it. This system is called quantitative realism.

(i) This is to be distinguished from the qualitative realism introduced previously. According to qualitative realism, the not-I has a reality in itself independently of the I; it gives rise to impressions on the I (affects the I) in such a way that the I's activity is diminished (limited, determined). According to quantitative realism, an independent reality of the not-I cannot be assumed. However, it does maintain that there is a real limitation of the I that is present without any contribution on the part of the I—that is, that there is a determination of the I the ground of which does not lie in the I, a determination that is just ungroundedly present. So, whereas qualitative realism maintains the independent reality of a determinant, quantitative realism maintains the independent reality of a mere determination.

(ii) Fichte says that this quantitative realism is identical with the "critical idealism" previously set forth (α, 3), according to which the interplay has its ground neither in the activity of the I nor in that of the not-I. Here we see clearly the course that the syntheses are following: what was previously put forth as a synthesis of other positions is now itself placed within a further opposition in which it proves to be not a synthesis of idealism and realism but a more subtle form of realism.

(iii) What is the relationship between quantitative realism and quantitative idealism? They agree in that both assume the I to be finite. They differ in that quantitative idealism maintains that finitude is absolutely posited, whereas quantitative realism maintains that finitude is contingent (i.e., is the result of an ungroundedly present limitation of the I). However, quantitative realism also encounters a peculiar difficulty: it cannot explain how a *real* determination can become a determination *for* the I (ideal)—that is, it cannot show how the I's absolute positing of itself could be determined by something extrinsic to that positing.

(c) A ↔ I

Both of the positions that have emerged maintain the mediacy of positing—that is, that it is a law for the I that the I and the not-I can only be posited mediately. In other words, the I can be posited only through the non-positing of the not-I, and the not-I only through the non-positing of the

I. This means that the I *as* posited (*not* as that which posits) is simply the counterpart of the not-I, and conversely. The I and the not-I, so regarded, are called *subject* and *object*, respectively. The difference between the two positions concerns the ground of this law of the mediacy of positing: quantitative idealism locates this ground in the I's positing (i.e., this law is simply made the law of positing in general); quantitative realism locates this ground in the passivity of the I. So, according to the former, the law has its ground in the I, whereas, according to the latter, its ground is not in the I. The synthesis that is now posed requires that the ground lie in both subject and object at once. However, there is no way of seeing how it could lie in both (this would require their unity, whereas it is their unity that is provided by the ground). Hence, Fichte says: "We confess our ignorance on this topic" (FW I, 190; SK 174). This position of established ignorance is called critical quantitative idealism.

(III, B). Substantiality

(α) A (f) ↔ A (m)
  (1) Identification of the items:
   (a) A (f) = non-positing by means of a positing—that is, positing of something as not posited through the positing of something else as posited.
   Comments: We have seen that, thus far, there is a certain ambiguity in the concept of substantiality. Specifically, it is not entirely clear what the components of this interplay are.
    (i) At first (section D), the components were: (1) the limited activity in the I, which, in relation to the totality of activity, is (2) a passivity (it is *not* the totality but is opposed to it; hence, it is passivity).
    (ii) Regarded in a different way, however, it can be said that the relation to the totality is essential to the interplay and that, in fact, the limited activity and the passivity are identical so that there can be no interplay between them. Thus, the components of the interplay can be taken as (1) the limited activity and (2) the absolute totality of activity.
    (iii) There is still a third way of regarding the interplay. To say that the interplay involves the positing of a limited activity over against the totality entails that a portion of the totality is excluded from the limited activity that is posited. That is, if the totality is A+B, then the positing of A involves the exclusion of B. Thus, a portion of the totality (B) is posited as not posited in the positing of the limited activity (A). Thus, the limited activity (A) and that which is posited as not posited in the positing of A (i.e., B) can be regarded as the components of the interplay.
     In this section, Fichte's formulations are in terms of this third way of regarding the interplay. He elaborates it as follows: What is posited as positing (A) is posited in a determinate sphere as completely filling

it. Thus, to say that B is posited as not posited means: it is not posited in the sphere of A. B is excluded from the sphere of A and posited in an indeterminate sphere outside it.

From this, two conclusions follow:
  (i) In contrast to efficacy, here the non-posited is not simply annihilated but only excluded from a certain sphere. If we apply this, it says: the limited I is not the sheer opposite of the not-I but merely excludes it.
  (ii) A (f) is an *exclusion* from a determinate sphere.
(b) To identify the activity that grounds the matter of the interplay, Fichte notes that: (i) The sphere of A is posited as totality with respect to A (i.e., it is completely filled by A). (ii) But B is also posited, posited in an indeterminate sphere outside the sphere of A, and thus with respect to B, the sphere of A is a non-totality. (iii) Thus, the sphere of A is the determinate part of a *higher sphere* that includes both the determinate (the sphere of A) and the indeterminate (the sphere of B). A (m) is the positing of this higher sphere.

(2) The synthesis:
  (a) A (f) → A (m)
  This means: insofar as something (B) is excluded (from A), a higher sphere (A+B) is posited. It is the exclusion, rather than the positing of the higher sphere, that is the ground.

  Application: The I (A) excludes the not-I (B); that is, it posits an object absolutely (on no further grounds). So the positing of the object is the grounding act, and the higher sphere (A+B) incorporating the I and the not-I is grounded on it. This is *quantitative idealism*. The I posits the not-I (as a non-positing of itself)—that is, the I posits mediately, simply because it does so (without any further ground).

  (b) A (m) → A (f)
  This means: The higher sphere (embracing both the I and the not-I) is absolutely posited, and only on this basis does exclusion become possible. In other words, what is fundamental is the opposition of the I and the not-I, and this does not first arise from a positing by the subject (by exclusion). This is *qualitative realism*. Positing activity is determined by the thing in itself.

  (c) A (f) ↔ A (m)
  This means: The positing of the higher sphere and the I's excluding activity determine one another—they are one and the same. In other words, there is a not-I opposed to the I because the I opposes it to itself, *and*, conversely, the I opposes something to itself because there is a not-I opposed to it. In other words, the not-I exists because it is posited by the I. But the I can posit the not-I only on the basis of passivity in itself, which presupposes that it is affected by the not-I. This is the same circle that we

found at the beginning of section E and in the α-stage of the investigation of efficacy. Here, too, the synthesis prescribes that the circle is to be retained. This means in the briefest formula: affection of the I by the not-I and positing of the not-I by the I are one and the same act. This is the position of *critical idealism*.

(β) I (f) ↔ I (m)
  (1) Identification of the items:
    (a) Each component excludes the other in a certain sense:
      (i) If A is posited (as totality), then B is excluded from it and hence excluded from the totality.
      (ii) If B is posited (or reflected on as posited), then A is excluded from the absolute totality—that is, the sphere of A is no longer the absolute totality but only part of the higher sphere (A+B).
         Thus, the form of the interplay is: mutual exclusion of the components from the absolute totality.
    (b) There are two totalities (A and A+B). Now Fichte says explicitly that it is between these two totalities that the interplay takes place—that is, these two totalities are the components of the interplay. (Note how this resolves the ambiguity discussed above.) For there to be an interplay between these two totalities, they must be distinguishable in such a way that one of them can be determined as the absolute totality. Thus, each must be determinable in order to be fit for serving as a component in the interplay. This *determinability* is the matter of the interplay.
  (2) The synthesis:
    (a) I (f) → I (m)
       This means: the mutual exclusion determines which of the two totalities is absolute. More specifically, if B is excluded by A, then A is the absolute totality. So whether the determinate totality (A) or the determinable totality (A+B) is the absolute, totality is purely *relative*.
    (b) I (m) → I (f)
       This means: determinability of the totality determines the mutual exclusion. Here the crucial point is: if the determinability of the totality (i.e., the possibility of determining which totality is absolute) is to determine something else, then this determinability must itself be granted. Thus, it must be possible to determine which totality is absolute. In other words, whether A or A+B is the absolute totality is *not* purely relative but has an absolute ground.
    (c) I (f) ↔ I (m)
       This combines the previous two conclusions and hence says that the determination of the absolute totality is (i) relative and (ii) absolute—that is, the ground for the determination of the totality is both relative and

absolute. Specifically, this means that the totality is determinable but that its determination does not involve setting up either of the previous totalities (A or A+B) as absolute. Rather, the determination involves the relation between these: the absolute totality consists of both of these totalities mutually determining one another. This means that the totality is the union of the two totalities in mutual determination: A determined by A+B and A+B determined by A. From this, it also follows that A+B and B are also mutually determining since, insofar as A+B is not determined by A, it is determined by B. This new totality, as synthesis of determinate totality (A) and determinable totality (A+B), is a determinate determinability. This totality is *substance*.

Comments: (i) This synthesis means that the I (as positing of itself) is not the absolute totality within that the distinction between subject and object would be determined and contained (contra idealism). But it also means that the conjunction of the sphere of the subject and that of the object does not constitute the absolute totality in such a way that the I would constitute only a part of the totality (contra realism). Hence, neither the I nor the conjunction of the I and the not-I constitutes the absolute totality. Rather, the totality consists in the mutual determination, the interplay, between the I *and* the limited I (in its opposition to the not-I). The totality is this complete interplay.

(ii) In terms of this synthesis, Fichte clarifies the concept of substance (following Spinoza) as the all-encompassing (the absolute totality, the absolute whole), not as an underlying substratum. If substance is, then, the complete interplay, then each of the items involved in the interplay is an accident. This entails that the accidents in their interplay (i.e., synthetically united) yield the substance and that, hence, the substance is nothing whatsoever beyond the accidents (and, in particular, not an enduring substratum, a bearer of accidents, as, for example, in Locke).

(γ) A ↔ I
   (1) Identification of the items:
      (a) A = the absolute conjoining and holding fast of opposites. This is the synthesis of A (f) (the mutual exclusion—hence opposition—of A and B) and A (m) (the positing of the higher sphere [A+B] in which A and B are conjoined). Here again, Fichte notes that the power of the I that is active in this synthesis is the *imagination* (cf. section E, I).
      (b) In the interplay, A and B are mutually exclusive, yet they are conjoined in a higher sphere. Hence, they must, as opposed, stand together, which they can do only insofar as they mutually destroy one another. Hence, the interplay (I), as synthetic unity, is the *clash*, the incursion of each on the other.

(2) The synthesis:
  (a) A → I
    This means: the activity by which the I opposes the objective and the subjective and unites them (the conjoining of opposites) determines the clash of the components—that is, the subjective and the objective become components only by virtue of this activity of the I. This proposition leads to *idealism*: the opposition between subject and object (hence, presentation, "experience") is grounded in an act of the I. This position is the same as quantitative idealism except that it replaces the concept of the mediacy of positing (i.e., the positing of the subject by the non-positing of the object and the positing of the object by the non-positing of the subject) with a single act in which both subject and object are posited. But this position leaves something unexplained: how the I (which posits only itself) could posit something objective.

  (b) I → A
    This means: the I's activity of conjoining opposites is determined by the mere clash of opposites (not by the actual presence of the opposites). The sheer encounter between the I and the not-I is the ground of the possibility of that activity of the I by which the subjective and the objective are conjoined in their opposition.

    Fichte elaborates this by regarding the clash (or encounter) as the presence of a *check* on the I. This means that for some reason that is not derived from the I's activity (for some reason that is not grounded in the I), the subjective sphere (posited by the I) proves to be extensible no further. In other words, the I's positing of the subjective (i.e., itself) is restrained (checked). This does not mean that a bound is set to the I's activity but rather that the I is given the task of setting bounds to itself—that is, the check merely indicates that bounds must be set but is not itself already a definite bound. To set these bounds, then, the I must oppose something objective to the subjective and conjoin them (hence the activity).

    This proposition leads to a *realism* that is even more abstract than quantitative realism. It presupposes neither a not-I existing independently of the I (qualitative realism) nor a determination (bound) present in the I but not derived from the I (quantitative realism), but merely a check indicative of the necessity for a determination to be made. Yet even this realism is inadequate, for like every realism, it fails to explain the transition from the not-I to the I. Specifically, it explains the requirement that the I be determined or bounded (i.e., the check to its activity) as something involving no assistance from the I. It does not explain how the check could be something *for* the I.

(c) A ↔ I

This means: the occurrence of the clash and the I's activity of conjoining subject and object are mutually determining. This final synthesis of section E can be explained as follows:

(i) This synthesis overcomes the one-sidedness of the previous synthesis (of abstract realism): on one hand, rather than regarding the check as something that occurs independently of the I's activity, the synthesis maintains that there can be a check only insofar as the I is active—that is, its possibility depends on the activity of the I. On the other hand, the activity is also conditioned by the check (they are mutually conditioned).

(ii) To understand the nature of the synthesis, we need to look more carefully at the activity. It is the activity of conjoining opposites in their opposition. To conjoin them means: to posit the boundary at which they come together. So the activity is a positing of the boundary. We can give still another formulation of this. The opposites at issue are the I and the not-I (subject and object). So the boundary that is posited is the boundary between the I and the not-I. But that which posits the boundary is the I. So the I's positing of the boundary is a bounding of itself, a self-bounding, a self-determination, a determination of the I as bounded (limited) over against the object.

(iii) The activity is conditioned by the check. The question is thus: What must be the character of the activity for it to be conditioned by the check? What is required is this: the activity must be such that, if the check did not occur, the activity would not posit a boundary—that is, it would not bound itself and thus would be unbounded, *infinite*. So in itself, the activity must be infinite.

(iv) The synthesis says: the activity is conditioned by the check. This means: if the check occurs, then this infinite activity posits the boundary between subject and object, thereby bounding itself and determining itself (over against the object). But to determine itself is to posit itself as *finite*.

(v) So the I posits itself as both finite and infinite. It posits itself as infinite (A+B) and as finite (A) and determines each by the other. It ascribes the infinite activity to itself: it determines A+B by A. But if the activity is determined, then it is not infinite. So it must be distinguished from the I—that is, it must be ascribed to, determined by, what is beyond the I (B). This means that A+B must be determined by B. Thus, we get that interplay between totalities that was described at the β-stage above. But now that interplay is identical with activity (according to the present synthesis).

(vi) The interplay in which the I posits itself as both finite and infinite, in which the I endeavors to unite the irreconcilable, is the *power of imagination*. Imagination is the power of holding together in their interplay the infinite and the finite.

(vii) So it is the imagination that makes it possible for the I to bound itself—to oppose an object to itself. Imagination is the *productive* power that brings forth the object: "The not-I is itself a product of the self-determining I, and nothing at all absolute or posited outside the I" (FW I, 218; SK 195). But the object is brought forth only on the condition that the check occur (even though, conversely, the check cannot occur without the concurrence of the I). Hence, we have the residual aporia of the theoretical *Wissenschaftslehre*: the possibility of the check remains unexplained.

Bibliography

Behler, Ernst, ed. *Philosophy of German Idealism*. New York: Continuum, 1987.
Beiser, Frederick C. *The Fate of Reason: German Philosophy from Kant to Fichte*. Cambridge, MA: Harvard University Press, 1987.
———. *German Idealism: The Struggle against Subjectivism, 1781–1801*. Cambridge, MA: Harvard University Press, 2002.
Descartes, René. *The Philosophical Writings of Descartes*. Translated by John Cottingham, Robert Stoothoff, and Dugald Murdoch. Vol. 1. Cambridge: Cambridge University Press, 1985.
Di Giovanni, George, and H. S. Harris, ed. *Between Kant and Hegel: Texts in the Development of Post-Kantian Idealism*. Rev. ed. Indianapolis: Hackett, 2000.
Fichte, Johann Gottlieb. *Early Philosophical Writings*. Translated and edited by Daniel Breazeale. Ithaca, NY: Cornell University Press, 1988.
Fichte, Johann Gottlieb, and Friedrich Joseph Wilhelm Schelling. *Fichte-Schelling Briefwechsel*. Edited by Walter Schulz. Frankfurt: Suhrkamp, 1968.
———. *Sämmtliche Werke*. Edited by I. H. Fichte. 8 vols. Berlin: Veit, 1845–46.
———. *The Science of Knowledge*. Edited and translated by Peter Heath and John Lachs. Cambridge: Cambridge University Press, 1982.
Hegel, Georg Wilhelm Friedrich. *The Difference between Fichte's and Schelling's System of Philosophy*. Translated by H. S. Harris and Walter Cerf. Albany: SUNY Press, 1977.
———. *Faith and Knowledge*. Translated by Walter Cerf and H. S. Harris. Albany: SUNY Press, 1977.
———. *Hegel: The Letters*. Translated by Clark Butler and Christiane Seiler. Bloomington: Indiana University Press, 1984.
———. *The Phenomenology of Spirit*. Translated by A. V. Miller. Oxford: Oxford University Press, 1977.
———. *The Science of Logic*. Translated by A. V. Miller. London: Allen & Unwin, 1969.
———. *Werke in zwanzig Bänden: Theorie-Werkausgabe*. Edited by Eva Moldenhauer and Karl-Markus Michel. Frankfurt: Suhrkamp, 1969–71.
Heidegger, Martin. *Basic Writings*. Edited by David Farrell Krell. Rev. and exp. ed. New York: HarperCollins, 1993.
———. *Gesamtausgabe*. Frankfurt: Klostermann, 1975–.
———. *Hegel*. Translated by Joseph Arel and Niels Feuerhahn. Bloomington: Indiana University Press, 2015.
———. *Identity and Difference*. Translated by Joan Stambaugh. Chicago: University of Chicago Press, 1969.
———. *Introduction to Metaphysics*. Translated by Ralph Manheim. New Haven, CT: Yale University Press, 1959.
———. *Schellings Abhandlung Über das Wesen der menschlichen Freiheit (1809)*. Edited by Hildegard Feick. 2nd ed. Tübingen: Niemeyer, 1995.

———. *Schelling's Treatise on the Essence of Human Freedom*. Translated by Joan Stambaugh. Athens: Ohio University Press, 1985.
Henrich, Dieter. *Between Kant and Hegel: Lectures on German Idealism*. Edited by David S. Pacini. Cambridge, MA: Harvard University Press, 2003.
Herrmann, Friedrich-Wilhelm von. "Fichte und Heidegger." In *Der Idealismus und seine Gegenwart: Festschrift für Werner Marx zum 65. Geburtstag*, edited by Ute Guzzoni, Bernhard Rang, and Ludwig Siep, 231–56. Hamburg: Meiner, 1976.
Hölderlin, Friedrich. *Hyperion and Selected Poems*. Edited by Eric L. Santner. New York: Continuum, 1990.
Jamme, Christoph, and Helmut Schneider, eds. *Mythologie der Vernunft: Hegels "ältestes Systemprogramm des deutschen Idealismus."* Frankfurt: Suhrkamp, 1984.
Jacobi, Friedrich Heinrich. *David Hume über den Glauben, oder Idealismus und Realismus, ein Gespräch*. Breslau: Löwe, 1787.
———. *Über die Lehre des Spinoza in Briefen an den Herrn Moses Mendelssohn*. Brelau: Löwe, 1785.
Kaufmann, Walter. *Hegel: A Reinterpretation*. Notre Dame, IN: University of Notre Press, 1978.
Kant, Immanuel. *Correspondence*. Translated by Arnulf Zweig. Cambridge: Cambridge University Press, 1999.
———. *Critique of Judgment*. Translated by Werner S. Pluhar. Indianapolis: Hackett, 1987.
———. *Critique of Practical Reason*. Translated by Lewis White Beck. Indianapolis: Liberal Arts, 1956.
———. *Critique of Pure Reason*. Translated by Norman Kemp Smith. New York: St. Martin's, 1965.
———. *Foundations of the Metaphysics of Morals*. Translated by Lewis White Beck. Indianapolis: Liberal Arts, 1959.
———. *Gesammelte Schriften*. Edited by the Preußische Akademie der Wissenschaften. Berlin: De Gruyter, 1900–.
———. *Prolegomena to Any Future Metaphysics*. Edited by Lewis White Beck. Indianapolis: Liberal Arts, 1950.
Kelly, George Armstrong. *Idealism, Politics, and History: Sources of Hegelian Thought*. Cambridge: Cambridge University Press, 1969.
Leibniz, Gottfried Wilhelm. *The Leibniz-Clarke Correspondence*. Edited by H. G. Alexander. Manchester: Manchester University Press, 1956.
Merleau-Ponty, Maurice. *Themes from the Lectures at the Collège de France, 1952–1960*. Translated by John O'Neill. Evanston, IL: Northwestern University Press, 1970.
Nietzsche, Friedrich. *"The Birth of Tragedy" and "The Case of Wagner."* Translated by Walter Kaufmann. New York: Random House, 1967.
———. *On the Genealogy of Morals*. Translated by Walter Kaufmann and R. J. Hollingdale. New York: Random House, 1967.
Reinhold, Karl Leonhard. *Beyträge zur Berichtigung bisheriger Missverständnisse der Philosophen*. Vol. 1. Jena: Mauke, 1790.
———. *Briefe über die kantische Philosophie*. Vol. 1. Leipzig: Göschen, 1790.
———. *Essay on a New Theory of the Human Capacity for Representation*. Translated by Tim Mehigan and Barry Empson. Berlin/New York: De Gruyter, 2011.
———. *Ueber das Fundament des philosophischen Wissens*. Jena: Mauke, 1791.

———. *Versuch einer neuen Theorie des menschlichen Vorstellungsvermögens.* Prague and Jena: Widtmann and Mauke, 1789.
Rousseau, Jean-Jacques. *Emile or On Education.* Translated by Allan Bloom. New York: Basic Books, 1979.
Sallis, John. *Chorology: On Beginning in Plato's "Timaeus."* Bloomington: Indiana University Press, 1999.
———. *Delimitations: Phenomenology and the End of Metaphysics.* 2nd ed. Bloomington: Indiana University Press, 1995.
———. *Elemental Discourses.* Bloomington: Indiana University Press, 2018.
———. *Force of Imagination: The Sense of the Elemental.* Bloomington: Indiana University Press, 2000.
———. *The Gathering of Reason.* 2nd ed. Albany: SUNY Press, 2005.
———. *Kant and the Spirit of Critique.* Edited by Richard Rojcewicz. Bloomington: Indiana University Press, 2020.
———. *Spacings—Of Reason and Imagination in Texts of Kant, Fichte, Hegel.* Chicago: University of Chicago Press, 1987.
———. *Transfigurements: On the True Sense of Art.* Chicago: University of Chicago, 2008.
Sassen, Brigitte, ed. *Kant's Early Critics: The Empiricist Critique of the Theoretical Philosophy.* Cambridge: Cambridge University Press, 2000.
Schelling, Friedrich Wilhelm Joseph. *Aus Schellings Leben: In Briefen.* Edited by G. L. Plitt. Vol. 1. Leipzig: Hirzel, 1869.
———. *Philosophical Investigations into the Essence of Human Freedom.* Translated by Jeff Love and Johannes Schmidt. Albany: SUNY Press, 2006.
———. *Sämmtliche Werke.* Division I: 10 vols. (= I–X); Division II: 4 vols. (= XI–XIV). Edited by Karl Friedrich August Schelling. Stuttgart: Cotta, 1856–61.
———. *System of Transcendental Idealism (1800).* Translated by Peter Heath. Charlottesville: University Press of Virginia, 1978.
———. *The Unconditional in Human Knowledge: Four Early Essays, 1794–1796.* Translated and edited by Fritz Marti. Lewisburg, PA: Bucknell University Press, 1980.
Schultz, Johann. *Erläuterungen über des Herrn Professor Kant Critik der reinen Vernunft.* Königsberg: Dengel, 1784.
Schulze, Gottlob Ernst. *Aenesidemus, oder über die Fundamente der von dem Herrn Prof. Reinhold in Jena gelieferten Elementar-Philosophie, nebst einer Verteidigung gegen die Anmaaßungen der Vernunftkritik.* 1792 [no place of publication or press given].
Spinoza, Benedict de. *A Spinoza Reader: The Ethics and Other Works.* Translated by Edwin Curley. Princeton: Princeton University Press, 1994.

Index

absolute, 107, 112; absolute, meaning of, 39–40; absolute difference, 57; absolute standpoint, 120–21; derived absoluteness, 123; I as absolute subject, 54
absolute identity, 57, 111, 113, 116–17
abstraction, 41, 43, 50, 56, 63; abstracting reflection, 55, 58
act (*Tathandlung*), 34, 45, 50, 51, 54–56
action, 9; action of mind, 56, 60–61, 63
activity: independent activity, 76–77; vs. passivity, 45, 66, 69–71
Aenesidemus, 25–28, 30, 33–35, 97. *See also* Schulze
aesthetic, the, 12–13, 15, 102. *See also* art; beauty
affection, 36–37, 69–70
Anstoß (check), 83–85, 90–91, 114, 116
antinomy (third), 9
antithesis, 61–62
appearance, 5–6, 7–8, 11, 17, 36; of the I, 35; as object of positing, 58
apperception. *See* transcendental apperception
a priori knowledge, 3, 4–6; of freedom, 9
architectonic, 38. *See also* foundation; system
Aristotle, 21, 43
art, 10, 15, 104–7; philosophy of, 102. *See also* aesthetic; beauty
atheism, 18, 31
Atheism Controversy, 31

Baggerson, Jens, 30
beauty, 10–11, 13, 14, 15, 106, 107. *See also* art
Beck, Jacob Sigismund, 115
becoming, 98, 127. *See also* creation; God: birth of
beginning: in German Idealism, 2–3, 15; of philosophy, 100, 107
being, 113; vs. act, 45; vs. becoming, 98; vs. seeing, 44

Berkeley, George, 16–17
Böhm, Wilhelm, 12–13

categorical imperative, 9, 89–90, 93. *See also* moral law
categories, 8, 11, 22, 51; derivation of, 33, 63
causality, 10, 26, 34, 36, 70, 92; dogmatism and, 44
certainty, 37–39, 51–52, 101, 102
check (*Anstoß*), 83–85, 90–91, 114, 116
chôra, 99, 118, 128, 134
circularity, 34–35, 40–41, 46, 59–60, 74, 76, 80, 81
cogito, 1, 102
common sense, 110
concepts 22; nature and, 101; philosophical method and, 47
consciousness, 8, 11–12, 19, 33; in art, 105–6; of freedom, 44; of moral law, 35; ordinary consciousness, 101, 110; representations and, 22–24. *See also* self-consciousness
consciousness, principle of, 24, 26, 33–34
content (vs. form), 39–40, 41, 52, 56, 57, 58–59, 97
contradiction, 57, 67, 70, 86, 104, 106. *See also* opposition
Copernican revolution (in Kant), 5–6, 32–33, 36, 115
copula, 123
creation (formation of nature), 129–30
Critical Journal of Philosophy, 21, 28, 110–12
critique (of reason), 3, 4, 10, 17, 37

deduction of categories, 8, 23
decree of reason, 59, 73
deed. *See* act
Derrida, Jacques, 6
Descartes, René, 1, 71–72, 102, 116
determination, 65, 67–68
determinism, 9, 123

165

Dionysian, the, 118
divisibility, 59–61, 67
dogmatism, 25, 32, 34, 37, 43–45, 46; in Fichte's critique of Schelling, 109, 114
doubt, 102
dualism, 126

efficacy (*Wirksamkeit*), 65–66, 70, 75
empiricism, 43
enactment, 12, 40, 42, 46, 48; reenactment, 103, 107
end of philosophy, 6–7
Enlightenment, 10, 18
Erhard, Johann Benjamin, 30
ethics, 12, 13–14. *See also* moral law
evil: possibility of, 131–32; problem of, 125–26
existence, 19–20; in relation to ground (Schelling), 117–18, 126–27, 129
experience, 5–6, 8, 11, 42–43; possibility of, 26–27, 35
explanation, 19–20

fact: vs. act, 50; of consciousness, 48, 51, 54, 56–57, 87–88; finitude as, 91; of reason, 9, 14
faith, 18, 20, 21, 112
fatalism, 18, 122, 123
Feder, Johann Georg Heinrich, 17, 25
feeling, 21, 41, 42; of freedom, 119, 122
Fichte, Johann Gottlieb, 21, 25, 27, 29–94; freedom, 15; Hegel and, 1, 111–12, 114; Jacobi and, 19, 20; Kant and, 3–4, 12, 16, 29–33, 35–37; nature of I, 8; Romantics and, 10; Schelling and, 47, 97–98, 99, 100, 102, 108–9, 112–14, 116, 120–21; subject-object relation, 115–16
finitude, 1, 34–35, 66, 75, 78–84, 91; finite subjectivity, 120–21; finite vs. infinite I, 59–60, 74, 84, 89; relation to the infinite, 98, 104, 106–7, 111–12
Flatt, Johann Friedrich, 27
Forberg, Friedrich Karl, 31
for itself, 35, 44
form: vs. content, 39–40, 41, 52, 56, 57, 58–59, 97; forms of pure intuition, 7–8, 33; systematic form, 37–39, 97; of *Wissenschaftslehre*, 62
formalism, 47
Förster, Friedrich, 12
foundation (of system), 22, 38. *See also* principle
freedom, 1, 14; in art, 105; centrality for Schelling, 95; concept of, 119, 124–25; consciousness of, 44; denial of, 18, 123; in Kant, 9, 10–11; vs. mechanism, 10, 15; vs. nature, 96; philosophy as work of, 95, 100; source of presentations, 42; system and, 119–20, 121–22
freedom of speech, 30
French Revolution, 30
Freundeskreis Hegels, 12

Garve, Christian, 17
Garve-Feder review, 16–18, 19
genius, 41, 105–6
German Idealism: outcome of, 1, 133, 135; end of, 1–2, 7, 15
God: birth of, 118, 127–32; concept of, 96; distinction within, 117–18, 126–29; divine understanding, 119, 128–30; evil and, 125–26; as postulate, 9, 15, 31; in Spinoza, 18, 72, 96. *See also* creation; pantheism; revelation
Goethe, Johann Wolfgang von, 10, 21, 30
goodness, 15
Göttingen Review, 16–18, 19
ground: of all knowledge, 4; of existence, 117–18, 126–28, 129–30, 133–34; of experience, 35, 43, 45, 50, 54; God as, 122–23, 125, 133; *Tathandlung* (act) as, 54. *See also* principle
grounding principle (*Satz des Grundes*), 61, 63

Hegel, Georg Wilhelm Friedrich, 4, 21; on art, 10; on *Aufhebung*, 86; author of "Oldest Systematic Program," 12–13; on end of philosophy, 6; on Fichte, 111–12, 114; on infinity, 112; on Kant, 111–12; on language of philosophy, 38; as outcome of German Idealism, 1, 95–96; progression

of ideas, 13; Romantics and, 10; Schelling and, 96, 99, 109–12, 116; on Schulze, 27–28, 110–11; transformation of spirit, 2
Heidegger, Martin, 6, 45; on German Idealism, 1, 7; on Hegel, 10, 117; on identity, 56; on Schelling, 1, 95, 117; on Spinoza, 124
Henrich, Dieter, 13, 21
Herbart, Johann Friedrich, 115
Herder, Johann Gottfried von, 21
Herrmann, Friedrich-Wilhelm von, 53n3
history, 15; of self-consciousness, 99, 103–4, 111
Hölderlin, Friedrich, 10, 11, 13, 21, 31, 96, 110
human beings. *See* man
Hume, David, 18, 20, 26, 27

I, the (*das Ich*), 8, 11–12, 43; as All, 96–97; nature of, 45–46, 51–52; vs. nature, 99; pure I, 92; self-intuition of, 35. *See also* consciousness; intelligence; self-consciousness; subject
idealism: vs. dogmatism, 37, 43–44; in Jacobi, 18; relation to realism, 124–25; Schelling's critique of, 116, 124–25; subjective vs. objective idealism, 112; stages within *Wissenschaftslehre*, 66, 75, 79–83. *See also* subjective idealism; transcendental idealism
ideas, 13–15, 104
identity, 33; within difference, 44–45; of the I, 51, 53, 55–56, 60; law of identity, 51–56, 63, 123; of subject and object, 45–46, 99–100, 103–4, 111, 114; synthetic identity, 55–56
imagination, 10, 74, 83, 84–86, 88, 104
imitation, 103
immortality (as postulate), 9, 15
indifference, 117, 134–35
individual (vs. the I), 51–52
infinite, the: in art, 106–7, infinite vs. finite I, 59–60, 74, 84, 89; relation to finite, 98, 104, 106–7, 111–12
inner sense, 11, 35
intellectual intuition, 35, 41–42, 47–48, 49, 54, 106–7
intelligence, 43, 44–45, 90–93; vs. nature, 101. *See also* I, the

interdetermination (*Wechselbestimmung*), 68–70, 76–77. *See also* mutual determination
interest, 43
intersubjectivity, 52
intuition (*Anschauung*), 8, 11–12, 88, 105. *See also* intellectual intuition
irreducible remainder, 118, 127–28

Jacobi, Friedrich Heinrich, 18–20, 21, 35–36, 58, 111–12, 115
Jamme, Christoph, 12–13
Jena, 21, 30–32, 110

Kant, Immanuel, 7–12, 13; Copernican revolution, 5–6, 32–33, 36; on end of philosophy, 6; Fichte and, 29–33, 35–37, 51, 89; on genius, 105; on imagination, 85; on nature, 10–11; new beginning in, 3; practical philosophy, 9, 14–15; reception of, 16–28; Schelling and, 97, 98, 102
Karl August, Duke of Saxe-Weimar Eisenach, 31
knowledge, 42, 99–100; absolute knowledge, 121; a priori knowledge, 3, 4–6; as finite, 78; self-knowledge, 11–12, 103; as systematic, 40

language (of philosophy), 38
law of identity. *See under* identity
Leibniz, Gottfried Wilhelm, 7, 20, 102, 116
life, 134
limitation (mutual), 59–61, 67
Locke, John, 20, 71–72
logic, 41, 51n2, 56; logical principles, 57, 61, 63
longing (*Sehnsucht*), 118, 127, 128–29
love, 129, 131

man (as culmination of nature), 101, 131
matter (Platonic), 99, 118, 128
mechanism, 10, 15
mediation, 45, 55, 66, 73, 78, 81–82
Mendelssohn, Moses, 19–20
Merleau-Ponty, Maurice, 6–7
metaphysics, 3, 12, 17–18, 22–23; after Kant, 4, 13–14; pre-Kantian, 1, 32

methodology, 22, 47–48, 78, 103–4
moral law, 9, 14, 29, 35, 48, 90, 98. *See also* categorical imperative
moral subject, 14
moral world, 15
mutual determination, 39, 68, 84, 97
mythology, 10, 12, 13, 107

nature, 10–11, 14, 99, 101; vs. freedom, 96; as ground (Schelling), 117, 126–27; vs. the I, 99; in Spinoza, 96
nature, philosophy of (*Naturphilosophie*), 1, 14, 111, 116; as point of contention, 113–14; vs. transcendental philosophy, 100–101, 108–9, 113–14, 124, 127
necessity: necessary connection (= X), 52–53; necessary thought, 36; in Plato's *Timaeus*, 99; source of presentations, 42
negation, 67, 68–69
negativity, 111
Newton, Isaac, 20
Nietzsche, Friedrich, 45, 118, 133–34
nihilism, 18
nonground (*Ungrund*), 134–35
Novalis, 10

object: of consciousness 8, 24; identity with subject, 45–46, 99–100, 103–4, 111, 113, 114; of knowledge, 5–6; movement toward the subjective, 100–101; as source of affection, 36–37; subject-object distinction, 99–100, 117
"Oldest Systematic Program of German Idealism," 12–15, 107
opposition (*Gegensatz*), 33, 56–63, 82; fundamental oppositions (Fichte), 61; imagination and, 85–86, 104. *See also* contradiction

pantheism, 96, 122–23
passivity (vs. activity), 45, 65–66, 69–71
peace, perpetual, 15
philosophy: beginning of, 100, 107; end of, 6–7; finitude of, 78; task of, 20; as work of freedom, 95, 100
Plato, 13, 15, 98–99, 118, 128, 134

poetry, 10, 12, 15, 107
Pöggeler, Otto, 13
politics, 14–15
positing: meaning, 58; absolute positing, 52–54; counterpositing, 56–57. *See also* self-positing
postulates, practical, 9, 13–15, 31
practical philosophy, 9, 14–15, 62–63, 64–65, 102, 104
practical reason, 9, 15, 21, 63; primacy of, 48, 65, 80, 93–94
preestablished harmony, 102
presentation (*Darstellung*) of system, 32, 33
presentation (*Vorstellung*). *See* representation
principle (*Grundsatz*): fundamental principle of philosophy, 4, 22–24, 33, 37–39, 97; the I as, 45–46; principles of the sciences, 38, 39, 40; principles of the *Wissenschaftslehre*, 8, 12, 39, 49–63
principle of ground. *See* grounding principle
principle of identity. *See* identity: law of identity
progression: of ideas, 13–14; history of self-consciousness, 99, 103–4, 111

quantity, 61, 67, 68, 76

realism: in Jacobi, 18; relation to idealism, 124–25; stages within *Wissenschaftslehre*, 66, 75, 79–84
reality (category), 56, 67–69
reason: as absolute, 121; attitude toward, 10, 18; critique of, 3, 4, 10; culmination of nature, 101; decree of, 59, 73; imagination and, 104; role of, 20. *See also* practical reason
receptacle (*chôra*), 99, 118, 128, 134
receptivity, 36
reciprocity, 68. *See also* mutual determination
reflection, 6, 41, 50, 100, 110, 113, 120; abstracting reflection, 55, 58
Reinhold, Karl Leonhard, 20–27, 30, 38, 44, 97; as developer of Kant, 3, 4; Fichte and, 33–34, 35–36, 42

religion, 10, 15, 30, 31
representation (*Vorstellung*), 8, 11–12, 16–17, 33–35; Fichte on, 42–43, 44, 87–88; Reinhold's theory of, 21–25, 44; Schelling on, 99–100
revelation, 29–30; of existence, 19–20; God's self-revelation, 127, 128–30
Romanticism, 10–11, 21
Rosenzweig, Franz, 12
Rousseau, Jean-Jacques, 10
ruleless (*regellos*), 118, 127–28

Sallis, John: end of philosophy, 6; on imagination, 86
Schulz, Johann, 16
Schulze, Gottlob Ernst, 25–28, 33–35, 43, 44, 46, 58, 115; Hegel's criticism of, 110–11
Schelling, Friedrich Wilhelm Joseph, 4, 21, 95–132; culmination of German Idealism, 1, 131; Fichte and, 32, 47; Hegel and, 1, 96, 99, 109–12, 116; Kant and, 4, 16, 96; "Oldest Systematic Program" and, 12–13; progression of ideas, 13; Romantics and, 10
Schiller, Friedrich, 10, 14, 15, 21
Schlegel, August Wilhelm, 21, 108
Schlegel, Friedrich, 10, 21, 108
Schneider, Helmut, 12–13
science: philosophy as, 2, 3, 4, 25, 27, 37, 95; *Wissenschaftslehre* as, 37–40
self. *See* I, the; subject
self-consciousness, 8, 14, 33; divine self-consciousness, 128–29, 131; history of, 99, 103–4, 111; the I as, 51. *See also* consciousness
self-knowledge, 11–12, 103; of absolute, 121
self-positing, 12, 46, 51, 53–56, 93–94, 97; as freedom, 124; as reality, 69
self-relatedness, 14
self-reverting activity, 45–46, 47–48, 54, 58, 92
skepticism, 18, 25–26, 27, 110–11
Socrates, 21, 134
speculative reason, 9. *See also* theoretical reason
Spinoza, Baruch, 18, 96–97, 98, 116, 123–25; Fichte and, 52, 71–74, 79; pantheism of, 122

spirit, 123, 131; of Kant's philosophy, 33; nature and, 11; transformation of, 2; as unity of God and longing, 129
state, the, 12, 14–15
striving, 89, 92–93, 112, 114
subject, 8; absolute subject, 54; as free, 14; identity with object, 45–46, 99–100, 103–4, 111, 113, 114; of knowledge, 5–6, 121; movement toward the objective, 101–3; passivity of, 36–37; representation and, 24; subject-object distinction, 99–100, 117. *See also* I, the
subjective idealism, 16–17, 112
substance, 1, 71–74; in Spinoza, 18, 72–73, 96
substantiality, 66, 70–71, 75
synthesis: concepts of, 75; of subject and object, 104; synthetic identity, 55–56; task of Fichte's third principle, 59–62, 64
system, 133–35; completion of, 107; as deed to be enacted, 42; evil and, 132, 133; in Fichte, 30, 37–38, 42, 62–63; as form of science, 37–38; knowledge as, 40; systematizing Kant, 21–22, 33, 97; system of freedom, 119–20, 121–22; system of ideas, 13–14; system of pure reason (Kant), 9

Tathandlung (act), 34, 45, 50, 51, 54–56
teleology, 102
theoretical philosophy, 63, 64–65, 86–87, 102
theoretical reason, 9, 15, 21
thing in itself, 5–6, 8–9, 17, 25, 34–35, 58, 115; criticism of, 19, 23–24, 35–37, 115; dogmatism and, 43, 114
thinking (*Denken*), 8, 11–12, 36, 46, 47, 54
Timaeus, 98–99
time, 8
transcendental apperception, 11–12, 33, 51, 68
transcendental idealism, 16–17, 18, 45
transcendental philosophy, 100–102, 105, 108–9, 113, 124, 127
transference, 80–81
truth, 15, 99
Tübingen, 96

unconditional. *See* absolute
unconscious, the: in art, 105–6

understanding (*Verstand*), 23–24, 35, 88. *See also* God: divine understanding
unity: of consciousness, 11, 57, 67, 69, 70; as demand of system, 126, 133; of experience, 11–12; identity as, 123; spirit as, 129
unruly (*regellos*), 118, 127–28

Von Herrmann, Friedrich-Wilhelm, 53n3

Wieland, Christoph Martin, 21
will (*Wille*), 9, 118, 127, 131, 132
willing (*Wollen*), 104, 124
Wissenschaftslehre, 8, 12, 37–94; concept of, 37–41; method of, 47–48; as term for philosophy, 30
Wolffians, 51n2
world, 14

JOHN SALLIS is Frederick J. Adelmann Professor of Philosophy at Boston College. He is author of more than twenty books, including *Chorology*, *Songs of Nature*, and *Kant and the Spirit of Critique*.

MARK J. THOMAS is Associate Professor of Philosophy at Central College in Pella, Iowa. He is author of *Freedom and Ground: A Study of Schelling's Treatise on Freedom*.

For Indiana University Press

Tony Brewer, Artist and Book Designer
Brian Carroll, Rights Manager
Gary Dunham, Acquisitions Editor and Director
Anna Francis, Assistant Acquisitions Editor
Anna Garnai, Editorial Assistant
Brenna Hosman, Production Coordinator
Katie Huggins, Production Manager
David Miller, Lead Project Manager/Editor
Dan Pyle, Online Publishing Manager
Pamela Rude, Senior Artist and Book Designer
Stephen Williams, Marketing and Publicity Manager

www.ingramcontent.com/pod-product-compliance
Lightning Source LLC
Chambersburg PA
CBHW021356300426
44114CB00012B/1257